The Politics of Food

The Politics of Food

Edited by
Marianne Elisabeth Lien and Brigitte Nerlich

Oxford • New York

English edition
First published in 2004 by
Berg
Editorial offices:
First Floor, Angel Court, 81 St Clements Street, Oxford OX4 1AW, UK
175 Fifth Avenue, New York, NY 10010, USA

Berg is the imprint of Oxford International Publishers Ltd.

Library of Congress Cataloging-in-Publication Data
A catalogue record for this book is available from the Library of Congress.

British Library Cataloguing-in-Publication Data
A catalogue record for this book is available from the British Library.

ISBN 1 85973 848 6 (hardback)
1 85973 853 2 (paperback)

Typeset by Avocet Typeset, Chilton, Aylesbury, Bucks
Printed in the United Kingdom by Biddles Ltd, King's Lynn.

www.bergpublishers.com

Contents

Contributors

Efrat Ben-Ze'ev is a Lecturer at the Department of Behavioral Sciences, Ruppin Academic Center and a fellow of the Harry S. Truman Research Institute at the Hebrew University, Jerusalem. She holds a doctorate in social anthropology from the University of Oxford. Her research has dealt with the Palestinian refugee experience, focusing on the interface between history and memory. Currently she is studying the memories of the 1948 Israeli war veterans.

Lawrence Busch is University Distinguished Professor of Sociology and Director of the Institute for Food and Agricultural Standards at Michigan State University. He has written widely on agriculture, agricultural research, agricultural policy, food systems, and food standards. His current work focuses on third-party certification of food and agricultural products and the growing global role of supermarkets.

Katarzyna J. Cwiertka is a post-doctoral Research Fellow of the Netherlands Organisation for Scientific Research (NWO), affiliated with Leiden University. She studies the modern history of Japan and Korea through the focus on food. She is the editor of *Asian Food: The Global and the Local* (RoutledgeCurzon/ University of Hawaii Press 2002), and is currently working on a monograph about dietary modernization of Korea under the Japanese rule.

Bente Halkier is Associate Professor at the Department of Communication, Journalism and Computer Science, Roskilde University, Denmark. She was trained in sociology and political science and did her PhD dissertation on how consumers deal with environmental issues in food consumption. She has done research on environmental consideration in consumption, political consumerism, risk and food consumption, and trust and distrust in food. Her current research interests are consumption in an every-day life perspective, social norms around food consumption, and the interplay between direct and mediated communication about food consumption. She is senior partner in the comparative EU project, "Trust in Food".

Keith Hart teaches anthropology at Goldsmiths College London and lives with his family in Paris. He has taught at numerous universities around the world, but especially at Cambridge, where he was Director of the African Studies Centre and was awarded the first ever teaching prize in the humanities and social sciences. He contributed the concept of the informal economy to development studies. His latest book is *Money in an Unequal World* (2001); see the related website www.thememorybank.co.uk.

Haldis Haukanes is a social anthropologist and a post-doctoral Researcher at the Centre for Women's and Gender Research at the University of Bergen, Norway. She has done research on social transformations in rural post-communist Czech Republic, including community dynamics, change in agriculture and property relations, and local and personal histories. Her current research focuses on issues of environmental risks, consumption and gender, studied in relation to the food practices of rural and urban families in the Czech Republic.

Chaia Heller is completing her PhD in anthropology at the University of Massachusetts in Amherst. She has taught environmental and feminist philosophy at the Institute for Social Ecology in Vermont since 1988, and is the author of *The Ecology of Everyday Life: Rethinking the Desire for Nature* (Blackrose Books 1999). Her research on the French debate over genetically engineered food was funded by the National Science Foundation and focuses on questions of globalization, agriculture, and the cultural limits of science hegemony.

Eivind Jacobsen is Head of Research in the Department for Market and Distribution at the National Institute for Consumer Research, Norway. Trained as a sociologist, he has done research on consumption, retailing, marketing, food politics and food safety. His current research interests include animal-welfare schemes, regulation related to consumer politics and consumers' roles in innovation processes. He has recently co-edited *The Politicization of Food* in Norwegian (*Politiseringen av maten*, Abstrakt Forlag 2003).

Marianne Elisabeth Lien is Associate Professor at the Department of Social Anthropology, University of Oslo. She is trained in anthropology, nutrition and nutritional anthropology and has done research on food, culture, consumption, food politics and marketing (*Marketing and Modernity,* Berg 1997). Her current research interests include economic anthropology, markets, globalization, aquaculture and biomigration. She is currently in charge of a research program funded by the Research Council of Norway focusing on transnational flows.

Anne Murcott is author of numerous articles in sociology on various aspects of food, health and culture. She has edited and co-authored six books and served as Director of the Economic & Social Research Council (UK) Research Programme '"The Nation's Diet": the social science of food choice' (1992–1998). She is now Honorary Visiting Professor at City University in London, Honorary Professor, Department of Sociology, University of Leicester, Professor Emerita in Sociology at London South Bank University and Special Professor at the University of Nottingham.

Brigitte Nerlich is a Senior Research Officer at the *Institute for the Study of Genetics, Biorisks and Society* (IGBiS) at the University of Nottingham. She studied French and philosophy in Germany and has published in the fields of semantics and pragmatics. In the past she has done research on the function of metaphor, metonymy and polysemy in language acquisition and language use. Her most recent research focuses on the cultural and political contexts in which metaphors are used in the public and scientific debates about cloning, genetically modified food, the human genome project, designer babies, and foot and mouth disease.

Acknowledgements

The idea for this book emerged from a workshop at the 2002 conference of the EASA (European Association of Social Anthropologists), in which six of the contributors took part. We thank Jon Mitchell at the EASA for inviting Marianne to convene a workshop, and Anne Murcott for bringing us together. This book is a result of interdisciplinary collaboration. Marianne would like to acknowledge mentors who have inspired and guided her interest in the anthropology of food over the past two decades: Eduardo Archetti, Wenche Barth Eide, Unni Kjærnes and Gretel Pelto. Thanks also to the Department of Social Anthropology, University of Oslo, for providing funds that made it easier for us to deal with some of the linguistic revisions, expertly carried out by Michael Gibson, and the indexing of the book. Sincere thanks to Kathryn Earle and Caroline McCarthy at Berg for the constant and kind assistance we received from them throughout the writing of this book. Brigitte would also like to express her gratitude to the Leverhulme Trust and the Economic and Social Research Council – without their funding she could not have carried out this joint project. Last, but not least, we would like to thank each other for mutual inspiration and smooth cooperation in the process of editing.

Marianne Elisabeth Lien and Brigitte Nerlich

-1-

The Politics of Food:
An Introduction

Marianne Elisabeth Lien

In recent years, food has emerged as a political topic par excellence. Capable of connecting individual bodies to abstract communities and techno-scientific innovations to moral concerns, food has become a highly charged and contested field. Recent food scandals, such as the outbreak of BSE (bovine spongiform encephalopathy) and the public debates over GMOs (genetically modified organisms) have shattered the idea that 'food is food' as we always knew it, and have exposed fundamental dilemmas of modern food production related to risk and control. At the same time, food is increasingly involved in controversies at a transnational level, in relation to issues of access, dominance, trade and control in what is seen as a shared global environment. Such controversies have placed food at the forefront of political debates both within and between nation-states.

Not long ago, the term 'Politics of Food' would have drawn notice to a fairly specific set of problems within a particular set of arenas. The politics of food would have taken place within the domain of state bureaucracy. The term would have denoted a range of issues such as food security, social inequality, nutrition policy, and agricultural policies. Focusing on the micro level, the politics of food could also involve the gendered and unequal distribution of food and labor within the household (Murcott 1982; Charles and Kerr 1988; Counihan 1999). Going beyond the level of the state, the term might have applied to the study of unfair trade, the dominance of multinational corporations and food as a human right (Eide et al. 1984). Most importantly, the term 'politics of food' would have focused attention on the access to food at different levels of scale and the problems of matching access to needs. In other words, seeing food as a source of nutrients, and politics essentially as what political institutions did (or ought to have done), the *politics of food* would have been located where the two came together.

1

Since then, the field has been extended in novel directions. In light of current controversies, a purely institutional approach to food politics is, in itself, no longer capable of capturing the vast array of connections that relate to food production, distribution and consumption. We do not argue here that institutional approaches to the politics of food are irrelevant, nor that the issues of need, access, nutrition policies and global inequalities are less important today than they were a generation ago (see Pottier 1999; Hart 2001). Rather, we argue that contemporary issues require that our notion of the politics of food is expanded to fields and arenas not traditionally thought of as 'political'. Accordingly, our aim is to draw attention to some of the less obvious ways in which food is politicized. Most contributions to this book are inspired by anthropological perspectives on food and eating, and many apply an ethnographic approach. Yet, this book is not strictly anthropological, as it draws on insights and methods that are central also to other disciplines in the humanities and social sciences, most notably linguistics, political science, history and sociology.

To indicate that the politics of food takes place both inside and outside the arenas normally designated as political is to draw attention to controversy, hegemony, resistance, and conflicts of interest that underlie both the structuring of food choice and the structuring of public and media agendas. But it also implies drawing attention to how food itself has become a political object. These issues are elaborated in the introduction. But first, let us briefly recapitulate some events that have changed the way we think about the food we eat.

What Happened? Transformations of Substance and Scale

A notion of risk has been introduced. When in 1996 a UK laboratory demonstrated the suspected link between BSE in British cows and the rare and mortal brain disease in humans called vCJD (a variant of Creutzfeldt Jacob's Disease), the event provoked chain reactions all over the world. Apart from making headlines in most European newspapers and causing a world-wide ban on British beef, the event epitomizes what, in hindsight, may be seen as the emergence of both a new awareness of risk and an increased distrust in political institutions as key issues in public debates about food in Europe, and subsequently also in the US.[1] The case of BSE in Britain demonstrated for many that government officials could not be trusted (a picture of the then UK Minister of Agriculture feeding his daughter a beefburger to prove its safety was circulated widely across Europe). It also exposed how the beef industry, seeking to cut expenses, had used bovine meat in the production of feed for bovine animals, thus transgressing the rule that, until then, had largely remained unspoken, namely that herbivores should not be forced to feed on species of their own kind – a type of cannibalism. This practice might never have become public knowledge had it not been for the fact that temperatures used in feed production were turned down (another cost-cutting measure), thus allowing the prions causing BSE to migrate from contaminated carcasses to healthy cows and, in turn, across species boundaries to human consumers (Franklin 1999). In this way, the case of BSE also became a vivid illustration of commercial greed, of inept food-safety authorities, untrustworthy politicians and a nature that, according to media coverage, had the ability to 'strike back'. Thus, in the case of BSE, the political implications of a food scandal have had significant and far-reaching consequences, even if the implications for human health are still being debated, as the number of people directly affected by vCJD is still relatively low (Zwanenberg and Millstone 2003).

The BSE scandal came in the wake of other scandals, such as salmonella and dioxins in chicken, so that the 1990s may be seen to represent a historical watershed with regard to the way food is thought about, talked about and handled. Food is no longer simply a much-needed material resource; its purchase is now linked to the need for consumers to balance monetary concerns with issues of risk and distrust. What could previously be left to food-safety authorities and nutrition expertise hit the head-lines of the news media and became a topic of expert controversy and public debate (see Nerlich, this volume). Where policy measures used to be dominant, a complex interplay of food producers, food control, state policies, news media and the public is now involved in defining food-safety. As a result, 'what's for dinner?' has become an issue of considerable concern, demonstrated yet again in the most recent food scare about carcinogens in salmon sparked by a food-safety report published in the United States (see http://www.foodstandards.gov.uk/news/pressreleases/sciencesalmon). Food is politicized, not only as a commodity for consumption, but all the way into the kitchen and the dinner table, with implications for cooking and family care (see both Halkier and Haukanes, this volume).

Genetic modification of food, which again hit the headlines in the 1990s, has meant that many of our most common foodstuffs can no longer be taken for granted. Since the emergence of GMOs on the food market, the material proper-ties of food itself have become subject of controversy. Some argue that genetic modification represents only a faster method of plant cultivation, and one with immediate benefits. Critics maintain that speed makes a difference, as it collapses qualitatively significant material changes into a time-span of a few years that would previously only be noticeable over several generations. Such changes expose the malleability of edible substances, and force us to realize that the foods we eat are the result of human manipulation, often with unintended consequences. No longer trapped in a 'black box' of conventional (agri-) cultural practices (Latour 1987), food is thus exposed as a hybrid phenomenon. As such, it immedi-ately enters the battlefield of conflicting agendas and interests (see Jacobsen, this volume). In this way, the politics of food has come to be implicated in the very notion of food itself, what food is and what it should be.

Genetic engineering has implications far beyond its actual implementation. Even in Norway, where GMO foods are still marginal and essentially banned, public awareness of the options inherent in genetic engineering has opened the food debate toward new problem areas, and has thus politicized the very substance of food, even though our tomatoes are still more or less the same. In this way, the politics of food is no longer confined to policy-making within the nation-state, but closely connected to innovations and discourses that take place on the transnational arenas of science, technology and trade (see both Heller and Busch, this volume).

Food on Transnational Arenas

Food is increasingly involved in controversies at a transnational level. The global politics of food involves not only the unequal distribution of access and rigged producer markets (see Hart, this volume), but also moral and political engagements in relation to what is seen by many as a single global environment (Franklin et al. 2000). In this way, politics of food is also politics at a distance, as exemplified by consumer boycotts, internet petitions and other examples of global-environmental activism (see Lien, this volume). Several factors constitute the background for this development. First, although the long-distance transport of food is far from new (cf. Pelto and Pelto 1983; Mintz 1985; Hart this volume), the delocalization of food has become more significant during the last decades, leading to what some scholars refer to as the 'globalization of food and nutrition systems' (Sobal 1999). Using the terminology of Held et al. (1999) one may reasonably argue with regard to food that we have witnessed an increase both in the extensity of global networks, in the intensity and impact of global interconnectedness, and in the velocity of global flows. This implies that the potential impact of local events on distant affairs have become even more significant (see Nerlich, this volume). This imbues some affluent consumers with a sense of responsibility for relations that are not only distant, but also extremely complex and hard to grasp, and thus brings world politics into the shopping cart. At the same time, as global consumers, we are vulnerable to shifts in practices, regulations and routines that take place in distant regions of the world. Negligence, fraud, and adulteration represent sources of risk to most of us, even if they happen elsewhere, just as corporate decisions that are made in New York, or policy decisions made in Brussels, may have dramatic consequences for the access to food and livelihood in rural India.

This is just another way of saying that as food systems are globalized, food becomes entangled in complex webs of political significance. It does not, by itself, make food a political object, but it vastly increases the number of diverse interests, relations and regulatory frameworks that are enrolled as each food item makes its way from production through to consumption (Fine and Leopold 1993). Hence, the potential for interests to diverge and come into conflict also rises exponentially, even if only a few of these conflicts ever surface on the political agenda of the public media.

In the case of food, therefore, its socio-political relations of production are always more significant than the food-item itself might reveal. What appears to be a carrot or a piece of meat is indeed a product with a history and implications more complex and profound than most of us even want to think about. This gap between what we actually know about the food we eat and what we could potentially know (and even act upon), makes transparency a key issue. Thus, the politics of food is also a politics of silence and exposure, a quest for the power to control what will be declared, what will be the focus of public debate and what will remain unspoken (Nestlé 2002). This issue has been in the forefront of the debate concerning GM food in Europe, where the issue of explicit and exhaustive labeling has brought European governments into conflict with the United States. Transparency is also a key theme in the debate in the wake of the first diagnosis of BSE in a cow in the United States in 2003 (cf. the *Guardian*, 12 January 2003; http://www.oie.int/eng/press/en_031224.htm).

The problem of safety and transparency is not new. It was the basis for the creation of regulatory systems for food control established as early as the nineteenth century. Yet, we argue that with more abstract relations[2] between producer and consumer, a weakening of expert authority (Beck 1992) and frequent exposures of food 'scandals' in public media, consumers sense even more strongly the impossibility of being 'fully informed'. As a result of what is experienced by some as a 'knowledge deficit', the politicization of food is more than ever a selective process of choosing to highlight one particular issue out of a myriad of potential candidates. Since the list is almost endless, the question of which items to politicize becomes a political issue in itself (see Lien, this volume).

At the same time, food is always locally embedded. The cultural, social and moral context for the provision and consumption of food is also a local context. As the following chapters show, such local contexts filter which food-related issues are to surface on the public agenda, and provide a framework within which such issues are constructed, interpreted, discussed and solved. In other words, all novel developments, from the impact of foot-and-mouth disease on the English countryside to new technologies of genetic engineering are always understood in the light of relations and distinctions that are significant in relation to a local and familiar framework. Thus, the discovery of BSE in the Czech Republic resonated with the prominent ambivalence about East–West boundaries in the post-Soviet states (see Haukanes, this volume), while the French campaign against GMO was absorbed in an anti-American, anti-globalization movement and expressed through promotion of French Roquefort (see Heller, this volume). Similarly, the British debate about the 'foot-and-mouth' epidemic tapped into a pre-existing framework of urban consumer guilt about the greedy capitalist exploitation of the local country-side (see Nerlich, this volume), while transnational anti-whaling campaigns draw upon Euro-American notions of individualism and family values to evoke sympathy for the whales (see Lien, this volume). In this way, controversies that may appear at first to be part of a discourse that some scholars refer to as 'transcultural' (Milton 1996: 170) turn out to be strongly embedded in values and distinctions that are, in fact, highly specific. Thus, in an era of so-called globalization, when it comes to food, the boundaries between local concerns and global affairs are not easily drawn.

Why Food?

Much of what has been said so far about transformed processes of production and globalized systems of provision could have been said about a whole range of material products, such as textiles, petroleum, hardwood, pharmaceuticals and more. Yet, as the following chapters demonstrate, several features make food a unique phenomenon, more profoundly absorbed in complex relations than any other product, and yet different from everything else. What is so special about food?

As a material substance with a crucial balance of nutrients and toxins, food has immediate biological implications. Unlike clothing, piercing, or body paint, food is literally transformed and becomes *part of* the human body. Thus, the saying 'you are what you eat', has several layers of meaning, from the symbolic to the material. But the absence of food has profound implications as well. The physiological need in humans to eat every day makes access to food a crucial issue, and has compelled human beings throughout history to develop social and technical systems of provision that aim to ensure stable food supplies through domestication, exploitation, reciprocity and trade. It also makes us vulnerable, weak and easy to control. In this way, food is entrenched in structures of subordination, governance and domination.

Secondly, as food and eating are routinized on an everyday basis, food becomes a convenient medium for the expression of social and ceremonial distinctions, and for naturalizing relations of community and hierarchy. As such, the symbolic meaning of food in any given context may be seen as sedimentation of historical structures of power and inequality that have been operating through generations (Bourdieu 1979; Mintz 1985). As a symbolic system of meaning, food is therefore both a structured and a structuring force.

Thirdly, humanity's attempts to enhance bodily functions and abilities through scientific means have paved the way for what in the field of food is captured by the term 'nutritional science'. As nutrition has become one of the most significant fields of preventive medicine, it serves also as a structuring agent in relation to food choice. In this way, scientific nutrition advice may run contrary to agricultural interests (Kjærnes 1993), food industry (Nestlé 2002) and even national food and nutrition policies (Lien 1990). In this way, connections between food and body also give rise to conflicts between policy interests, business and science.

The Legacy of Anthropology

As anthropologists have demonstrated since the inception of the discipline, food is a profound medium of reciprocity that marks and distinguishes persons and relations through acts of sharing, giving and receiving (Malinowski 1922; Mauss 1925). Add to this the significance of food in systems of classification (Douglas 1966, 1975; Leach 1964; Lévi-Strauss 1970), the social organization of labor in food production (Richards 1939; Evans-Pritchard 1940), food in religious and healing rituals (Archetti 1997), and the precarious interplay between the extraction of food resources and the environment (Rappaport 1968), and we have a rough idea of the various ways in which food would make its way into holistically oriented anthropological monographs of the twentieth century (for an overview, see Douglas 1984; Murcott 1988; Sutton 2001). Food's importance as a social mediator, a cultural symbol and a natural resource is readily apparent in holistic studies of small-scale societies.

Yet, as anthropologists' attention shifted from small-scale exotic societies to post-industrial societies closer to 'home', the holistic approach has become more difficult to realize. At the same time, there has been a tendency toward analytical specialization through subfields since around the 1970s. Today, food is no longer an indispensable component of a social and cultural analysis. Rather, in more recent publications, food tends to be either the paramount topic of analysis, or hardly mentioned at all. Thus, the 'anthropology of food' has emerged as a distinct subdiscipline,[3] widely popular but often also somewhat detached from more general research issues. What we witness here is partly an attempt at cutting problems 'down to size' (such as 'food and gender', 'systems of provision', 'food production', 'food and risk', 'food consumption' and so on) in order to address urgent challenges in applied research, or to link food to topical concerns. However, as a result of such delineations, the complex entanglements that were the hallmark of more holistic anthropological accounts tend to be lost.

Furthermore, the way we choose to cut the problem down to size is often informed by the way we order and classify food generally, that is deeply entrenched in Western ways of thinking about and ordering the world. Certain Euro-American cultural distinctions have therefore – almost unnoticed – slipped into our theoretical apparatus and provided us with approaches to food that split apart dimensions of food that are, in fact, closely connected. Thus, broadly speaking, food is approached as either nature or culture, either production or consumption, either as an aspect of the private *or* the public domain. Although this is a common problem and difficult to escape, it is perhaps more problematic in the field of food than in other areas, because it often implies that we cut our analyses precisely at the most interesting junctions. As a result, the analytical possibilities inherent in the multiplicity of food, i.e. the analytical potential of food as a mediator between domains commonly set apart, is often lost.

What we need is not a return to meticulous accounts of villages as in the anthropological classics, but rather a re-evaluation of an underlying premise that has shaped the anthropological structure of inquiry: the fundamental assumption that relevant connections cannot be defined in advance, but emerge as a result of empirical research. This inductive approach lay at the heart of functionalist anthropology and went hand in hand with the holistic approach. Today, in an academic world already ordered by neat and sharp subcategories (risk, globalization, embodiment, etc.), a more holistic approach may seem impossible to achieve. Research projects must to be formulated in relation to culturally pre-defined domains, and food studies are no exception. Yet, I would suggest that precisely in this situation, more widespread intellectual disobedience in relation to the overarching categories would allow food studies to move a step forward. The degree of entanglement of a phenomenon can never be ascertained in advance, and this is especially the case in relation to food. In a world of global systems of provision, abrupt material transformations and complex layers of governance, most efforts at compartmentalizing food in accordance with pre-defined categories are bound to be too narrow. Malinowski claimed in 1922 that:

> An Ethnographer who sets out to study only religion, or only technology, or only social organisation cuts out an artificial field for inquiry, and he will be seriously handicapped in his work. (Malinowski 1922:11)

Malinwoski's advice to anthropologists in the early 1920s captures what could be seen as the most significant lesson to be learnt from anthropology in the field of food studies today: one who sets out to study food only as consumption, production, globalization, embodiment, nutrition, family life or economics is likely to be trapped by the same boundaries that structure the very field that she or he tries to illuminate. Fresh insight into contemporary dilemmas requires research that challenges such sectorial boundaries. I am proposing an approach to food which resists such preconceived distinctions and follows instead the connections that food allows humans to make. Just as Appadurai (1986) suggests we might study the 'social life of things', food may be followed through its various entanglements, across boundaries both legal and moral, beyond and between nations, bodies, persons and nutrients. If we do that, we will find that what appears as controversies about food often turns out to be controversies about something else.

Mary Douglas once said, referring to consumption more generally, that 'the essential function of [food] is its capacity to make sense' (Douglas and Isherwood 1979: 40). I argue that the essential function of food is its capacity to make connections. Approached holistically, food effectively dissolves most preconceived distinctions between nature and culture, production and consumption, morals and markets, family and society, the individual and the collective, body and mind. At the same time, it remains a profound medium of reciprocity, constituting meaningful relationships at different levels and of different kinds. It is precisely through this capacity to make connections that food has become a highly charged political object.

To state that food is a political object is another way of drawing attention to the fact that many relations that are constituted by and through the medium of food are also power relations, and should be analysed as such. Our approach to power relations goes beyond, or even bypasses, a focus on the formal institutions of the state (Gledhill 1994, Vincent 2002). In light of the crisis of legitimacy characterizing political life in general, and the deregulation and liberalization currently affecting food in particular, a focus on policies, bureaucracies and politicians would simply be too narrow to grasp significant issues and changes. Politics, like food, is embedded in social practice, discourse, controversy and conventions that are not always labeled 'political'. Thus, our approach to the politics of food is based on the premise that 'action which contests existing power relations may take many forms', and that much of this is 'in constant danger of slipping from view, simply because of its everyday and inchoate quality' (Gledhill 1994: 23). Drawing attention to some of the less obvious ways in which food is politicized, we seek to contribute to a more nuanced understanding of both politics and food.

Governmentality, Risk, Embodiment, Nature

What connections are illuminated through an empirical focus on food? The following section highlights some dimensions that are particularly relevant to the chapters that follow. Most issues below have been developed theoretically by other scholars and from other topical angles. They are included here because they are particularly relevant for analyses of contemporary power relations surrounding food.

One such connection is captured by the term governmentality (Foucault 1991; Coveney 2000) referring to the emergence in Europe of a concern for the governance of a complex of 'men and things' through a range of techniques for knowing about populations (statistical surveys, medicine, demography) and for managing populations through such knowledge (see both Halkier and Cwiertka, this volume). In the book *Food, Morals and Meaning*, John Coveney makes a powerful link between a Foucauldian concept of governmentality and the twentieth-century discourse on food and nutrition, arguing convincingly that nutrition is a government of food choice which situates the individuals within a field of knowledge for explicit objectives, and, at the same time, provides them with a way of constituting themselves as ethical subjects through a decipherment of their pleasures and fulfilments. (Coveney 2000: 177)

Coveney's use of Foucault helps us to trace how food mediates relations between the state and the individual, or between the nation and 'its' human bodies. Most importantly, he demonstrates how governmentality in relation to food involves the socialization of family members as 'good' parents, 'good' children and 'good' citizens, and thus involves the construction of ethical subjects. As the following chapters demonstrate, these relations can take many different forms (see chapters by Cwiertka, Haukanes, Ben-Ze'ev and Lien).

Another set of issues relevant to the study of food and social connections is captured by the recent emphasis on institutional reflexivity (Giddens 1991), risk-society (Beck 1992) and related terms like radical doubt, uncertainty and (lack of) trust. Although these descriptions of high modernity are somewhat eurocentric and hardly applicable on a global scale (Nugent 2000), they draw attention to a range of dilemmas that are strongly felt along the North Atlantic rim. Because they transcend the physical boundaries of the body, food and eating practices are highly sensitive to shifting configurations of risk and trust (Fine and Leopold 1993). Furthermore, since what is harmful in food often escapes the senses (i.e. toxic substances cannot always be seen, smelled or tasted), trust in relation to food is abstract, involving social relations that are often distant, and often more imagined than real (Lien 1997). Consequently, changing configurations in the relation between the state and its citizens, or between supplier and consumer, are likely to be expressed as uncertainty about food and risk. Similarly, as the case of BSE has shown, food scandals can bring about significant changes in the organization of safety regulations and systems of provision. In recent years, scientific authorities have been losing public trust. Although European countries differ greatly in this respect (Poppe and Kjærnes 2003), there is a general trend in which science and experts no longer offer the sense of certitude they once did. One aspect of this 'post-enlightenment' turn is the transformed role of the media from that of being disseminators of expert knowledge to becoming virtual battlefields of conflicting expert claims. In this situation, the politics of food is also a 'politics of discourse' in which the power to set the public agenda, to frame the debate, and to silence opponents become a key resource. Such politics of discourse may be analysed as the strategic use of food metaphors (see Jacobsen, this volume), the distribution of blame and shame (see both Nerlich and Lien, this volume), and the role of the media in framing abstract risks in such a way that they are perceived as 'real' or relevant to ordinary consumers (see both Haukanes and Heller, this volume).

A third set of issues that emerge from the connections that food help us make relates to the sensory and experiential dimensions of food and eating. As an anchor of embodied experience, food often plays a key role in collective or individual acts of remembrance (cf. Karen Blixen's *Babette's Feast*, or Marcel Proust's account of 'La petite Madeleine'). David Sutton has explored these dimensions by drawing attention to the often ignored potential of food to evoke memory. In his book *Remembrance of Repasts* (Sutton 2001), he makes a fine attempt to bridge the Cartesian dualism of mind and body by analysing food in a Greek village as both semiotics *and* embodied experience. Drawing on the works of Paul Connerton (1989) on commemoration and Thomas Csordas (1994) on embodiment, he demonstrates how worlds of experience and interpretation are contained in food. Here, we take this further, showing how eating as a commemorative act highlights the role of food in political conflicts regarding land-claims and displacement of refugees (see Ben-Ze'ev, this volume). Food thus emerges as a material link that confirms and establishes, in a very sensual manner, the felt connections between a people and a place. Such connections reveal important nuances to the alleged ability of globalization to weaken ties of kinship and place (Eriksen 2003). The fact that food politics is also body-politics has also been developed in other directions, through explorations of food and gender (Counihan and Kaplan 1998; Counihan 1999) and of food, body image and self-identity (Lupton 1996; see both Haukanes and Cwiertka, this volume).

Finally, a view of food as nature draws attention to the connections that are made between food and the natural environment, and between food and an idealized image of nature as opposed to culture and technology. Today, when science and technology can more than ever before refashion what we used to see as nature, the concept of nature appears to retain an even greater capacity to capture our imagination and to encapsulate notions of what is good, sound and true. Thus, even though the foods we consume are shaped, adjusted and manipulated by human intervention, references to nature abound in food advertising, culinary discourse and public debate (Lien 1995, 1997). This obsession with nature affects the way we think about food both in relation to environments of production (e.g. organic farming methods), in relation to food products themselves (e.g. processed foods vs 'natural' foods), and in the way we envisage the way food shapes our body and health (e.g. popular 'Paleolithic' diets). We need to pay attention to a 'politics of nature' which, in contemporary discourse, goes beyond what is traditionally captured by the term environmentalism. As Macnaghten and Urry (1998) note, there is not one single nature, only a diversity of natures that are contested and constituted through a variety of social, cultural and political processes. When we envisage food and diets as more or less 'natural', or argue for schemes of production that are more (or less) sustainable or harmoniously adapted to our notions of nature, we latch on to these debates, and thus find ourselves in a field which is already highly charged with assumptions of a rather dubious kind.

Bruno Latour (1987) offers a way out by suggesting a symmetrical approach in which nature and society are analyzed on equal terms. In his analysis of modern practices of purification and translation between nature and culture (Latour 1993), he provides us with a theoretical framework which is fruitful for understanding the hybrid nature of food, and its contemporary oscillation between the natural and cultural domains (see Jacobsen, this volume).

Outline of the Chapters

Drawing on case studies that are both ethnographic and historical, the book focuses on continuities as well as contemporary turns, and on national as well as transnational issues. The following chapters are structured and presented in relation to some overarching topics that draw attention to the types of connection that are involved. In Part I we explore the mediations between individuals and society as expressed through our role as food consumers, and by looking at food as a commodity. Is shopping for food a political act? To what extent may we analyse food consumers as political agents? These questions are posed by Bente Halkier in Chapter 2 about the handling of food-related risks. Drawing on research among consumers in Denmark, she argues that consumers are often called upon to solve political problems concerning food and risk. She shows how consumers use food purchasing and food consumption as strategies for political activity, while at the same time forming part of a particular governmentality of risk-management. Brigitte Nerlich also addresses the issue of consumer agency in Chapter 3 through an analysis of the media debate that followed in the wake of the foot-and-mouth epidemic in the UK. Her critical examination reveals that the focus on 'cheap food' as the primary cause of the epidemic, which was so prominent in the media, was not self-evident. Why did a tragedy for farmers become such a big issue for consumers? Why did consumers literally blame themselves? Focusing on the framing of the FMD debate in 2001, Nerlich discusses the policy outcome of the crises, and draws attention to some dilemmas of modern agriculture that appear, as yet, to be unresolved. Eivind Jacobsen in Chapter 4 addresses similar issues from a theoretical perspective. Pointing to the significance of rhetorical tropes, he elaborates the notions of food as nature, food as commodity and food as culture as metaphors that are particularly prominent in food discourse. Focusing on controversies and conflicts of interests, Jacobsen demonstrates how such tropes are closely interwoven with the basic structures of power in society, and strategically used by various actors to invoke or challenge established connotations. Thus, a focus on rhetorical tropes exposes underlying struggles over what food production and food consumption are and what they should be.

In Part II we draw attention to the role of food as a mediator between body, place and nation. In her Chapter 5 discussion of French peasants and the transformation of a debate about GM crops, Chaia Heller draws attention to the framing of risk and competing forms of expertise. Based on ethnographic research of the GMO controversy in France between 1997 and 2000, she shows how an objectivist risk frame was replaced by a focus on peasant 'savoir faire', food quality, productivist agriculture and globalization, and how the debate about risk became embedded in ongoing transnational controversies about local peasant expertise, and foreign trade. Heller's account demonstrates how food, precisely through its capacity to collapse nature and culture, may allow a debate to transcend its initial scientific boundaries and become, essentially, a debate about something else. Debates about risk and national boundaries are also the focus of Haldis Haukanes' account in Chapter 6 of the case of BSE in the Czech Republic. Based on ethnographic field-work in a Czech village, she discusses the emerging awareness of BSE among the Czech people as a process of BSE 'becoming real', a process in which the media played an important role. Her chapter focuses on ways in which food scandals like BSE have the capacity to realign the boundaries between what is perceived as edible and what is not, and she demonstrates how such realignments are resisted, both by state policies aimed at securing confidence and trust, and by individuals with their capacities to shift attention from risk to enjoyment in the context of food consumption. The nation-state figures prominently in Katarzyna Cwiertka's Chapter 7 historical analysis of the role of Western food in the making of the Japanese nation-state. Arguing that the mutual interdependence between politics and food has never been as great as since the rise of the nation-state, she examines the involvement of the Japanese state in the matter of public nutrition throughout the late nineteenth and first half of the twentieth century. Cwiertka highlights the connections between nation and nurture by drawing attention to the way Japanese military rations were modeled after Western diets with the aim of ensuring nutritional efficiency, and shows how these, in turn, were propagated as efficient solutions to dietary deficiency for the nation as a whole. While Cwiertka focuses on the attempts of national authorities to shape citizens' diets, Efrat Ben-Ze'ev takes an opposite approach in Chapter 8 as she describes the way food helps displaced Palestinian refugees in their attempts to construct and preserve memories of Palestine. Based on fieldwork among Palestinian refugees, she demonstrates how the picking, eating and sharing of edible plants collected at village ruins are both an act of remembrance and an act of protest against the Jewish-Israeli rendering of the landscape. The role of food, she argues, is to form the basis for a language that commemorates and constructs Palestine, a Palestine that is an all-encompassing symbol while at the same time being reinserted into mundane commensality.

Part III focuses on the role of food in global relations of inequality and equalization. Lawrence Busch draws attention in Chapter 9 to the roles of grades and standards in the social construction of safe food. He examines how the food system has changed as a result of the political realignments and reformulations collectively known as globalization. Why is it that food safety has become a political issue just as food has become safer? Busch demonstrates how grades and standards are implicated in food safety, and how they are used to impose a new discipline on food producers and processors, while often concealing the origins of the problem. The case of HACCP (hazard analysis and critical control point) is used to clarify the points. Marianne E. Lien focuses in Chapter 10 on transnational activism that seeks to prevent the transformation of certain animals to meat through the commodity chain. Comparing transnational campaigns against consumption of dog meat in Korea, against Norwegian and Japanese whalers, and against the consumption of kangaroo in Australia and the UK, her chapter is a critical examination of the role of hegemony and marginalization in transnational 'grass-root' activism. As such, the campaigns represent the enforcement of food taboos on a global scale. Keith Hart addresses in Chapter 11 what is probably the most acute problem of all, the political economy of food in an unequal world. He demonstrates how food and agriculture still hold the key to reducing economic inequality on a world scale. Yet, rural–urban exchange in the poor countries is being stifled by subsidized and more efficient Western food producers. Hart argues that the rhetoric of neo-liberalism masks what are still mercantilist policies on the part of rich and powerful nations. A more just economic order would require a new political framework for world markets, capable of mediating the interests of rich and poor, much as the redistributive policies of the 1930s sought to redress economic inequality at the national level. Anne Murcott's short end piece to the book takes the long view. With selective reference to contributions to the politics of food over the last half century (the earliest example was published in 1941), it provides a sketch of the present collection's distinctive place in the field. Continuities are clearly identifiable. As important, however, are new intellectual approaches and analytic stances notably exemplified in the examination of rhetorics and the discourse of 'riskification'. The epilogue ends by urging readers to pick up on these innovative lines of enquiry to refresh continuities and to renew efforts that open up underresearched topics in the politics of food.

Acknowledgements

Thanks go to Keith Hart and Brigitte Nerlich for their careful comments and constructive criticism.

Notes

1. We do not argue that BSE in the only factor contributing to this awareness – several other food scandals played a part. Nor do we argue that food distrust was caused by the BSE event in a straightforward manner; in the UK such dis-

trust had in fact been 'simmering' for years. What we argue is that the case of BSE was significant, both in bringing about political change and in serving as a model for exposing controversies in media, even in countries that remained uncontaminated by the disease itself. In this way, it represents a case in which, afterward, things were never quite the same.

2. Abstract relations refers both to the distance, socially, culturally and spatially, between production and consumption, and to the processes of abstraction that characterize the ways in which suppliers and consumers are made apparent to each other (through market surveys, sales statistics, and through the emphasis on brand name at the expense of structures of ownership and agency in food production, cf. Lien 1997).

3. This is exemplified by the development of nutritional anthropology as a distinct subfield in the US. In Europe, we find similar developments toward compartmentalization under the heading 'anthropology of food'.

References

Appadurai, A. (1986), 'Introduction', in A. Appadurai (ed.), *The Social Life of Things*, Cambridge: Cambridge University Press.

Archetti, E. (1997 [1986]) *Guinea-Pigs: Food, Symbol and Conflict of Knowledge in Ecuador*, Oxford: Berg.

Beck, U. (1992), *Risk Society: Towards a New Modernity*, London: Sage.

Bourdieu, P. (1979), *Distinction: A Social Critique of the Judgment of Taste*, London: Routledge.

Charles, N. and Kerr, M. (1988), *Women, Food and Families*, Manchester: Manchester University Press.

Connerton, P. (1989), *How Societies Remember*, Cambridge: Cambridge University Press.

Counihan, C. M. (1999), *The Anthropology of Food and Body: Gender, Meaning and Power*, London: Routledge.

Counihan, C. M. and Kaplan, S. L. (eds) (1998), *Food and Gender, Identity and Power*, Amsterdam: Harwood.

Coveney, J. (2000), *Food, Morals and Meaning: The Pleasure and Anxiety of Eating*, London: Routledge.

Csordas, T. (1994), 'Introduction: The Body as Representation and Being-in-the-World', in T. Csordas (ed.), *Embodiment and Experience*, Cambridge: Cambridge University Press.

Douglas, M. (1966), *Purity and Danger*, London: Routledge.

—— (1975), 'Deciphering a Meal', *Implicit Meanings*, London: Routledge.

—— (1984), 'Standard Social Uses of Food: Introduction', in M. Douglas (ed.), *Food in the Social Order*, New York: Russel Sage.

Douglas, M. and Isherwood, B. (1979), *The World of Goods*, London: Routledge.

Eide, A., Eide, W. B., Goonatilake, S., Gussow, J. and Omawale (1984), *Food as a Human Right*, Tokyo: United Nations University.

Eriksen, T. H. (ed.) (2003), *Globalisation: Studies in Anthropology*, London: Pluto.

Evans-Pritchard, E. E. (1940), *The Nuer: A Description of the Modes of Livelihood and Political Institutions of a Nilotic People*, Oxford: Oxford University Press.

Fine, B. and Leopold, E. (1993), *The World of Consumption*, London: Routledge.

Foucault, M. (1991), 'Governmentality', in G. Burchell, C. Gordon and P. Miller (eds), *The Foucault Effect: Studies in Governmentality*, Sydney: Harvester/Wheatsheaf.

Franklin, A. (1999), *Animals and Modern Culture*, London: Sage.

Franklin, S., Lury, C. and Stacey, J. (2000), *Global Nature, Global Culture*, London: Sage.

Giddens, A. (1991), *Modernity and Self-Identity*, Cambridge: Polity.

Gledhill, J. (1994), *Power and its Disguises: Anthropological Perspectives on Politics*, London: Pluto.

Goody, J. (1982), *Cooking, Cuisine and Class*, Cambridge: Cambridge University Press.

Hart, K. (2001), *The Memory Bank: Money in an Unequal World*, New York and London: Texere.

Held, D., McGrew, A., Goldblatt, D. and Perraton, J. (1999), *Global Transformations: Politics, Economics and Culture*, Oxford: Polity.

Jerome, N. W., Kandel, R. F. and Pelto, G. H. (1980), *Nutritional Anthropology: Contemporary Approaches to Diet and Culture*, Pleasantville, NY: Redgrave.

Kjærnes, U. (1993), 'A Sacred Cow: The Case of Milk in Norwegian Nutrition Policy', in U. Kjærnes et al. (eds), *Regulating Markets, Regulating People: On Food and Nutrition Policy*, Oslo: Novus.

Latour, B. (1987), *Science in Action*, Cambridge, MA: Harvard University Press.

—— (1993), *We Have Never been Modern*, New York: Harvester.

Leach, E. (1964), 'Anthropological Aspects of Language: Animal Categories and Verbal Abuse', in E. H. Lenneberg (ed.), *New Directions in the Study of Language*, Cambridge, MA: MIT Press.

Lévi-Strauss, C. (1970), *The Raw and the Cooked: Introduction to a Science of Mythology*, London: Jonathan Cape.

Lien, M. E. (1990), *The Norwegian Nutrition and Food Supply Policy: Accomplishments and Limitations of a Structural Approach*, Working Paper P-90–204. Berlin: Wissenschaftszentrum Berlin für Sozialforschung (WZB).

—— (1995), 'Fuel for the Body – Nourishment for Dreams: Contradictory Roles of Food in Contemporary Norwegian Food Advertising', *Journal of Consumer Policy*, 18: 157–86.

—— (1997), *Marketing and Modernity*, Oxford: Berg.

Lupton, D. (1996), *Food, the Body and the Self*, London: Sage.

Macnaghten, P. and Urry, J. (1998), *Contested Natures*, London: Sage.

Malinowski, B. (1922), *Argonauts of the Western Pacific: An Account of Native Enterprise and Adventure in the Archipelagoes of Melanesian New Guinea*, London: Routledge.

Marsden, T., Flynn, A. and Harrison, M. (2000), *Consuming Interests: The Social Provision of Foods*, London: UCL Press.

Mauss, M. (2002 [1925]), *The Gift: the Form and Reason for Exchange in Archaic Societies*, London: Routledge.

Milton, K. (1996), *Environmentalism and Cultural Theory*, London: Routledge.

Mintz, S. (1985), *Sweetness and Power: The Place of Sugar in Modern History*, New York: Penguin.

Murcott, A. (1982), 'On the Social Significance of the Cooked Dinner in South Wales', *Social Science Information*, 21(4/5): 677–96.

—— (1988), 'Sociological and Social Anthropological Approaches to Food and Eating', *World Review of Nutrition and Dietetics*, 55: 1–40.

Nestle, M. (2002), *Food Politics*, Berkeley: University of California Press.

Pelto, G. H. and Pelto, P. J. (1983), 'Diet and Delocalization: Dietary Changes since 1750', *Journal of Interdisciplinary History*, 14: 507–28.

Petrini, C. (2001), *Slow Food: the Case for Taste*, New York: Columbia University Press.

Poppe, C. and Kjærnes, U. (2003), *Trust in Food in Europe: A Comparative Analysis*, Report No. 5. Lysaker: National Institute for Consumer Research.

Pottier, J. (1999), *Anthropology of Food: The Social Dynamics of Food Security*, Oxford: Polity.

Rappaport, R. A. (1968), *Pigs for the Ancestors: Ritual and Ecology of a New Guinea People*, New Haven: Yale University Press.

Richards, A. (1939), *Land Labour and Diet in the Northern Rhodesia: An Economic Study of the Bemba Tribe*, London: Oxford University Press.

Sobal, J. (1999), 'Food System Globalization, Eating Transformations and Nutrition Transitions', in R. Grew (ed.), *Food in Global History*, Boulder: Westview.

Sutton, D. E. (2001), *Remembrance of Repasts: An Anthropology of Food and Memory*, Oxford: Berg.

Vincent, J. (2002), 'Introduction', in J. Vincent (ed.), *The Anthropology of Politics*, London: Blackwell.

Zwanenberg, P. van and Millstone, E. (2003), 'BSE: A Paradigm of Policy Failure', *Political Quarterly*, 74: 27–38.

Part I
Food, Risk and Blame

Handling Food-related Risks:
Political Agency and Governmentality

Bente Halkier

In the Nordic countries, it has become increasingly popular to call upon the so-called 'ordinary consumer' in order to solve different societal and political problems. Food politics and environmental politics have been particularly prone to this. Public debate and public information services pay a great deal of attention to consumers' handling of different risks connected with foodstuffs. In the Danish media, there are frequent discussions about food and risk, and how they are related to the environment. These discussions revolve, for example, around additives in manufactured goods, pesticide residues in vegetables and fruit, straw-shortening chemicals in wheat and rye,[1] growth hormones in meat, 'mad cow' disease, dioxin in poultry products and genetically modified organisms in beans and corn. Both environmental risks and health risks are mentioned as important factors by a majority of the Danish consumers who buy organic foodstuffs, and this indicates the food-related risks are part of at least some of the Danish consumers' understanding of everyday life – 60 per cent of Danish consumers report that they always or sometimes buy organic dairy products when shopping, and the numbers for vegetables and meat are similar: 60 per cent for vegetables and 40 per cent for meat (Danmarks Statistik 2002).[2]

The issues associated with food-related risk are frequently debated in the public sphere and in political institutions, and there are attempts to manage these issues in terms of instrumental rationality. It is often assumed that if consumers obtain enough of the correct information, they will handle risks properly or participate in implementing solutions to environmental problems by changing their behavior accordingly. However, a number of studies show that consumers relate to issues of food-related risks in ways that are socially and culturally more complex and diverse (see for example Holm and Kildevang 1996; Kjærnes 1999; Sellerberg 1991; Slovic 1992). Handling risks in food consumption has become a part of the ambivalent experience of modern everyday life. More generally, handling risks in food consumption have become an integral part of the ongoing negotiations of social norms. There are crucial differences in how these issues are seen by researchers, politicians and administrators on the one hand, and the public on the other; whereas the first group sees questions of food quality, food safety and food ethics, the second group sees issues that are related to the practical social norms that govern food consumption. Hence, the practices of ordinary food consumers are entangled in the societal politics of food. The apparently most trivial activities of everyday life can be politicized. However, the question is how we can better understand the politicization of risk-handling in the area of food consumption. What kind of political processes are involved when responsibility for helping to solve political problems is explicitly and actively imposed on consumers? This chapter discusses primarily the type of agency involved in ordinary and unorganized consumers' activities in the politicized area of food; such consumer activities are also discussed as simultaneously forming a part of society's ways of governing problems relating to the food sector.

The chapter begins by examining the theoretical links between risk in food consumption, political activity and the political processes of governing. Next, it briefly presents the methods employed and the main results of an empirical study of some Danish consumers' handling of food-related risks. Thirdly, the chapter discusses in what ways the activities of these consumers might constitute political consumer agency and in which ways such activities might express a particular governmentality of food.

Food Consumption, Risk-handling and Politics

Consumption is a particular field of practices within the sociality of everyday life, which combines the satisfaction of needs with expressions of identity (Falk 1994; Gronow 1997; Warde 1997). Consumption not only includes the activities of buying goods and services, but also the social relations connected to the provision, allocation and use of goods and services. Thus, consumption is part of the social space in which people participate by creating and reproducing meanings about the occurrences of everyday life through attempts to knit together the experiences and roles which they encounter on a daily basis (Gullestad 1989; Luckman 1989). Consumers' experiences are the basis of and the result of their practices and interpretations in interaction with or in relation to important others (Berger and Luckmann 1987: 33–48; Goffman 1959: 245; Lave 1988: 178–9; Schütz 1975: 23–41).

Food-consumption practices constitute a particular kind of consumption since food is literally incorporated into the body – or indeed kept out of it (see Lien, this volume). Analysing food consumption thus means dealing with everyday life experiences and with practices that are characterized by the material and sensate experiences of taking things into the body and keeping things out of the body. Symbolically, these processes are linked to interpretations of social belonging and distancing (Falk 1994: 24–7, 134–7). Furthermore, food practices belong to a mundane sphere of consumption and, as such, are characterized by predominantly habitual activities (Warde 1997: 199) and by practices that are remembered by the body and routinely carried out (Hastrup 1995: 182–4).

Risk points to 'the possibility that an undesirable state of reality may occur' (Renn 1992: 56). Thus risk represents something threatening; something that those who feel at risk must handle. In order to understand risk and risk handling, sociologists have made a distinction between risk and danger. Risk refers to people's intentional and systematic ways of dealing with threats and insecurities, whereas people are exposed to danger irrespective of their own choices. Risks are taken, whereas dangers happen to you (Beck 1992: 21). When consumers attempt to tackle environmental risks related to their food, risk-handling becomes immersed in the social experiences of food consumption, and expert definitions and administrative criteria for risk become mixed into people's everyday experiences. Thus, risk-handling becomes part of a set of practices, interpretations and relations that may not have anything to do with risk in the first place, and can include things such as preparing tasteful meals. Risk handling is related to existing interpretations or changes to them. In relation to food, risk handling can, for example, change people's understanding of what 'good' food is. Risks are also used to express social relations, such as how one's family works. Hence, consumers produce their own ways of understanding and handling risks in food consumption (Sellerberg 1991: 196). This might be the reason why many studies that examine public beliefs about different types of risk show that laypersons actually have a fairly broad understanding of risk, one which expresses values and relations of social trust and distrust (Simmons 1997: 253; Slovic 1992: 150; Wynne 1992: 281–3).

When consumers attempt to handle risk-problems in their food consumption, they step into an arena of societal problems that is currently quite politicized, and is characterized by a number of food scandals and conflicts of control and regulation across Europe (Berg 2000; Kjærnes 1999). There are also a number of conflicting discourses about the links between food and politics. Some consumers have constructed ordinary food consumption as a strategy for political activity, referred to as political consumerism or political consumption (Micheletti et al. 2003). In such cases risk-handling can be regarded as a type of political activity, albeit one that is more an individualized, micro-local and solution-oriented type. This may be contrasted to, for example, membership in organizations or grassroots political activism, which are the main types of political activity in Denmark (Goul Andersen et al. 2000).

There are three themes in political sociology that are traditionally debated when assessing whether some type of activity constitutes political activity: agency, community and influence. The theme of agency deals with the capacity of citizens to act (Giddens 1984; Held 1987). The theme of community deals with the degree to which citizens experience a sense of belonging to a collectivity that is related to their actions (Anderson 1983; Eyerman and Jamison 1991; Maffesoli 1996). Finally the theme of influence deals with the ways in which citizens are capable of making a difference to societal problems by their actions (Clegg 1989; Hirschman 1970). These themes will be addressed in the discussions of how consumers' risk-handling in relation to food might be understood as a type of political activity.

As a part of assessing the potential political character of consumers' food activities, it is important to discuss the configurations that such food activities have in relation to larger societal processes. The complexities of risk-handling in food consumption are, however, not just experienced, negotiated and acted upon as part of everyday life. There are societal rules and regulations that govern the environmental, safety and quality issues related to food, and these aim to influence consumers' practices. Such activities can take the form of public information campaigns on risk-handling and campaigns that suggest norms for consumption – such as buying organic foodstuffs, avoiding additives and buying local products.

These types of 'governing problems' which are encountered in society can be understood as what Foucault has labeled governmentality (Foucault 1991). Foucault argues that the ways in which power is exercised in society have changed over time. Earlier forms of governing were based upon absolute demand and the power over subjects by the sovereign ruler. Later, a number of regulating authorities tried to exercise power over their subjects. In modern societies, this control has changed so as to make people monitor and direct their own behavior, bodies and thinking. Hence, governing social and political problems becomes 'the conduct of conduct' (Dean 1999: 10). This type of governing is focused on normalising and disciplining people's bodily practices at a micro-level (Hewitt 1991: 228–30).

Thus, to look at consumers' food activities from the perspective of governmentality is to look at 'how thought operates within our organised ways of doing things, our regimes of practices' (Dean 1999: 17–18). Signs of governmentality in the area of food-related risks can be detected in consumers' attempts to shape their own practices to conform to particular patterns which are regarded as less risky (for example to health and environment). As such, when consumers negotiate the practical social norms that govern risks in food consumption, they actually negotiate the control of their own consumption practices.

In contrast to general values, norms are always bound up with concrete social practices. Norms are expressions of how people engaged in social interaction develop and use mutually accepted regulations of their practices – or regimes of practices. Often, the actual use of norms takes place as a situated negotiation of what it is acceptable to do (Mortensen 1992: 197–8). Norms are no longer (if they ever were) just conventional rules; they are also social and reflexive negotiations of acceptable practices. But negotiations of norms are intimately related to larger discursive repertoires in society, enhanced by the use of mass media (Thompson 1995: 26–37). This is how consumers' norms in handling risk in food consumption can be seen as part and parcel of the operation of particular societal bodies of knowledge and opinion (discursive repertoires) in the management of risk in the food sector.

An Empirical Study of Risk-handling and Food

The empirical work that informs the discussions in this chapter is based on the research project 'The risks of consumption'.[3] This is a qualitative in-depth study of how consumers handle environmentally related[4] risk in food consumption, using parents with small children as a sample of consumers. The data-material consists of analyses of a number of focus-group interviews (Coffey and Atkinson 1996; Morgan 1997; Potter 1996) with Danish parents and their small children. The interview material focuses on food and risk and there is also a textual analysis of public documents that deal with food, risk and the environment.

This chapter focuses on the first part of the data-material. The study, which was carried out in 1999, convened six focus groups with three pairs of parents in each group. The focus-group participants differed in their levels of education as well as within their contexts of living.[5] In this section, I will present some of the main empirical results regarding the systematic variations of consumer practices across the different focus groups. I present these results in a highly condensed form, by constructing a typology of risk-handling. I have chosen this method as it allows the very complex empirical results to be simplified and structured in a way that makes it easier to follow the discussion in the rest of the chapter. The different types of risk-handling are only briefly described, and presented without direct quotes, in order to save this for the discussion of the political dimension of risk-handling in food consumption in the remaining sections.[6] The three types of risk-handling are (1) worried risk-handling, (2) irritated risk-handling and (3) pragmatic risk-handling.

In worried risk-handling, consumers follow the public debate on health and environment closely, and they obtain information about the different matters that they see as problematic. Emotionally, they feel intimidated by the risks discussed in the mass media, and in their homes and their social networks risk in food consumption is a subject of negotiation and conversation. The parents attempt to use foodstuffs that they perceive as less risky – for example, organic products, and bread without straw-shortening chemicals. These are individual or family ways of managing the perception of this sort of risk in daily life. In worried risk-handling, consumers typically see themselves as societal actors that are capable of acting and making a difference through their role as consumers. However, relations of trust and mistrust are divided. Sometimes great confidence is expressed in, for example, declarations of content and the state-controlled organic products labeling scheme. Sometimes mistrust is expressed in public authorities, producers, retailers, experts and the media. In other words, trust is placed in different relations in society, most typically in institutional relations versus social-network relations (Misztal 1995: 101).

In irritated risk-handling, risk is primarily associated with risk communication in the media, campaigns and leaflets, but also risk communication in interpersonal communication. Consumers experience risk communication as a threat to other relations of everyday life – such as personal autonomy, or eating what you feel like eating. This type of risk-handling is divided between the two imperatives of modern commodity cultures: to be liberated from control and to impose self-discipline (Featherstone 1990: 13). Food is enjoyed and is an important part of social relations with others, and as such consumers talk about food in their social networks. The public debate about the environment, risk and foodstuffs is followed from the sidelines. But consumers are frustrated by the ways in which risk communication creates dilemmas in their everyday life, dilemmas to which they often cannot see any solutions. When we analyse the irritated practices, we see that consumers have difficulties in seeing themselves as societal actors through their role as a consumer. A diffuse lack of trust is expressed in the accumulated amount of risk-knowledge in society, rather than simply expressing mistrust in particular actors and institutions. Irritated risk-handling can be expressed in various ways. The issue of risk can be dismissed most of the time. Or, for example, one week the risks related to food and shopping are dismissed, and people may cook and eat what they want to. In the next week the media, family or friends may remind consumers about risk, and they might, tentatively, change their practices to something that is perceived as less risky for a short while.

In pragmatic risk-handling, risk is understood as a daily life-problem along the lines of all other daily problems. Consumers don't necessarily think about environmentally related risks in consumption, unless there is a television program (for example) about something that they regard as such a risk. Food in general is not something that is necessarily talked about, food is simply something to make and eat together. Hence risk is – potentially – a problem with which one must have a 'sensible relationship' in a busy everyday life. Within pragmatic risk-handling, parents do not emphasize their involvement in risk issues at the expense of other priorities in their daily family lives. Neither, however, do they neglect risk, when they perceive it as important, for example in relation to the health of their children. They place their trust in risk-handling either with public authorities or with people they know personally. Either way, pragmatic risk-handling requires the establishing of practical routines that allow the parents avoid reflecting too much upon it or becoming too involved emotionally (Ilmonen 2001: 13–14). There is more emphasis placed upon making daily life function in a satisfactory fashion than upon trying to influence society via their role as consumers.

The Politics of Risk in Food Consumption

This section discusses food-related risk-handling in relation to political activity and to governmentality. In addition to examining these empirical patterns of risk-handling, it also deals with social norms that govern Danish consumers' behavior in relation to food. It will focus on the three aforementioned dimensions of citizens' political action: agency, community and influence. I will discuss governmentality as it is particularly related to agency and influence.

Agency

The degree of agency involved in people's everyday life practices suggests something about whether and in what ways citizens can be seen to be engaged in political activity. Hence, the concept of agency separates active and socially directed actions from all other actions. In principle, everything that people in society do every day can create consequences for each other and for overall social dynamics. In this sense, we are all actors all of the time. But most of us do not drive in our car to work in order to aggravate the CO_2 problem. Neither do most of us buy conventionally produced fruit in order to support the use of pesticides. Most of our actions have unintended consequences (Giddens 1984: 27) on an aggregated, and hence political, level. Thus, one important conceptual element of agency is intentionality: do citizens carry out particular actions with the intent to achieve certain consequences? Another important element of agency has to do with the conditions for action; are they structured in such a way that makes them more likely to be carried out? This other part of agency is often discussed under the heading of autonomy in relation to political activity (Held 1987: 290–1): do citizens have resources and the space for action to carry out their actions with intended consequences?

When we look at the three ways of handling food-related risks, there seems to be a number of central patterns that are relevant to questions of agency. Worried risk-handling implies intentionality with a shifting experience of autonomy. In pragmatic risk-handling, a relative degree of autonomy is experienced, but without much intentionality of practice. In irritated risk-handling, consumption practices are not experienced as autonomous actions.

In worried risk-handling, consumers intentionally choose particular consumption practices which they see as being less risky to health or the environment. Examples include buying organic foodstuffs of all sorts, buying Danish fruit, using goods with as few additives as possible, and a number of other specific choices. This attitude is expressed in the following quote from one of the women:

> I don't know ... you know, I think I have a tendency to have ideological taste buds ...
> someone once told me ... [*laughter*] ... I simply BELIEVE that organic tomatoes taste
> better than the traditional ones ... so if they have something organic for sale ... in the
> shop today ... you know, if they for example have organic cauliflower, that can make
> me feel like eating cauliflower soup. I don't feel like it all winter, because ... I don't
> know, I AM quite selective, because you know ... I just pass by the vegetable shelves
> cause never mind about the traditional ones, it's about organic things, right ... now they
> had cucumbers, right, so we are going to get tzattiki this week ... so I go after the
> organic label a lot in this manner ... then now and then we get a tin of non-organic
> sausages and guilty consciences.

When the parents express worried risk-handling, they tend to underline consumption practices as existing within a space where ordinary people can take an active stance. In that sense, they express confidence in consumption as a type of agency in society which involves the autonomy to act. This is well illustrated in another quote from one of the women interviewed:

> But ... all right, I do believe that you can do something by talking about it, you know
> ... in your workplace or what you do ... even though it is ... small things, you can do
> something in that way ... get your own vegetable garden.

In pragmatic risk-handling, food-consumption practices are mainly embedded in routines, which are rarely reflected upon and not necessarily explicitly discussed within the social network – this is different from worried risk-handling. Routine practices draw upon tacit knowledge, and are often remembered semi-consciously or by the body. Thus, it is very difficult to assess the degree of intentionality involved in such practices, other than by examining the rationalizations that informants make of their practices in discussions with each other. Here is an account of one of the women:

> I think about such things as fruit and the like, you can't assess when they say that it's
> not sprayed, but I don't believe very much in that, you know. I think it's sprayed in some
> degree all of it, you know. But really, you can't do anything else than, then you have to
> buy it and wash it and ... eat it.

In irritated risk-handling, food-consumption practices are experienced as embedded in a web of everyday dilemmas, related to different structural conditions for choosing between alternatives. This typically results in an understanding of the ordinary consumer as possessing only a quite weak type of agency in society, a perception which is illustrated by a quote from one of the men:

> But I am also tired of the way that . . . something is being taken up, right, and then I actually sit and get worked up about it and say that it's too bad . . . but my possibilities for doing ANYTHING AT ALL about it are not really there, hng? You know . . . the fish doesn't improve because they make such a television show, does it? I have just got yet another problem thrown in my face, right?

From another point of view, the various ways of handling food-related risks can also be seen as signs of social steering via the consumers' self-discipline and social control. Across the three types of risk-handling, a number of social norms and norm-negotiations for handling food risks are expressed in the narratives that circulate in the network groups of interviewed consumers.[7] Such norms and negotiations construct the mutually accepted regulations of what it is acceptable and unacceptable to do (Mortensen 1992: 197). Looking at the ways in which consumers negotiate the norms for handling food-related risks from the perspective of governmentality (Foucault 1991), we can argue that consumers negotiate the different ways of applying a risk-oriented discipline to their food practices. Rationalizing food-consumption practices, for the purpose of limiting risk, can be regarded as part of self-discipline and social control. In the empirical material, we can see both norms and negotiations that endorse such rationalizations, as well as norms and negotiations that react against the rationalizing of everyday life. The empirical examples cover both expressions of convention ('one ought to do this or that') and expressions of reflexive norm-negotiation or drafts for norms ('could we do this or that?'). The sociology of norms acknowledges that a sense of norms is not just bound by rules and conventions, but consists also of normative reflections and situationally bound negotiations of how normative choices should be understood and regulated socially (Garfinkel 1967; Mortensen 1992).

Some examples of where the rationalization of norms and norm-negotiations seems to be accepted as a part of regulating satisfactory behavior toward risk-handling includes the following:

1. Can we trust the information about the food we buy?
2. You should not eat food that seems too artificial.
3. Should we trust organic foodstuffs?
4. You should buy foodstuffs with as few additives as possible.
5. How can we as consumers evaluate individual foodstuffs?

It seems to be taken for granted that consumers need expert knowledge and administrative criteria to help regulate their food practices in order to usefully handle the risks of consumption.

Examples of norms and negotiations that express a reaction against the rationalization of food practices include the following:

1. Daily prioritizing hinders environmental consideration.
2. It's okay that our practices in relation to the environment are shifting, because there are good reasons for this.
3. Keep you fear of impurity in check.

What seems to be taken for granted here is that everyday life carries burdens and responsibilities, and includes things other than worries about food-related risks. Thus, it does not make sense to attempt overly to rationalize such practices and social relations.

Turning back to the different types of risk-handling, worried risk-handling may not merely express a consumer's intentionality or attempts at autonomous activism regarding the politics of food. It may also form part of the processes from which certain kinds of power and societal order emerge in the area of food and risk. Likewise, irritated risk-handling may not only express consumers' experiences of their lack of autonomy when particular risk-handling practices are rejected. It may also be regarded as a kind of resistance against the overrationalization and social control of one's own personal and intimate food practices.

Community

In relation to political activity, community traditionally means that politicized practices take place together with others in a group of people (however this group is defined) (Eyerman and Jamison 1991; Melucci 1989), be it as part of concrete organization or movement or an imagined community (Anderson 1983). One of the reasons that political consumption and politicized consumption choices are seen as problematic as a type of political activity is exactly that they seem to be so individualized, taking place in the intimate sphere and the market place (Gabriel and Lang 1995; Micheletti et al., 2003).

The parents interviewed for this study referred to 'community' in this sense. This was especially the case for worried risk-handlers, but it was also true for pragmatic risk-handlers. These consumers seem to feel associated with a diffuse and imagined community of consumers who handle food risks similarly in their daily lives. This imagined community of active co-consumers helps them to understand their own individual practices as useful or meaningful in relation to improving the conditions for food safety and quality or for environmental considerations. This can be illustrated by the use of an inclusive 'we' by one of the men participating in the focus group:

> It's obvious to see what is happening in American farming at the moment, how incredibly many American farmers who have restructured their production to genetically modified products . . . and now they have found out that the consumers don't want it . . . and now they try to change production back again, cause it's not profitable for them . . . to produce genetically modified crops, and that's clearly the pressure from consumers who

boycott the products. And I think that this is the strongest weapon we have got, it's simply to boycott things that we say, that we won't touch.

Worried risk-handlers usually make references to other people that they know personally who also choose particular consumption practices or uphold particular routines, such as buying organic goods. These are people from their social network, with whom the more worried parents also discuss some of the dilemmas of acting as a conscious consumer. In this sense, the community around the risk-management practices is not only imagined but also concrete.

These kinds of reference to imagined or concrete community are far more rare among the irritated risk-handlers. Here, parents find it difficult to understand themselves as food consumers who can act together with other consumers. One of the men said:

> Yes maybe exactly because there is so much, that no matter what the hell you do, no matter WHAT you buy, it is infested with some sort of risk of one thing or another. Maybe something is added, maybe it's sprayed, growth hormone is added, you can't see through it anyway.

The relation between 'community' and 'food-related risk-handling' is too complex to discuss fully in this short space. However, the empirical results from the focus-groups study seems to indicate a mixture of patterns, just as in the case of the relation between food practices and 'agency'. Consumers don't necessarily understand their practices as part of a community of co-consumers, be that a concrete or an imagined one.

Influence

In order to discuss the degree of political influence that risk-handling consumers might achieve, it is necessary to discuss the different types of influence they can exert in their role as consumers. The ordinary consumer strategy for influencing society works directly via two dynamics. An 'exit' dynamic (Hirschman 1970), which can have influence on a globalized food market, and a highly localized 'voice' dynamic which is integrated in the social networks of consumers. When the influence of ordinary consumers is discussed and assessed, the focus is usually on the exit dynamics, or how consumers can influence market mechanisms by moving their purchasing power around. However, precisely because consumption is *not* merely reducible to the purchasing act, but also includes the different social and symbolic uses of food in everyday life (Warde 1997), it is important to study the local-voice dynamics as well.

Based on the empirical findings of this study one can establish certain relations between the types of risk-handling and the types of influence that consumers can exert. They form relatively obvious patterns: worried risk-handlers use both exit dynamics and local-voice dynamics, since particular goods are bought intentionally to fight food risks. Food risks are also something that is discussed in the families and in the social networks. Pragmatic risk-handlers use exit dynamics but not local-voice dynamics, since particular goods are bought and particular cooking habits are established to fight food risks, but in routine and tacit ways. Irritated risk-handlers do not necessarily use exit voice dynamics, and the use of the local-voice dynamic wavers.

When parents as consumers attempt to influence food safety, food quality and environmental solutions via exit dynamics, the market opens up a space for fast and easy action where people are already present. They don't have to become a member of an organization or devote time to meetings, and they can influence concrete solutions in society directly by supporting or boycotting instead of going the long way around through representative political institutions. This pattern of influence seems at least partly responsible for the growth of the organic market in Denmark (Michelsen et al. 2001). Furthermore, a recent Danish survey shows, for example, that for milk, vegetables and meat/poultry, organic products are considered to be the safest or second safest type of product bought by consumers concerned about food safety (Halkier and Holm, in print).

On the other hand, the only signals sent via the exit dynamics are responses to retailers and producers that there is a demand for specific goods. This results in diffuse political signals for 'less foreign fruit', for example, whereas consumers do not participate in a public debate about what the content of the alternatives should or could be. They are crucially dependent upon what producers supply (Keat 1994: 27–30), and in many cases such alternatives do not exist. Furthermore, the demands and activities of ordinary consumers remain scattered and unorganized. Hence, they remain invisible to a public sphere dominated by the mass media, to NGOs (non-governmental organizations) and to the political system. This makes it difficult for consumers' demands to reach societal or political agendas and to influence food policy and food regulations – unless, that is, consumers can establish alliances with organized political actors in order to highlight their activities and demands. This means that trying to exert influence via the market is not always very successful.

The other dynamics that ordinary consumers can use to exert influence are the voice dynamics in social networks where decisions about purchases are discussed, where uses of particular foodstuffs are identified as elements of a lifestyle, and where norms are negotiated. This dynamic is a more long-term one that does not necessarily influence short-term policy-making, but rather influences the social and cultural norms and the political legitimacy of different solutions in the areas of food and environmental policies. When consumers handle food risks and talk about it with each other in their everyday lives, they participate in the formation of political experiences related to the political conflicts in the policy areas about (for example) which actors and institutions should be responsible for different problems and solutions. Such formations of political experience can be seen as part of the normal procedures of a democratic public sphere (Kaare Nielsen 1991).

In other words, the social-network voice dynamic relates to the larger debates about supplementing the traditional 'governmental' understanding of political processes, where politics is seen as something that takes place in the political system and between parliamentary assemblies, administrative institutions and political interest organizations. The traditional understanding of politics should be supplemented by a 'governance' understanding (Bang et al. 1997). Here politics is seen as sets of processes taking place on all levels of society, including those operating in the everyday lives of citizens, building on (among other things) a Foucauldian concept of power as constructive and transformative (Clegg 1989: 153–9).

This brings the discussion back to governmentality. When consumers negotiate food-related risks and negotiate norms relating to food risk and food consumption, using a micro-local voice dynamic of influence, they reproduce, legitimize and reject particular repertoires of thinking about handling food-risks in their own regimes of practices. But one should not assume that consumers are simply oppressed by the dominant dynamics that govern the food area. Consumers also express their subjectivity and agency in worried risk-handling and risk-rationalized norms as well as in irritated and pragmatic risk-handling and anti-rationalizing norms. The social order is not inflicted upon consumers; they themselves participate in establishing, reproducing and perhaps challenging this order by drawing upon and contributing to larger discursive repertoires in society (Dean 1999: 12–13).

This can be seen in all of the earlier examples concerning norms and norm negotiations. For example the norm 'You should buy foodstuffs with as few additives as possible' constructs a subjectivity, a position of agency in which consumers know what to do if they want to participate in minimizing this food-risk for themselves as well as for society. The attempts to use foodstuffs with fewer additives can be interpreted as both a political activity on the level of the individual consumer who is trying to influence the politics of food, and at the same time as part of a larger governmental strategy regarding the politics of food.

Conclusion

Ordinary consumers are frequently called upon in modern society to solve different political and societal problems. In Denmark, this is especially true for the handling of food-related risks. In the public sphere, issues of environmentally related risk in food consumption are often debated, and attempts are made to manage them in terms of instrumental rationality. But consumers relate to risk issues in ways that are socially and culturally more complex and diverse, because food consumption is a part of modern everyday life in all its complexity. Hence, public discourses and regulations of risk attempt to order the complexities of consumption in order to govern political problems of food, such as quality, health risks, environmental risks and the like. This takes place via suggesting norms for consumers to discipline their food practices as 'the conduct of conduct' (Dean, 1999: 10). When consumers practically and discursively handle food-related risks in their daily lives and become entangled within the politics of food, they are potentially both carrying out political activities and creating political regulation in this domain.

What kind of political agency is society dealing with when ordinary consumers have ascribed to them political responsibility in their capacities as consumers? Using the Danish example of consumers' food-related risk-handling as an instance of politicized consumption, a mixed picture seems to emerge that clusters around each of the three themes of political activity discussed above: agency, community and influence. Risk-handling can be but is not necessarily intentional, and it varies drastically depending on whether consumers experience themselves as having sufficient autonomy to act in society. Some consumers interpret their risk-handling practices as part of a community of co-consumers acting together, whether concrete or imagined, but others do not necessarily experience their practices in this way. Finally, although ordinary consumer strategies might be limited in their ability to exert a direct influence on the substance of policy-making, they might at the same time have a stronger indirect influence on social and cultural norms.

Precisely because consumers' handling of food-related risks implies negotiation and the use (or rejection) of social and cultural norms, such practices can also be regarded as entailing risk-oriented self-discipline and social control. Such self-discipline and social control in food practices can be seen as constituting the backbone of a guiding political rationality in modern society, labeled governmentality. Thus, in the various ways of handling the risks connected to food, consumers do not simply use food consumption as a strategy for political activity; consumers also form a part of a particular governmentality of risk-management in the areas of society related to food.

Notes

1. Straw-shortening chemicals are used in the growth period for wheat and rye in order to keep the straws shorter to allow for larger and heavier growth of the grain without the wheat or rye falling to the ground. In Denmark, the use of such chemical substances applied directly to crops and used for very basic foodstuffs caused controversy in the 1990s. Several producers of bread –

conventional as well as organic – supply bread labeled 'not produced with straw shorteners'.

2. Denmark has a state-controlled labeling scheme for organic products, and there are an increasing number of food products that are less damaging to the environment available in the retail sector.
3. The study is called 'The Risks of Consumption: Environmental Norms and Consumer Practices', and it is financed by The Strategic Programme for Environmental Research in Denmark. The study was carried out at the Center for Social Scientific Environmental Research in Denmark (CeSam).
4. By environmentally related food risks I mean risks where environmental effects are part of what is considered problematic. Thus, such food risks are not only about the health effects for an individual, but also about the problems for larger portions of the eco-system. A good example concerns pesticide residues in fruit. In Danish food regulation, there are limit values for the content of such residues in order to protect the health of individual consumers. At the same time, the use of pesticides in modern farming is considered an environmental problem. Furthermore, when consumers talk about such food risks, collective environmental and individual health considerations are often intermingled with each other. Hence, the empirical data-material covers a broader range of food risks, but has evolved around environmentally related food risks.
5. The study has exchanged focus-group interview guides with a Norwegian research project on consumer trust and distrust, headed by Unni Kjærnes, SIFO, Oslo (Nygård 1999).
6. More detailed accounts can be found in Halkier 2001a and 2001b.
7. The norms and norm-negotiations were interpreted by means of techniques in conversation analysis (Antaki 1994), discourse psychology (Potter 1996) and a three-fold concept of normativity (Mortensen 1992).

References

Anderson, B. (1983), *Imagined Communities*, London: Verso.

Antaki, C. (1994), *Explaining and Arguing: The Social Organization of Accounts*, London: Sage.

Bang, H., Dyrberg, T. B. and Hansen, A. D. (1997), 'Elite eller Folkestyre: Demokrati fra Oven og/eller Neden?' [Elite or populism: Democracy from above and/or below], *Grus*, No. 51.

Beck, U. (1992), *Risk Society*, London: Sage.

Berg, L. (2000), *Trust in Food in Europe*. Working Paper no. 17. SIFO [The State Institute for Consumer Research], Oslo.

Berger, P. and Lockmann, T. (1987), *The Social Construction of Reality*, Harmondsworth: Penguin Books.

Clegg, S. R. (1989), *Frameworks of Power*, London: Sage.

Coffey, A. and Atkinson, P. (1996), *Making Sense of Qualitative Data: Complementary Research Strategies*, London: Sage.

Danmarks Statistik (2002), *Nyt fra Danmarks Statistik: Familiernes Miljøvaner* [News from Denmark's Statistics: Environmental Habits of Families]. No. 379. Copenhagen.

Dean, M. (1999), *Governmentality: Power and Rule in Modern Society*, London: Sage.

Eyerman, R. and Jamison, A. (1991), *Social Movements: A Cognitive Approach*, Cambridge: Polity.

Falk, P. (1994), *The Consuming Body*, London: Sage.

Featherstone, M. (1990), 'Perspectives on Consumer Culture', *Sociology*, 24: 5–22.

Foucault, M. (1978), *The History of Sexuality*, Volume 1, Harmondsworth: Penguin.

—— (1991), 'Governmentality'. In G. Burchell, C. Gordon and P. Miller (eds), *The Foucault Effect: Studies in Governmentality with Two Lectures by and an Interview with Michel Foucault*, Chicago: Chicago University Press.

Gabriel, Y. and Lang, T. (1995), *The Unmanageable Consumer: Contemporary Consumption and its Fragmentations*, London: Sage.

Garfinkel, H. (1967), *Studies in Ethnomethodology*, Engelwood Cliffs NJ: Prentice Hall.

Giddens, A. (1984), *The Constitution of Society*, Cambridge: Polity.

Goffman, E. (1959), *The Presentation of Self in Everyday Life*, New York: Anchor Books.

Goul Andersen, J., Torpe, L. and Andersen, J. (2000), *Hvad Folket Magter: Demokrati, Magt og Afmagt* [What the People are capable of: Democracy, power and powerlessness], Copenhagen: Jurist – og Økonomforbundets Forlag.

Gronow, J. (1997), *The Sociology of Taste*, London: Routledge.

Gullestad, M. (1989), *Kultur og Hverdagsliv* [Culture and Everyday Life], Oslo: Universitetsforlaget.

Halkier, B. (2001a), 'Consuming Ambivalences: Consumer Handling of Environmentally Related Risks in Food', *Journal of Consumer Culture*, 1: 205–24.

—— (2001b), 'Risk and Food: Environmental Concerns and Consumer Practices', *International Journal of Food Science and Technology*, 36: 801–12.

—— and Holm, L. (in print), 'Tillid til Mad: Forbrug mellem Dagligdag og Politisering' [Trust in Food: Consumption between Everyday and Politicization], *Dansk Sociologi*.

Hastrup, K. (1995), 'The Inarticulate Mind: The Place of Awareness in Social Action', in A. P. Cohen and N. Rapport (eds), *Questions of Consciousness*, London: Routledge.

Held, D. (1987), *Models of Democracy*, Cambridge: Polity.

Hewitt, M. (1991), 'Bio-politics and Social Policy: Foucault's Account of Welfare', in M. Featherstone et al. (eds), *The Body: Social Processes and Cultural Theory*, London: Sage.

Hirschman, A. O. (1970), *Exit, Voice and Loyalty*, Cambridge, MA: Harvard University Press.

Holm, L. and Kildevang, H. (1996), 'Consumers' Views on Food Quality: A Qualitative Interview Study', *Appetite*, 27: 1–14.

Ilmonen, K. (2001), 'Consumption and Routine', in J. Gronow and A. Warde (eds), *Ordinary Consumption*, London: Routledge.

Kaare Nielsen, H. (1991), *Demokrati i Bevægelse* [Democracy in Movement], Århus: Århus Universitetsforlag.

Keat, R. (1994), 'Scepticism, Authority and the Market', in R. Keat et al. (eds), *The Authority of the Consumer*, London: Routledge.

Kjærnes, U. (1999), 'Food Risks and Trust Relations', *Sosiologisk Tidsskrift*, 7: 265–84.

Lave, J. (1988), *Cognition in Practice*, Cambridge: Cambridge University Press.

Luckmann, T. (1989), 'On Meaning in Everyday Life and in Sociology', *Current Sociology*, 37: 17–30.

Maffesoli, M. (1996), *The Time of the Tribes: The Decline of Individualism in Mass Society*, London: Sage.

Melucci, A. (1989), *Nomads of the Present*, London: Hutchinson Radius.

Micheletti, M., Follesdal, A. and Stolle, D. (2003), *The Politics behind Products: Using the Market as a Site for Ethics and Action*, Piscataway NJ: Transaction.

Michelsen, J., Lyngaard, K., Padel, S. and Foster, C. (2001), 'Organic Farming Development and Agricultural Institutions in Europe: A Study of Six Countries', *Economics and Policy*, 9.

Misztal, B. (1995), *Trust in Modern Societies: The Search for the Bases of Social Order*, Cambridge: Polity.

Morgan, D. L. (1997), *Focus Groups as Qualitative Research*, London: Sage.

Mortensen, N. (1992), 'Future Norms', in P. Gundelach and K. Siune (eds), *From Voters to Participants*, Århus: Politica.

Potter, J. (1996), *Representing Reality: Discourse, Rhetoric and Social Construction*, London: Sage.

Renn, O. (1992), 'Concepts of Risk: A Classification', in S. Krimsky and D. Golding (eds), *Social Theories of Risk*, Westport: Praeger.

Schütz, A. (1975), *Hverdagslivets Sociologi* [*The Sociology of Everyday Life*], Copenhagen: Hans Reitzel.

Sellerberg, A. (1991), 'In Food We Trust? Vitally Necessary Confidence – and Unfamiliar Ways of Attaining it', in E. Fürst et al. (eds), *Palatable Worlds: Sociocultural Food Studies*, Oslo: Solum.

Simmons, P. (1997), 'The Construction of Environmental Risks: Eco-Labelling in the European Union', in P. Sulkunen et al. (eds), *Constructing the New Consumer Society*, London: Macmillan.

Slovic, P. (1992), 'Perception of Risk: Reflections on the Psychometric Paradigm', in S. Krimsky and D. Golding (eds), *Social Theories of Risk*, Westport: Praeger.

Thompson, J.B. (1995), The Media and Modernity: A social theory of the Media, Cambridge: Polity Press.

Warde, A. (1997), *Consumption, Food and Taste*, London: Sage.

Wynne, B. (1992), 'Risk and Social Learning: Reification to Engagement', in S. Krimsky and D. Golding (eds), *Social Theories of Risk*, Westport: Praeger.

—3—

Risk, Blame and Culture: Foot and Mouth Disease and the Debate about Cheap Food

Brigitte Nerlich

Introduction

Foot-and-mouth, like BSE and salmonella, swine fever and the GM food debate, reproduces once again the sensation that the food chain is currently a scene of crisis and confusion. This strikes home because food is a commodity we consume not only as purchasers, but as eaters: this is about breakfast, lunch and dinner. The politics comes to us on a plate.

Franklin, 'Sheepwatching'

In 2001 Britain suffered the worst epidemic of foot and mouth disease (FMD) in its history. The first case was confirmed in pigs in an abattoir in Essex on 20 February 2001.[1] The possible source of the infection was traced to a small pig unit in Northumberland, Burnside Farm, where it is thought that the disease was introduced at the beginning of February through the use of waste meat products, probably illegally imported airline food (cheap food), mixed into pigswill. From then onward the disease spread quickly throughout the UK. The Ministry of Agriculture, Fisheries and Food (MAFF) (now Department for Environment, Food and Rural Affairs, DEFRA) made efforts to trace the spread of the disease and eliminate it, applying the traditional methods of slaughter and livestock-movement restrictions (see Woods 2002). By the end of March 2001, however, FMD cases were still on the increase. The Prime Minister, Tony Blair, postponed a general election, the countryside was closed down to stop the spread of the virus, and tourism suffered as the public stayed away. By the end of September the epidemic had abated and in January 2002 the UK regained disease-free status. During the epidemic approximately 8 million animals were killed and disposed of on massive funeral pyres and in huge burial sites. The purely financial cost of this epidemic for British farming, tourism and industry as a whole is estimated to exceed £15 billion (see Blake et al. 2002); the human cost cannot really be calculated.

Throughout the height of the epidemic the media asked consistently whether this tragedy was to some extent the cost of a so-called 'cheap food' policy. The argument went that pressure for the production of cheap food, or, as one commentator later called it, 'the insatiable and unsentimental search of world markets for cheaper and safer food' (Thomson 2002), was a factor in many negative developments, including intensive industrial farming and the emergence and spread of animal diseases, such as FMD.

One of the most striking findings that will emerge from the analysis of a corpus of newspaper articles reporting on FMD and commenting on the causes for the disease and its spread is how quickly and consistently the whole FMD debate enrolled the issue of 'cheap food', explicitly blaming the move toward efficiency in the entire food chain for the outbreak of FMD and implicitly blaming the individual consumer for initiating a chain of (food) events that lead to FMD. This was in spite of the fact that most cases of FMD occurred in rurally deprived areas in the northeast and southwest of the country (such as Cumbria, Northumberland and Devon) and on smaller farms, not in places where the symptoms of industrialized farming would be expected to be felt, such as the East Midlands for example, where only two cases were reported.

Even though long-distance animal movements in a globalized marketplace may have played an important role in spreading the disease more quickly,[2] and even though the virus may have entered the country through imported (cheap) meat, this mismatch between alleged 'causes' and observed 'symptoms' was puzzling and needed to be investigated further. The questions I wanted to answer in this chapter therefore were: why was 'cheap food' so consistently considered to be the probable source of the disease, why was it regarded as the major causal or risk factor for the origin of FMD, and why did practically all commentators agree to construct the problem in this way?[3]

To answer these questions, I will examine in some detail the main arguments in the 'cheap-food' debate as it unrolled chronologically on the pages of the *Guardian*. The corpus studied is small, consisting of only eight articles published between 21 February and 17 March 2001 (covering a period from the beginning of the FMD outbreak until its peak), which dealt prominently with the cheap-food issue, but they provide enough food for thought and mirrored many arguments and debates played out in other media.[4] I also searched websites during the first two months of the outbreak so as to get a better picture of the wider debate these articles stimulated among politicians, policy-makers and NGOs.

Although broadsheet articles (especially those published in the *Guardian* with its green, anti-big-business and anti-Blair agenda) do not reflect the perceptions of

Table 3.1 Collocations and argumentative structures

(Focus of food and farming debate)		
the big issue is going to be	CHEAP FOOD	
whole notion of	CHEAP FOOD	
concept of	CHEAP FOOD	
in the name of	CHEAP FOOD	
the myth of	CHEAP FOOD	
the mantra of	CHEAP FOOD	
the chimera of	CHEAP FOOD	
(On the one hand)		
we prefer	CHEAP FOOD	
we like	CHEAP FOOD	
we are seduced by the delight of	CHEAP FOOD	
we enjoy	CHEAP FOOD	
we love	CHEAP FOOD	
	CHEAP FOOD	at all costs
abundance of	CHEAP FOOD	
(We therefore have)		
policy of	CHEAP FOOD	*whatever the cost*
sacrifices on the alter of	CHEAP FOOD	
(On the other hand we should think of)		
realistic price of	CHEAP FOOD	
true cost of	CHEAP FOOD	
real price of	CHEAP FOOD	
real cost of	CHEAP FOOD	
what price	CHEAP FOOD	
hidden costs of	CHEAP FOOD	
added costs of	CHEAP FOOD	
	CHEAP FOOD	is expensive
(therefore)		
	CHEAP FOOD	*looks less and less like a good deal*
(but)		
	CHEAP FOOD	is here to stay
(Central problem)		
how to provide good	CHEAP FOOD	

Collocations collected from *Guardian* articles, published between 21 February 2001 and 17 March 2001 and websites dealing with the cheap food issue during the same time (website items are marked by italics) – the height of the FMD crisis.

the entire UK population, I assumed that I would find a variety of perspectives from which the issue of cheap food would be debated, principally because 'cheap food' or 'quantity food' is a contested concept that is inherently complex, vague and difficult to define, just as its counterpart 'quality food' (see Morris and Young 2000).

There was, however, a surprising absence of dissenting voices among journalists, politicians, organic farmers, vegetarian organizations, vets and left-wing organizations, who all seemed to agree on the fact that cheap food was the root of all evil in farming and health. This consensus was summed up neatly in the repeatedly asked question: 'What price cheap food?' (see Green Party 2001; What Price Cheap Food? 2002; Environment Observer 2001; Vetstream 2001; The real cost of cheap food?', Trewin 2001a). This rhetorically loaded question will be studied in the framework of its semantic collocations and in the argumentative contexts in which it was used (see summary in Table 3.1). It should be stressed from the outset that the question implies a contrast between (open) cheapness and (hidden) cost that invites further, mainly negative, inferences and comparisons, which are mostly in line with an anti-capitalist and green agenda.

What Price Cheap Food?

A day after the first case of FMD had been announced, on 21 February, Derek Brown reported in the *Guardian* that 'Digby Scott, commenting today on the estimable national pig association website, puts down the FMD outbreak to "supermarket greed and the drive for globalisation *at all costs* [which] has turned this country into *a cesspit for the world's cheapest meat and meat products*"' (Brown 2001, italics added). This reflects a typical self-image of the British as obsessed with buying cheap food at all costs, an issue to which I will return in my more detailed analysis of the cheap food debate in the next section. After this opening shot, the issues of globalization, intensification of agriculture, especially after the Second World War and the introduction of the so-called 'cheap-food policy', and the role of supermarkets were discussed again and again by journalists and also by politicians, such as the UK Prime Minister, Tony Blair, with the issue of cheap food as an important argumentative anchor point.

On 25 February Matthew Fort, the food editor for the *Guardian*, wrote a first article using the phrase 'cheap food' in a headline for the *Observer* that reverberated in various cognate forms through the whole cheap-food debate: 'Paying the price for cheaper food' (Fort 2001a).[5] This resonated with images of FMD as a plague visited on the UK as a price we had to pay for our craving for cheap food, our mismanagement of the countryside, our overindulgence and greed, or, as George Monbiot, professor of politics, *Guardian* columnist and author of *Captive State* (Monbiot 2000), wrote in his seminal article, published on 27 February:

'These practices [intensive farming], we are told, permit us all to enjoy cheap food. In truth, they merely force us to *pay by other means*, such as disease eradication programmes. The thousands of animals being burnt today are being *sacrificed on the altar of supermarket profits*' (Monbiot 2001, italics added).[6] Sin and sacrifice became themes that were taken up again in later contributions to the debate, adding religious and ritualistic overtones to the discussion of FMD and cheap food.

The 'paying the price' cliché, used in Fort's headline, became the stereotypical hook onto which many standard arguments against cheap food and about the hidden costs of cheap food were attached throughout the FMD outbreak. But Fort not only used clichés such as *paying the price* and *counting the true cost* skillfully, he also captured the nation's mood in a rhetorical nutshell. Using repetition, a major rhetorical strategy for producing emphasis, clarity, amplification, or emotional effect, he wrote:

> *Once again* British farming is in a state of shock. *Once again* consumers are in a state of bewilderment. *Once again* consumers are being asked *to pay the price for* a system of agriculture and food production which, time after time, has shown itself to be deeply flawed.
>
> We have had, and continue to have, listeria, salmonella, BSE, E. coli, swine fever and infectious anaemia in farmed salmon. We now have foot-and-mouth for the first time since 1981. And yet the root cause of each of these disasters is the same: *the policy that we must produce as much food as we can, as cheaply as we can.*
>
> So ingrained has the *concept of cheap food* become that it seems impossible now to eradicate it from the political process, institutional planning and the public mind. Yet no one seems to stop *to count the true cost of 'cheap food'.* (Fort 2001a, italics added)

During the whole of the cheap-food debate, UK consumers were either accused of triggering the farming crisis by demanding cheap food, or warned that they were paying directly or indirectly for a policy of cheap food, or they were exhorted to change their attitude toward cheap food, or else they were advised that if they wanted to live healthy, ethical and environmentally friendly lives they would have to pay more for their (organic) food. The farmers were generally portrayed as the victims of the cheap-food policy or its perpetrators. The supermarkets were stereotypically depicted as evil, money-grabbing and greedy, giving a 'bad deal' to farmers and consumers alike. The fate of the animals in all this was rarely discussed.

As already mentioned, Monbiot published his widely cited article 'Disease and Modernity' two days after Fort's article (a title that echoes Ulrich Beck's seminal book *Risk Society: Towards a New Modernity*, Beck 1992). Like Fort, Monbiot employed well-established rhetorical devices, such as repetition, contrast, and personification to hit the message home about what is, in his view, wrong with British food and agriculture:

Foot and mouth is an ancient disease which thrives on modernity. It loves the black holes into which farm animals are crammed, and the debilitated condition in which they stagger through their miserable lives [probable cause of FMD, BN]. But even more than that, *it loves* the long-distance economy which now governs the distribution of nearly all our food [spread of FMD, BN].

The long-distance food economy is a *disaster* for farmers, a *disaster* for the environment, a *disaster* for consumers and a *disaster* for animal welfare. But it's a *bonanza* for big business. (Monbiot 2001, italics added)

A day later, going beyond mere rhetoric, an article entitled 'From farm to plate – a sick industry' set out in some detail what price consumers pay for cheap food (in terms of food miles, supermarket profits, wasteful packaging, and so on). I can only quote a few salient lines:

Farming has become increasingly intensive, large scale and globalised in the *drive for cheaper food.*

Processed food may be of high nutritional quality, but it can add to *environmental and social costs.*

The drive for agricultural efficiency has produced high yields and *low prices* – but the benefits have come *at a price.* (Anonymous 2001, italics added)

The same day Felicity Lawrence, the *Guardian* consumer-affairs correspondent, published an article entitled '*Hidden Costs* behind the Checkout Prices' (Lawrence 2001a), in which she pointed out: 'Although food appears *cheap at the checkout,* there are *huge hidden costs*'. She quoted Jules Pretty, an agriculture economist at the University of Essex, as saying: '"We *pay three times over* – once at the till, then again through tax for EU subsidies and then again through hidden subsidies"', (Lawrence 2001, italics added). The hidden costs include cleaning up polluted water, cleaning up after disasters, such as BSE and FMD, and having a sick and obese population (see Pretty et al. 2000).

Following Lawrence's article, Pretty's figures about the hidden cost of cheap food were quoted on several websites as well as in a report published by the *Food Ethics Council* (after FMD 2001). One contribution to a website maintained by an organic farming organization used Pretty's work to turn the argument about cheap food and expensive food on its head, saying on 8 March that, taking all the hidden costs into account, so-called cheap food is actually expensive, whereas so-called expensive, i.e. organic food is relatively cheap (see Craigfarm 2001; see also Friends of the Earth's vision for the future of farming in the UK, published in 2001, see Diamand 2001).

On 2 March, the Prime Minister, Tony Blair, jumped onto the argumentative bandwagon pulled by the cliché 'paying the price for cheap food', but tried to pull it in a slightly different direction – the price of sustainable agriculture. He 'used a public meeting in Gloucester to signal his readiness to examine the wider problems facing farmers'. He also 'told farmers in the audience that supermarkets had "pretty much got an arm-lock on you people at the moment". Mr Blair said: "I think we need to sit down with the industry and really work out what is the basis on which we want sustainable farming for the long-term . . . And in a sense, *what price are we all prepared to pay for that as well*"' (BBC News online 2001, italics added). From then on the debate surrounding cheap food was more closely linked to the long-standing debate about sustainable agriculture, the advantages of organic food and the negative aspects of the European Common Agricultural Policy (CAP).

The same day, the *Guardian* published an article by Patrick Wintour, their Chief Political Correspondent, entitled 'Rethink on Cheap Food Policies', in which two other government officials were quoted: Elliot Morley, the then Parliamentary Under-Secretary at MAFF, and Michael Meacher, the then Environment Minister. Like Tony Blair they demanded a rethink of an agricultural policy based on postwar demands for cheap food, especially meat (see Wintour 2001).

Exploiting the emerging opposition against 'the mantra of cheap food' (Freestone 2001), Blair, Morley and Meacher all began to argue for a more sustainable agriculture, for a reform of postwar food and farming policies, especially the CAP, and they started to stress the importance of producing, distributing and buying local or regional food, instead of transporting animals, food and ultimately disease over long distances.

On 4 March Fort wrote an article in the *Observer* echoing Monbiot's phrase 'sacrificed on the altar of supermarket profits', entitled 'Sacrifices on the altar of cheap food', in which he argued against the economically based decision to slaughter millions of animals instead of opting for vaccination in the fight against FMD (see also 'Who is to blame?' 2001). He argued that 'the deceitful chimera of cheap food' had structured agricultural policy for too long and that 'we consumers have gone along with it, as we have gone along with all the other consequences of *cheap-food policies*: centralised production and retailing, and the control of the food chain by a few very powerful companies', being lured by '*[b]argain-basement beef*, nicely trimmed and packaged; *cut-price new potatoes* in December; and butter-basted chickens at 95p per kg' (Fort 2001b). The issue of blame, especially of blaming the consumer, becomes more prominent and is, as we shall see, linked to an 'ethical' food ideal, which is opposed to the 'economic' food agenda.

The author Jeanette Winterson pointed out in an article published on 6 March: 'The *real price of cheap food* is a sickly, obese population and a chemically maintained countryside where disease flourishes, while habitat and species diversity is destroyed . . . Nick Brown says he wants to look again at the effects of intensive farming. *The big issue is going to be cheap food'* (Winterson 2001, italics added). This reflects a growing concern with consumers' food choices as relating to issues of health, environment and risk. Here, consumers are not only blamed for 'causing' FMD, but also for bringing up a generation of obese children and for destroying the countryside in which future generations want to live and enjoy themselves.

In a speech entitled 'Environment: The next steps', made on 6 March (prior to going to the Rio+10 Environment Conference in South Africa), Tony Blair rejoined this chorus of anti-cheap-food campaigners. He echoed not only the arguments put forward in the *Guardian*, but also Monbiot's rhetorical stance ('The long-distance food economy is a disaster for farmers, a disaster for the environment, a disaster for consumers and a disaster for animal welfare.') when he called for 'greater emphasis on environmental good practice, *quality food* and high standards of care for farm animals' (Blair 2001).[7]

> We have long backed cuts in production-linked support, which consumes 90 per cent of the CAP budget, and is *bad for taxpayers, bad for consumers, bad for the environment and ultimately bad for farmers*. And a policy that simply pays farmers more for producing more cannot respond to environmental concerns, changing consumer tastes or regional needs. (Blair 2001, italics added)

This reflects to some extent the views of green organizations, such as Friends of the Earth who wrote in 2001: 'Much of the food we produce now contains unhealthy chemicals, we need to produce high-quality foods which are affordable to all' (Diamand 2001: 24).

A few days later, on 11 March, Fort wrote yet another article on cheap food. The headline he chose this time, 'Yes, food is cheap, and so is our talk', blends two clichés neatly and effectively: 'talk is cheap' (talking about something is easier than doing something) and 'paying the price for cheap food' (the actual price of cheap food does not reflect the real costs of cheap food). In the article itself, Fort set out in rhetorically apt form (again using repetition), what he thought that we as a nation *have* done wrong in the past and what we *should* be doing in the future:

> *We have* seen large-scale industrialised agricultural complexes and small-scale units that seem modeled on Cold Comfort Farm.
>
> *We have* suddenly learned about the centralised slaughter of animals brought about by the huge reduction in the number of abattoirs. *We have* become experts in cross-contamination brought about by having to ship animals vast distances across country. *We have* discovered a complex internal trade in animals which involves them being bought in a market in one part of the country and transported to another where they will fetch a higher price . . .
>
> Food production *should* be de-intensified. The food chain *should* be decentralised. We *should* cease to treat animals simply as if they were machines and the land as if it

were a factory. The cartel of food retailers needs to broken up. Food prices *should* rise four- or five-fold. We *should* eat less. We *should* initiate a state-funded process of education about food . . . starting in schools and continuing through the retail chain. (Fort 2001c, italics added)

This article contributes to the construction of an ethical food ideal, to which other *Guardian* writers contributed by urging readers to

- be prepared to pay for food that is produced *up to quality, not down to price*
- scrap *false economies of scale* and ensure that a *realistic price* is charged for the results
- switch to local suppliers
- change our attitude to food
- change our shopping habits

There is a major obstacle, however, to achieving this ideal state of food production and food consumption: this new ethical approach to food can only be afforded by the well-off who have the time and money to be 'worried about BSE and slaughterhouses, globalisation and ruthless agribusiness, food miles, genetically modified wheat and downtrodden teapickers in Nepal' and want to 'assuage their anxieties' and moral guilt by buying good (ethical and healthy) and more expensive food (Wheatley 2002). In short: 'If people want safer, nutritionally better, ethically better food, they will have to pay more' (Lawrence 2001). Lawrence quoted Michael Hart, a farmer in Cornwall who leads the Small and Family Farm Alliance as saying: 'people have to choose between *mass-produced, intensively farmed food* or *high quality produce which comes with animal welfare attached*, at prices which might well be out of reach of the poor'.

Through the debate of the cheap-food issue, FMD has become something of a stick with which to beat middle-class readers of the *Guardian* and middle-class food consumers, who are urged to take a moral stance on food consumption and to atone for their past sins of buying mass-produced cheap meat, acts of sin that have led, it seems, to the crisis in food and farming they are now witnessing. This exploits a trend in modern consumer society where people in the Western world have no longer to worry about how to get food, but about what type of 'ethical' food they consume, whether it's good or bad for their bodies, their children, the world – a topic studied by John Coveney in his book *Food, Morals and Meaning: The Pleasure and Anxiety of Eating* (Coveney 2000).

In a summary of the cheap-food-debate, which had up to then taken place mainly on the pages of the *Guardian*, Sandy Starr, writing for *spiked-online* magazine on 12 April (which publishes article that buck the general trend), put the finger on the problem:

Trying not to look as though he was blaming the farmers, Tony Blair passed the buck on to UK supermarkets, accusing them of holding the farmers in an 'armlock' to produce *cheap food* . . . Agriculture minister Elliot Morley followed up the charge by announcing a rethink of common agriculture policy away from overproduction . . . Few people seemed to spare a thought for those consumers who are less well off, and few people seemed to notice the sneering undertones of the *tirade against 'cheap food'*. The dietary options of many would be severely reduced if there were no cheap meat or supermarkets. (Starr 2001, italics added)

Jennie Bristow, also writing for *spiked-online*, had pointed out on 29 March:

Why pass up an opportunity – any opportunity – to extol the virtues of 'good' (fresh, locally-produced, organic or wannabe-organic, sold in little shops, *expensive*) food over 'cheap' (frozen or could-just-as-well-be frozen, imported or mass-produced, super-market-stocked, *cheap*) food? (Italics added by Bristow)

'The real price of cheap food', opines writer Jeanette Winterson [*Guardian* 6 March, 2001], 'is a sickly, obese population and a chemically maintained countryside where disease flourishes, while habitat and species diversity is destroyed'. Maybe in her world. But for many, many other people, *the real 'price' of cheap food* is the ability to eat meat every day if they want to; the ability to buy fresh fruit and vegetables all year round; the ability not to starve . . . (Bristow 2001, italics added)

These were lonely voices in a debate where cheap food was generally regarded as being at the root of all problems besetting agriculture and food production and where moral food consumption took precedence over issues of affordability.

The final contribution to the cheap-food debate that appeared in the *Guardian* was a humorous one – always a sign that a serious debate has run its course – in which Sue Townsend, author of the *Adrian Mole Diaries*, published two entries from his fictional diary, from 11 and 12 March 2001. One of them nicely summarizes the supposed links between FMD and cheap food in the form of Mole's neighbor, Vince Ludlow, an 'Animal Incineration Operative'. He operates at both ends of the morally tainted food chain, burning animals suspected of carrying FMD on the one hand and enjoying it, and selling cheap cuts of beef from the back of his van and profiting from it (Townsend 2001).

At the end of March the cheap-food debate fizzled out in the *Guardian*, but it was continued in other media and it had policy repercussions that reverberated throughout the following year (see Curry report 2002).

Rhetoric, Blame, Science and Morality

This summary of the cheap-food debate as carried out in the *Guardian* has given us some clues about why cheap food was so easily adopted as the 'culprit' or major risk factor responsible for the outbreak of FMD in Britain. There are three reasons: rhetorical, cultural, historical and semantic – three types of reason that interacted with the scientific uncertainties surrounding the cause of FMD in the UK in 2001.

Most commentators argued that cheap food was bad, indeed evil, in various ways, and expensive food was good in various ways (good for your health, good for the environment, good for the animals, ethically good) in a very stereotypical and dichotomous fashion, using polar adjectives such as good/bad, safe/unsafe, healthy/unhealthy, and so on which are very efficient ways of polarizing an argument (see Figure 3.1).

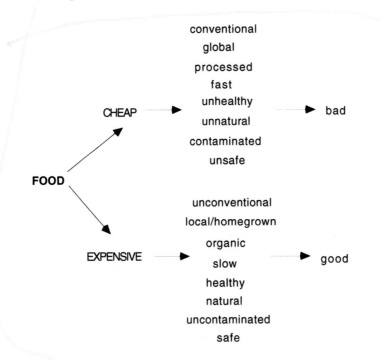

Figure 3.1

A few argued that cheap food was good, at least for those who couldn't afford any other food, and indeed better than cheap food had ever been. Many argued that cheap food was expensive in terms of environmental, animal-welfare and human-health costs and that, in the long run, expensive food, such as local and organic food, would be cheaper. All those arguments rotated around one central question: 'What price cheap food?' As this question was framed in a very clichéd and stereotypical way, it successfully focused the general debate about food, farming and politics and established a (moral and moralizing) link between (*Guardian*) journalists and (*Guardian*) readers, as well as journalists, politicians and NGOs, who all reacted to this question in a more or less uniform way, some because they genuinely cared, some perhaps because they thought it 'political'.

This rhetorical framing of the 'cheap-food' issue can, however, not entirely explain why 'cheap food' became the pivot around which the debate about FMD turned for a while. There are other reasons, less rhetorical and more cultural ones. According to the anthropologist Mary Douglas all societies have their own culturally specific ways of constructing risk and blame. In the book *Risk and Culture* (Douglas and Wildavsky 1982), she examines how particular kinds of danger come to be selected for attention' (p. 8). Her theory is that 'the choice of risks to worry about depends on the social forms selected. The choice of risks and the choice of how to live are taken together' (ibid.). Cheap food brings together a risk factor associated with the emergence of FMD and the way people in the UK choose to live – and eat. Risk is therefore not only scientifically, socially and culturally constructed in this case, it also becomes an issue of individual and, most importantly, of consumer choice and ultimately an issue of morality.

As the causes of the outbreak of FMD were unclear, as the rapid spread of the disease was devastating, as a debate raged between scientists and policy-makers about how best to eradicate the disease, and as previously unanticipated (environmental) risks associated with the slaughter policy began to emerge, cheap food became a cultural filler used to plug some of the holes left by scientific and political uncertainty. Just as the fires burning on every TV screen came to symbolize the catastrophic effects of the FMD crisis, the mismanagement of the crisis by the government or, for some, the thousands of animals that would normally be killed every day anyway, cheap food came to symbolize the cause of FMD. Both together, the (sinful) consumption of cheap food on the one hand and the burning (hell) fires of animal carcasses on the other, became symbols for the whole food chain, which began to unravel from both ends in front of people's very eyes.

This then sparked questions about the effects of intensive, industrial farming practices (which were themselves seen by many as the result of the postwar British agricultural policy and the later European CAP), about the possible advantages of sustainable agriculture and organic farming, about the problems of the (over-)production of food, the long-distance food economy, globalization, the role of supermarkets in food distribution ('the extensive, just-in-time, supply systems required by the supermarkets', Trewin 2001b: 18), and the issue of animal welfare. As newspapers reported extensively on these topics, people suddenly knew much more about the provenance, distribution and safety of their food than ever before, more than they might ever have wanted to know. In the process, FMD became a very personal issue.

Consumers as individuals can neither control the whole food chain nor control the governmental slaughter policy. In adopting (via the popular press) 'cheap food' as a major risk and causal factor they could, however, at least 'control' its cause.

And since they could or would not blame the farmers for causing FMD, cheap food gave them and the popular press a way of blaming themselves and their sinful behavior in British supermarkets. This issue of blame ties in neatly with deeply rooted religious and ritualistic thinking, according to which moral misdeeds can lead to the spread of disease, sins lead to disasters (see Douglas 1992: 26), and those who have perpetrated these sins have to pay for them in one way or another. In the case of FMD, greed for cheap food was the sin and the price consumers had to pay for their greed was FMD. Religion stepped in where science had left a vacuum.

In Western culture, science normally 'rescues' us from too much moral blame, but in complicated cases, such as BSE and FMD, other less 'scientific' and more ritualistic patterns of reaction and interpretation emerge (see Nerlich on 'natural attitude', 2004). FMD struck the UK suddenly and the policy of slaughter, chosen as the established 'cleansing ritual', turned it into a tragedy of quite epic proportions. People and especially the popular press needed some sort of explanation for this tragic event. Cheap food provided the press with an explanation in which issues of farming methods, consumption and the whole food chain met issues of risk, culture, society, morality and blame. This worked well in a society and culture where consumers have become morally responsible for their food choices and for the risks they take with their food choices, not only for themselves but for society at large, as well as the environment (see Halkier, this volume). In the case of the debate surrounding FMD, blame was therefore not only attributed to 'the system' of industrial food production – the food chain – and with it the government, but also to cheap food as the consumer's choice – the 'first' link in the chain.

So far we have seen that the rhetorical structure of the cheap-food argument was very pervasive and therefore made cheap food one of the pivots around which the debate about FMD turned. We have also seen that cheap food and with it culturally specific modes of attributing blame filled to some extend the vacuum left by scientific uncertainty surrounding the cause, spread and eradication of FMD. But to understand why cheap food became so important in the British media, we also have to examine the semantic value and connotations of cheap food and how they emerged historically.

Fifty years ago, *cheap*, when associated with food, had probably quite positive connotations in the UK. The so-called cheap-food policy promoted after the Second World War was generally seen as positive, as consonant with a sense of social justice. It meant that even people with less money could still afford to buy decent food. *Cheap* may have taken on more negative connotations much more recently, especially for those who can afford to count (hidden) costs as including environmental cost, animal welfare cost and cost to people's health rather than solely the (overt) cost to their purse and wallet. For those who can afford it, shopping habits have changed from being a straightforward act of buying something to eat to being an agonizing conundrum of choices.

In his book *The Dialectics of Shopping* (2001) Daniel Miller explores the many contradictions faced by shoppers on a typical street in London, and what this reveals about our relationships to our families and communities, as well as to the environment and the economy as a whole. Miller writes about shoppers confronted with multiple contradictions and dilemmas: should they buy food at the local store where it is more expensive or at the big supermarket where it is cheaper; should they have sympathy with environmental concerns or should they put 'ethical shopping' out of their minds, should they buy cheap food for their family and feel guilty about the environmental costs or buy expensive food and feel guilty about spending too much money, should they think about class or family, themselves or others, health or enjoyment and so on.

These and many other questions have become more prominent in the UK because of a wave of food scares such as *E. coli*, *Salmonella*, BSE and FMD.[8] From being a straightforward solution to a social and dietary problem, cheap food has become riddled with ambiguities and uncertainties. Cheap food has turned into a multivocal symbol (see Turner 1967) that connects, like the food chain for which it stands metonymically, a wide range of different concerns and expresses them, but not in a very clear and consistent way. However, precisely because of this vagueness and because cheap food can be interpreted in so many different ways, it works for all, it has a resonance among many, especially among middle-class readers of the *Guardian*, who can all agree that cheap food is terrible – it 'causes' FMD, it 'causes' the death of British agriculture, it 'causes' the burning of innocent sheep and lambs. When seen through the lens of 'cheapness', food thus became a major moral and political issue during the FMD outbreak in 2001, leading to a reappraisal of food and farming by the general public and policy-makers alike.

Conclusion

Although based on the questionable premise that FMD was caused by intensive agriculture and ultimately 'cheap food', the media debate about FMD and cheap food might have contributed to a rethink (by policy-makers, journalists, NGOs and some consumers) of current practices of agriculture, food production and food consumption, including issues of globalization on the one hand and individual consumer responsibility on the other, of scientific judgement on the one hand and socio-economic pressures on the other. Just as the BSE crisis provoked significant institutional changes regarding food safety and led to the creation of the Food Standards Agency, the FMD crisis might yet lead to even more radical policy changes regarding farming and food. What was a major animal and human tragedy might become a window of political opportunity in the arena of food policy, but an opportunity that is already on course to being a lost opportunity. As Winter notes:

> Perhaps at first sight a growing emphasis on food seems an unlikely policy conse-
> quence of FMD. After all the disease itself, not withstanding the occasional scare story
> in the media regarding alleged cases of humans contracting FMD, poses no dangers
> within the food chain. Moreover, the epidemic, for all its gravity for the farming com-
> munity, had no significant impact on the price and availability of meat products in the
> nation's shops. Indeed, it might be argued that the undisrupted supply of food during
> the crisis provided a powerful validation of global and European trading networks.
> Britain could withstand a crisis of the scale of the 2001 FMD outbreak because of the
> capacity of its large retailers to source overseas and because of a highly developed food
> distribution infrastructure. It is, therefore somewhat paradoxical that one of the main
> policy outcomes of the crisis was a renewed and highly critical scrutiny of our systems
> of food provision resulting in a number of policy initiatives designed to shorten and
> simplify food chains. (Winter 2003: 55)

This might seem less paradoxical when taking the activity of the media into account, as I have tried to do in this chapter.

Acknowledgement

This chapter was written with the support of the Leverhulme Trust, a British Academy travel grant and an ESRC Science in Society programme grant (L144 25 0050). I would like to thank Marianne Lien and Anne Murcott for their inspiring comments on a first draft of this chapter.

Notes

1. The best way to 'picture' the spread of the disease can be found on: http://www.guardian.co.uk/footandmouth/flash/0,7365,443772,00.html
2. Some argue, however, that even the initial spread of the disease cannot readily be blamed on animal movements brought about by supermarket demands (see Cumbria Foot and Mouth Disease Inquiry 2002).
3. See also the debate between Sean Rickard, an agricultural economist and George Monbiot, published in *Prospect* magazine, April 2001: http://www.monbiot.com/dsp_article.cfm?article_id=401.
4. By comparison, *The Times* only published two articles that dealt with the cheap food issue *en passant* (on 5 March and 6 March) and one leading article on 22 March. The *Independent* only published two articles that dealt promi-nently with this issue. Both appeared on 4 March, and one of them featured a

headline displaying a rhetorical device similar to the ones I will analyse in the *Guardian* sample: 'Cheap food is exacting a terrible price' (Budden 2001). The *Daily Telegraph* published four articles that dealt with the cheap-food issue, but not very prominently. Caution will obviously be necessary when trying to generalize from such a small sample and further research will be needed to test my provisional conclusions. Two important articles on the cheap food issue appeared in a regional newspaper, the *Western Morning News* (see Trewin 2001a and b).

5. A day before, on 24 February, Carol Trewin, the Farming Editor of the regional newspaper *Western Morning News* had published an article entitled 'The real cost of cheap food?', in which she discussed very similar issues. 'As each new twist of the foot and mouth saga unravels and the nation starts to come to terms with the impact it will have on agricultural businesses and rural life, there is a growing awareness that this catastrophe raises some fundamental questions about the nature of our food buying habits, the weakness of our Government on the international trading stage, and the global market place.' (Trewin 2001a: 8)

6. This article was quoted on the following websites:
   http://www.flora.org/fao/Ottawa/AgriFood/3/
   http://www.monbiot.com/dsp_article.cfm?article_id=392
   http://www.sus-tec.freeserve.co.uk/past/sustec92/92-15.html
   http://www.zmag.org/sustainers/content/2001-03/04monbiot.htm
   http://www.commondreams.org/views01/0301-05.htm

7. Quoted in: http://www.ivillage.co.uk/food/fruitveg/Organic/articles/0,10103, 164321_175612,00.html

8. Consumers worried initially that they were dealing with yet another food scare and a short period of panic buying, especially of meat and milk, began (see Poortinga et al. 2003 and Hutton 2001). It soon became clear, however, that FMD – a flu-like disease that causes quite horrible blisters on animals' feet and in their mouths – only affected cloven-hoofed animals, but posed no risks to human health, an issue amply discussed by all the media. But despite reassurances by the government and the *Food Standards Agency*, the epidemic had sparked off renewed worries about the safety of food.

References

After FMD (2001), *After FMD: Aiming for a Values-Driven Agriculture*, Food Ethics Council: The Independent Council for Ethical Standards in Food and Agriculture: www.users.globalnet.co.uk/~foodeth

Anonymous (2001), 'From Farm to Plate: a Sick Industry', *Guardian*, 28 February: http://www.guardian.co.uk/country/article/0,2763,444143,00.html

BBC News online (2001), 'Blair Offers Hope to Farmers', 2 March: http://news. bbc.co.uk/hi/english/uk_politics/newsid_1197000/1197301.stm

Beck, U. (1992), *Risk Society: Towards a New Modernity*, London: Sage.

Blair, T. (2001), 'Environment: The Next Steps', Speech, 6 March: http://www.pm.gov.uk/output/page2810.asp

Blake, A., Sinclair, M. T., and Sugiyarto, G. (2002), 'Quantifying the Impact of Foot and Mouth Disease on Tourism and the UK Economy', Nottingham University, Business School: http://www.nottingham.ac.uk/ttri

Bristow, J. (2001), 'Supermarkets are – Super', *spiked-online*, 29 March: http://www.spiked-online.com/Articles/00000000552E.htm

Brown, D. (2001), 'Pig Farmers Penned in', *Guardian*, 21 February: http://www. guardian.co.uk/food/Story/0,2763,441026,00.html

Budden, J. (2001), 'Cheap Food is Exacting a Terrible Price', *Independent*, 4 March: http://www.independent.co.uk/story.jsp?story=58955

Coveney, J. (2000), *Food, Morals and Meaning: The Pleasure and Anxiety of Eating*, London: Routledge.

Cumbria Foot and Mouth Disease Inquiry (2002), *Inquiry Report: An Independent Public Inquiry into the Foot and Mouth Disease Epidemic that Occurred in Cumbria in 2001*, URL:http://www.cumbria.gov.uk/elibrary/view.asp?ID=2003

Cunningham, J. (2002), 'Fruitful Talks', *Guardian*, 17 April: http:// society.guardian.co.uk/Print/0,3858,4395009,00.html

Curry Report (2002), *Farming & Food: a Sustainable Future*, Report of the Policy Commission on the Future of Farming and Food, January 2002, Cabinet Office: http://www.cabinet-office.gov.uk/farming

Diamand, E. (2001), 'Get Real about Food and Farming: Friends of the Earth's Vision for the Future of Farming in the UK'. Researched and written by E. Diamand and P. Riley, ed. by H. Baron. Friends of the Earth.

Douglas, M. (1992), *Risk & Blame: Essays in Cultural Theory*, London/New York: Routledge.

—— and Wildavsky, A. B. (1982), *Risk and Culture*, London: Routledge.

Environment Observer (2001), 'What Price Cheap Food: Overview and Animal Welfare', 3 April: http://www.iatp.org/EnviroObs/News/news.cfm?News_ID=419

Fort, M. (2001a), 'Paying the Price for Cheaper Food', *Observer*, 25 February: http://www.guardian.co.uk/Archive/Article/0,4273,4141953,00.html

—— (2001b), 'Sacrifices on the Alter of Cheap Food', *Observer*, 4 March: http://www.observer.co.uk/uk_news/story/0,6903,446139,00.html

—— (2001c), 'Yes our Food is Cheap – and so is our Talk', *Guardian*, 11 March: http://www.guardian.co.uk/food/Story/0,2763,450021,00.html

Franklin, S. (2001), 'Sheepwatching', *Anthropology Today*, 17: http://www. comp.lancs.ac.uk/sociology/sheepwatching.pdf

Freestone, P. (2001), 'Foot and Mouth Disease – Time for Action', *The Oven*: http://www.ivu.org/oxveg/Publications/Oven/Articles_General/fmd.html

Graigfarm (2001), *Graig Farm Organics*. 'Who is to Blame for the Spread of Foot & Mouth? A Personal View by Bob Kennard', 8 March: http://www.graigfarm.co.uk/f&mblame.htm

Green Party (2001), 'What Price Cheap Food?', July: http://greenparty.ennis.ie/press/column/cheap-food_jul01.html

Hutton, D. (2001), 'Socio-Economic Consequences of FMD for the Agricultural Sector': http://cmlag.fgov.be/eng/Deirdre_Huttons_abstract.pdf

Kirby, A. (2001), 'The Pointless Slaughter', *BBC News online*, 25 February.

Lang, T. and Raynor, G. (2002), 'Why Health is the Key to the Future of Food and Farming': http://www.ukpha.org.uk/health_key.pdf

Lawrence, F. (2001a), 'Hidden Costs behind the Checkout Prices', *Guardian*, 28 February.

—— (2001b), 'Switch to Local Suppliers Urged to end Crisis', *Guardian*, 28 February: http://shopping.guardian.co.uk/newsandviews/story/0,5804,443986,00.html

Lowe, P. (2002), 'After Foot-and-Mouth: Farming and the New Rural Economy', in J. Jenkins (ed.), *Remaking the Landscape*, London: Profile.

Miller, D. (2001), *The Dialectics of Shopping*, Chicago: University of Chicago Press.

Monbiot, G. (2000), *Captive State: The Corporate Takeover of Britain*, London: Macmillan.

—— (2001), 'Disease and Modernity', *Guardian*, 27 February: http://www.guardian.co.uk/Archive/Article/0,4273,4143089,00.html

Morris, C. and Young, C. (2000), '"Seed to Shelf", "Teat to Table", "Barley to Beer" and "Womb to Tomb": Discourses of Food Quality and Quality Assurance Schemes in the UK', *Journal of Rural Studies* 16: 103–15.

Nerlich, B. (2004). 'Towards a Cultural Understanding of Agriculture: The Case of the "War" on Foot and Mouth Disease', *Agriculture and Human Values*, 21(1): 15–25.

Poortinga, W., Bickerstaff, K., Langford, I., Niewöhner, J., and Pidgeon, N. (2003), 'The British 2001 Foot and Mouth Crisis: A Comparative Study of Public Risk Perception, Trust and Beliefs about Government Policy in Two Communities', *Journal of Risk Research*, 6: 1–18.

Pretty, J., Brett, C., Gee, D., Hine, R., Mason, C. F., Morison, J. I. L, Raven, H., Rayment, M. and van der Bijl, G. (2000), 'An Assessment of the Total External Costs of UK Agriculture', *Agricultural Systems*, 65(2): 113–36.

Starr, S. (2001), 'Sheep, Pigs and Scapegoats', *spiked-online*, 12 April: http://www.spiked-online.com/Articles/000000005574.htm

Thomson, G. R. (2002), 'Foot and Mouth Disease: Facing the New Dilemmas',

Scientific and Technical Review, 21(3): http://www.oie.int/eng/publicat/
RT/a_RT21_3.HTM#sommaire

Townsend, S. (2001), 'Foot in Mouth: Adrian Mole, age 33', *Guardian*, 17 March.

Trewin, C. (2001a), 'The Real Cost of Cheap Food?', *Western Morning News*, 24 February, 2002, reprinted in: *Foot & Mouth: How the Westcountry Lived through the Nightmare*, published by the *Western Morning News*, Manchester: Henry Ling, p. 8.

—— (2001b), 'Will British Consumers be Willing to Pay the Price to Help Farmers Survive?', ibid., pp. 17–18.

Turner, V. (1967), *The Forest of Symbols*, Ithaca, NY: Cornell University Press.

Vetstream (2001), 'What Price Cheap Food?' 1 March: http://www. vetstream.co.uk/v2000/community/opinion_cheap_food.htm

Watson, R. (2002), 'Battle Lines are Drawn over Farm Reforms', *The Times*, 28 June, p. 1.

What Price Cheap Food? (2002), Conference organized by the British Society of Animal Science & Scottish Centre for Animal Welfare Sciences, Exhibition Centre, University of York, Monday, 8 April 2002: http://www. bsas.org.uk/meetings/ann02/cheapfd.pdf

Wheatley, J. (2002), 'Eating to be Good', *The Times*, 15 June, Weekend, p. 1.

'Who is to Blame?' (2001), *Observer*, 4 March: http://www.observer. co.uk/uk_news/story/0,6903,446137,00.html

Winter, M. (2003), 'Responding to the Crisis: The Policy Impact of the Foot and Mouth Epidemic', *Political Quarterly*, 74(1): 47–57.

Winterson, J. (2001). 'Purse Power', *Guardian*, 6 March: http://www. guardian.co.uk/food/Story/0,2763,447143,00.html

Wintour, P. (2001), 'Rethink on Cheap Food Policies', *Guardian*, 2 March: http://www.guardian.co.uk/Archive/Article/0,4273,4144869,00.html

Woods, A. (2002), 'To Vaccinate or Vacillate? The British Response to FMD, 1920–2001'. Ms.

–4–

The Rhetoric of Food:
Food as Nature, Commodity and Culture

Eivind Jacobsen

Introduction

Different definitions of food are associated with specific rhetorical repertoires, and hence different questions, risks, roles and conflicts of interest. Distinct tropes imply differing degrees of influence for groups and individuals, as different sets of interests and points of view are made relevant and legitimate. If one can make one's own interpretations and constructions of reality hegemonic, then one's power and influence is increased (Bråten 1973; cf. also Bourdieu 1984: 479–82). This is reflected in constant struggles about what food, food production and food consumption are and should be. In this chapter I will take a closer look at three tropes that are often applied in relation to discussions about food, and question who benefits from their dissemination and possible domination.

Rhetorical tropes are essential for the conceptualization of food, food production and consumption. According to Lakoff and Johnson (1980: 39), metaphors and metonyms help us to structure thoughts, attitudes and actions. Metaphors are used to comprehend phenomena through reference to something else – through mental leaps between different conceptual domains (Lakoff and Johnson 1980: 5). In this way a surplus of meaning is produced, and this meaning may be used to explore and investigate the phenomenon in focus (Heradstveit 1992: 74). For instance, food is often referred to as 'fuel for the body' (implying that the body is a machine); the media sometimes discuss 'food as weapon' (implying that someone is denying someone access to food); others express worries related to juvenile eating habits by reference to the word 'grazing' (something which animals do, not humans). Metonyms imply a more direct and evident connection between signifier and signified (ibid.: 39), for example as when a whole is represented by a part (e.g. 'plate' for meal), effects by a cause (get 'filled up' for having a meal) or place for an action ('a look in the fridge' for having a small meal). However, tropes do not have 'innate, monosemic meanings that determine the mindset of those who use them' (Condit et al. 2002: 303; see also Stern 2000). Instead they offer sets of 'diverse potential meanings' where 'specific components . . . are activated in different contexts' (Condit et al.: 303). Nonetheless, tropes do constitute a textual frame within which the interpreter understands the meaning.

Tropes are often linked, referring to some kind of shared base-metaphor or connotative field of meaning, often with what Fernandez (1974: 42) calls performative consequences. Words are given metaphorical or metonymical meaning by being used in wider contexts. For instance, if 'the body is a machine' then 'food is fuel' (an input). It also follows that digestion produces 'output' and some kind of 'waste products'. Food as fuel may be 'more or less uncontaminated', it may be infused with extra properties in order to 'enhance efficiency' or perform 'supplementary functions'. These interlinked metaphors draw attention to the more or less amoral utilities of food for the body/machine. To take another example: if elks are 'game' they may be shot by a hunter, not slaughtered or murdered by a butcher or a murderer, and they consequently belong to another moral universe than farm-animals.

The use of rhetorical tropes is never arbitrary. Michel Foucault (1974: 117) claims that the dominant tropes of a historical period determine what can be known and comprehended – the basic episteme of the age. Hence tropes are closely interwoven within the basic structures and grids of power in a society. Annemarie Mol (1999: 75) brings this one step further by introducing the term 'ontological politics'. This is a composite term, where 'ontology' – what belongs to the real – is combined with 'politics' – the exercising of active choice. The combined term implies that reality cannot be taken for granted, but rather is open and contested, such as through conceptual and rhetorical manipulation. Related to the subject of this chapter, it means that what food is, and how it should be understood, is contested, and that this contestation is subject to political processes between different actors and interests.

Some tropes are part of a semiotic heritage we seldom reflect upon. However, they can also be deliberately and strategically applied wherever power is contested, as they serve to emphasize certain connections and dimensions at the expense of others. The persuasion of others is emphasized by Heradstveit: 'Rhetoric likes to employ various forms of figurative speech or tropes so as to engage the audience in dialogue and persuade it to accept a message' (Heradstveit 1992: 72; Fernandez 1974: 42). In this connection, Fiumara (1995: 42) points to the fact that 'an underlying assumption which structures most linguistic expressions of our argumentative culture is a latent oppositional metaphor whereby we strive to gain approving allies . . .' (see also Lakoff and Johnson 1980: 4). Hence rhetoric is employed in order to gain dominance by means of our definitions. In this way tropes are used as strategic vehicles in struggles over definitions of reality. They serve to frame the context of arguments, and hence can predispose specific views and understandings (see Nerlich, this volume). Heradstveit adds 'The aim of rhetoric is invoking (these) established and emotionally loaded connotations in the recipient's mind, in order via metaphorisation to transfer them to a new political context' (1992: 76). An important task for social research is to make evident whose understanding of reality, whose points of view and whose interests are privileged by specific tropes and figures of speech (Bråten 1973; Chandler 2002).

However, one important reservation should be made. Tropes have their limitations; you cannot stretch them too far. Politicians often experience this in their rhetoric, as they get caught in their own colorful metaphors or stumble in conflicting images. Metaphors sometimes backfire, for instance by committing their user to a conduct coherent with the metaphors applied. In certain situations this may impose unwanted restrictions on available actions, or function as 'trap wires' (to use a metaphor) that might be stumbled over. For instance, if you sell your strawberry jam by means of a Norwegian flag and a picture of a Norwegian mountain icon, you do have a problem when consumers or others find out that the strawberries are picked and parcelled in Poland. Besides, as I have argued above, tropes may be interpreted somewhat differently in different contexts (Stern 2000; Condit et al. 2002). These limitations apply to the strategic usefulness of tropes. Nonetheless, they do not discourage actors from trying to use them this way.

Food as Rhetoric: 'Nature', 'Commodity' and 'Culture'

Food is a domain in which the use of metaphors and metonyms is abundant. Food is closely linked to the human body and to basic life maintenance. In the food-related public debate several basic tropes from different connotative fields tend to be applied to represent what food is and should be. Without claiming to offer an exhaustive list, I would like to point to three connotative fields that are frequently referred to by different actors and interest groups in Western societies: First, food is presented as part of nature, as plants or animals, or as nutrition. Plants and animals are used (and misused) to produce food in more or less domesticated settings. As a vehicle for nutrients, food interacts with the human body and helps provide the physiological requirements that sustain life. Secondly, food is presented as a commodity for sale and purchase. In Western societies food is mainly produced, distributed and sold through markets. Food is often transported across long distances and sorted, put together, processed and distributed through several middlemen, each with his or her own economic interests and institutional agendas. Thirdly, food is presented as culture. Food is culturally embedded, perceived and interpreted along socially defined dimensions. Food is sensed, processed, presented and consumed in accordance with culturally defined categories and regulated and distributed through normatively sanctioned institutional systems. But food is also subject to creative cookery and display, and may serve as a material representation of individual or collective identities.[1]

Tropes from these three connotative fields are also frequently referred in the social science-related literature on food, as different disciplines tend to lean on different tropes. Economists tend to see food exclusively as a commodity. Social anthropologists and sociologists tend to see it mostly as a part of culture (Douglas and Isherwood 1979), while its status as a part of nature has been the focus of nutritional science and the agricultural sciences.

The three tropes may be understood as metonyms as well as metaphors, depending on the contexts within which they are used. They may be used as metonyms, or more precisely they belong to a sub-group of metonyms, so-called synecdoches – when a whole (for example nature) is represented by a part (such as beef). Referring to White (1979), Chandler (2002) claims that synecdoches point to the essentiality of a phenomenon. In this way, each of the three tropes of commodity, nature and culture points to a specific dimension of food that is highlighted as the most essential, suggesting what food 'really is' and should be comprehended as.

However, references to these three connotative fields may also be used as metaphors, pointing to something else that is qualitatively different, and to other contexts and connections (Heradstveit 1992: 79). Food as nature refers to a wide array of values, sentiments, associations and scripts of action arising from a broader set of meanings than those associated with human nutrition. Nature is a multi-vocal symbol, and is heavily loaded ideologically and emotionally (cf. Macnaghten and Urry 1998; Franklin 2002). As a commodity, food is given a status alongside napkins, washing powder and nails. The concept of a commodity is also multi-vocal, but (these days) perhaps not as emotionally loaded as the concept of nature. On the other hand, it might still have strong ideological bearings, where it is used to point to specific political and moral positions. The concept of culture is also multi-vocal and laden with symbolism, as it refers to expressive human activities (for example art), as well as to major signifiers of national, regional, local and ethnic identity.

References to various tropes and connotative fields imply different conceptions of time and relevant spaces. This opens up possibilities for different ethical or moral considerations, as it makes different consequential universes relevant. Hence, different rhetorical strategies evolve from different tropes, along with distinct discourses, networks and institutional structures. In this way specific tropes become institutionalized within distinct lines of conflict and habitual practices.

The three connotative fields are inseparably linked in the physical shape and substance of food. They share the same signifier – the material substance of food. In this way, as a signifier, the fields are 'linked' in the mundane practices of

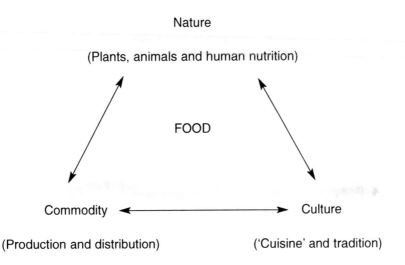

Figure 4.1 Food as a rhetorical field: Nature, commodity and culture.

farmhouses, kitchens, dining rooms and restaurants, places where food is produced, prepared and consumed. Hence, food is and will always be a genuine hybrid, a social-natural mix (Latour 1993).

Despite being enmeshed in different human practices, actors engage in argumentative wars over which connotative field, which trope, and therefore which language game, should dominate. Actors seek hegemony for their perspectives, their preferred rhetorical field and associated metaphors and metonyms, because they are more comfortable with them in their argumentative strategies. Actors tend to purify distinct aspects of food (as a signifier), claiming a specific trait to be its essence, and hence ignoring other aspects or taking them for granted. The definition of what food is and should be thus serves as an argumentative premise in struggles over economic and political resources of different kinds. Getting others to accept your definitions gives you an advantage in these struggles as it frames decisions and outcomes.

Despite this, adjustments often take place in order to handle an obstinate reality (Bateson 1972). For instance, food hardly has any value as a commodity if it is conceived of as inedible or dangerous. Similarly, cuisine and traditions evolve within the limits imposed by nature (biology) and its commodity potential (the market economy). As for nature, the biology of food is also culturally and economically fashioned and adjusted. Hence, the process of product development is aimed at targeting specific markets of potential buyers. Due to these adjustments, the argumentative wars tend to be wars over ranking, weighting and adaptation, and not so much questions about total exclusion. This implies that there may be room for compromises and strategic alliances. Yet, as tropes and connotative fields,

they tend to purify certain aspects and ignore others: food is translated and puri-
fied respectively as 'nature', 'commodity' and 'culture'.

In the following pages I will discuss each of these connotative fields and some
of their practical and political implications. I will specifically discuss taken-for-
granted assumptions about food as a material substance, and how food as 'nature',
'commodity' and 'culture' imply different ways of approaching this substance.

Food as Nature

Most actors in the food sector make references to nature and the naturalness of
food. Food is naturalized, understood as and presented as nature (Franklin 2002).
However, some do this more consistently and with higher credibility than others.
Environmental NGOs are among those who most consistently refer to this connotative field. They tend to paint a picture of a nature tortured by human ignorance, exploitation and misuse, a gloomy picture of paradise lost. Poisonous
foods and famines are part of the price we pay for our scientific and technological hubris, and things will only get worse unless we change our course of action.
Farmers and their organizations also refer to nature in their self-presentation.
However, this seems to be another nature, a domesticated and manageable nature.
Food is 'improved nature', nature tamed and cultivated through generations of
embodied experience. This quality is worth paying for, or else 'improved nature'
will deteriorate.

But there are also others who eagerly refer to the nature in food: brand-builders
place pictures of animals, mountains and waterfalls on their products, and tell us
that their products are 'natural' or 'pure'. Public bureaucrats are concerned about
a sustainable future with sustainable food, and also a nature of quality for future
generations. Hence, nature and society must be reasonably balanced through the
application of knowledge and precaution. Nutritionists also relate to nature, but
this is the nature of medicine, chemistry and physics. Food is understood through
the lenses of science. Scientists in biology and genetics regard nature as raw material for their transformation of food and the human project. They regard nature
as a manipulable and controllable resource.

In accordance with these examples, and in line with Macnaghten and Urry
(1998), there is not one single Nature but many natures (cf. also Braun and Castree
1998). Different images of nature follow from different experiences and positions
in society. Whenever food is referred to as nature, one should therefore ask what
nature, and possibly also whose nature. Whose image of nature is presented, and
what are the underlying assumptions and implications?

Macnaghten and Urry (1998) describe three common notions of Nature that all
imply a singular, universal Nature external to society: environmental realism leans
heavily on the notion of a neutral, rational science as the only legitimate interpreter

of nature. Nature is there for society to discover, use and exploit, and science tells us how. Environmental idealism has in many respects developed out of a reaction to the realist position. Here nature is understood as a subject, and the carrier of underlying, stable and consistent values of its own, values often considered to be superior to those found in a 'corrupted' human society. There is also a third position called environmental instrumentalism. Here the responses of humans to nature and the environment are in focus. It seeks to explain human motivations to engage in sustainable practices by means of simple calculations of individual and group interests. However, these considerations are based on the notion of a radical separation of humans from non-humans, subjects from objects (cf. also Tester 1992).

Focusing on food as nature almost automatically implies a long-term perspective. Nature is mostly considered to be beyond all human measures, in time as well as in space. The Norwegian freeholder has traditionally thought about landscape, arable land and soil in a generational perspective. He has inherited the farm from his father, and his father's father, down through the generations, and his son or daughter, and their sons and daughters, are supposed to continue this 'never-ending' project. Macnaghten and Urry (1998) denote this as 'glacial time', where actions and their consequences are evaluated with reference to timeframes exceeding the span of single human lives. In this perspective, nature is embodied in the productive activities of farming, where bodily skills and experiences are just as important as theoretical scientific knowledge of nature (Franklin 2002). This kind of traditional farming can be contrasted with modern industrialized farming methods, with its mechanized production and abstract, partly disembodied, codified, techno-scientific knowledge base (Morgan and Murdoch 2000). In this kind of farming, the time-perspective may be guided by more temporary concerns. The latter perspectives may often involve a rational or instrumental understanding of nature.

Public politics for a sustainable future employs a long-term time perspective in its rhetoric, if not always in praxis. Resources, pollution and biological diversity are supposed to be evaluated in a glacial time perspective, where they seek a kind of 'natural' balance in order to assure for the needs and qualities of future generations (Macnaghten and Urry 1998).

A focus on nutrition also involves a long-term perspective, though this is limited to the span of the human life. A time perspective that exceeds the sunset follows from acknowledging that food prepared and eaten today may have consequences for our lives several decades from now. Hence, food is fundamentally related to future health, and therefore also to risk. We have to eat, but the food we consume may be harmful to us and even kill us. This risk is increased by the human need for a diversified composition of foods (Fischler 1988).

The nutritional perspective may be seen as split between a medical-scientific based approach, and a more lay- and embodied version found among most consumers. The scientific notion of nutrition probably fulfills all the characteristics of realistic environmentalism as described above (Macnaghten and Urry 1998). However, consumers have to digest the food, thereby experiencing food and risk, in ways that go beyond scientific understanding. This also implies that the trust or mistrust in scientists and scientific judgements is framing consumers' risk assessment and understanding of nature. If this trust fails, they may search for other sources of knowledge concerning food as nature and the interactions between food and society.

In the above-mentioned examples an anthropocentric perspective has been employed, in which future generations, humanity or human life represents the relevant time horizon. A more radical approach focuses on animals, 'nature' or even 'mother earth' as subjects and points of reference. In such a perspective, human food and food production have to be evaluated in relation to eternity, where the human species and 'history' may be seen as a minor affair in terms of Darwinian evolution or the geological development of our planet. Some of the environmental NGOs and certainly some of the animal-rights NGOs are obviously propagating an idealistic notion of nature where ordinary divisions between humans and nature, and subjects and objects are blurred (cf. Kalland 1993; Lien, this volume). This opens the field for rather sharp and fundamentally ethical conflicts, one in which lives (human and animal) have been lost in actions against abattoirs and animal-transport facilities. It also opens up the possibility for what has been called 'environmental imperialism' – imposing Western (or perhaps American) ideas about nature and the interface between nature and society on the rest of the world. If Nature is a carrier of intrinsic values, and if Nature is essentially the same all over the world, it follows that it should be treated alike everywhere. Consequently, other people's food habits become a legitimate cause for concern and for global sanctions (cf. Lien, this volume).

Nature and 'naturalness', often linked to local or national idioms, are frequently used rhetorically in order to promote food products. In this way *Milka* chocolate is 'Swiss nature' and Norwegian milk is 'natural'. But even here the definitions of nature and 'naturalness' are contested. Organic and biodynamic products have gained market shares in parts of Europe in the last decade, thereby challenging traditional definitions or what it means to be natural (Bjørkhaug and Flø 1999). However, when the food industry makes an appeal to nature, they tend also to be accompanied by references to a scientific understanding of nature. Science justifies and legitimizes references to nutritional value, food safety and possible claims of functional qualities (Diplock et al. 1999). On this point, organic or biodynamic food represents a marketing challenge, as there is sparse scientific proof that these kinds of product are healthier than ordinary products.

Different authorities and public agencies have different regulatory roles in relation to food as nature. Nutritional policies are supposed to promote the health of their citizens. In this context risk monitoring, risk evaluation and risk communication are central tasks. By means of scientific expert evaluation, monitoring routines, and the enforcement of different kinds of standard, public authorities seek to ensure that food is safe and is perceived as such by the population (cf. Busch, this volume). The expert-based systems central to this regulation are heavily founded on what Macnaghten and Urry (1998) call an environmental realistic understanding of nature, implying a sharp divide between nature and society. The role of scientifically based expert systems in relation to solving trade disputes between countries may explain the endurance of this position. Juridical trade disputes have to be solved with reference to some kind of universal Truth that cannot be disputed.

Environmental policies are supposed to contribute to sustainable food production, nationally as well as internationally, while different kinds of industrial politics (farming, forestry and manufacturing) seek to make sure that definitions of nature do not come into conflict with short- and longer-term economic interests (Macnaghten and Urry 1998; Franklin 2002). Nevertheless, different regulatory ambitions and roles are often contradictory, as are different interests and public regulatory goals, hence different definitions of nature clash. For instance, a policy promoting 'green tourism' (green hills with white sheep) implies a different definition of nature than a farming policy favoring cheap food (intensive farming) or an international promotion of nations as wilderness areas (wolves, deer, primeval forests).

Food as Commodity

The commodity status of food is prominent in our capitalist society, although in the rhetoric of actors this is more often referred to indirectly rather than directly. One possible exception to this is in discount stores, which willingly refer to the one single feature relevant in commodities – their price. Today, in Western societies, retailers tend to control the market access of food. This has given them a strategic position of control and power, whereby they seek to transform the distribution system and the commodities themselves for their own purposes (cf. Marsden et al. 2000). It should be noted that nowhere else is the commodity character of products more dominant than among these intermediaries (Lien and Døving 1996). They have little 'loyalty' to the particular food products in their shelves, and practice so-called 'sourcing', whereby products and producers are taken in and out according to where the products can be acquired at the lowest price. Products are considered as fungibles, entities totally exchangeable with each other. Apart from price, a retailer's preoccupation with food is dominated by the need for effective logistics, storing and the mostly visual presentation of food for sale. This possibly creates an abstract and disembodied notion of food, very much in contrast to the embodiment implied in production (farming) and consumption.

A relatively similar notion of food is found in the mass-producing food-processing industry. By means of standardized and mainly mechanized production processes, raw material is meshed, heated or in other ways processed to produce ready-packed products, which are given a new design and identity as 'branded products' by means of packaging (Lien 1997). This may also involve an active denaturalization of the food. Related to this, Noelïe Vialles (1994) describes how animals are 'deanimated' and 'deanimalized' through the slaughtering process. Thereby the butcher, the industry and even the consumer are spared from the moral difficulties related to taking lives or 'eating lived lives'.

Because the food-processing industry and the retailers dominate the distribution system, the commodity character of food products is heavily disseminated and instituted in society. Thereby, the trope of food as commodity is projected into the economic structure of society. The different national retailers, their transnational counterparts as well as the major industrial producers, are furthering this commodification through joint initiatives toward standardization. Quality and safety requirements and technical systems are standardized, thereby reducing transaction costs and promoting trade and interchangeability of producers as well as products (cf. Brunsson 2002; Busch, this volume). This is also a way for these transnational agents to try to restrict the various creative national efforts to establish so-called technical barriers to trade. An auditing industry has grown up in order to monitor, support and certify these processes (Power 1997). Public authorities do also take part in this standardization, as active promoters and participants (cf. Brunsson and Jacobsson 2002).

Other actors are also actively promoting an understanding of food as a commodity. This includes industrial farming all over the world, as well as the (transnational) mass producers of food. However, first and foremost are the international trade-promoting agencies such as the World Trade Organization (WTO), and in some respect the European Union. The international trade regime resulting from The Uruguay Round (The General Agreement on Tariffs and Trade, or GATT) is based upon the traditional principle of non-discrimination, and these institutions are for the moment actively trying to impose a neo-liberal understanding of economics and trade on the world, thereby defining food as a commodity that can, and should, be traded globally (for example Klein 2000). They can effect this agenda by means of economic incentives (such as favorable loans or guarantees) and political instruments, and thereby more or less 'force' reluctant governments to apply to a universalistic understanding of food as a globally exchangeable commodity. In this way national protective agricultural regimes come under pressure, and are gradually forced to open up for imports of foods.

These policies are of course based on the political support of dominant nation-states, and first and foremost by the USA. However, they are also based on an institutionalized international system for risk assessment and monitoring. This way an international system for food safety is partly established defining rules and procedures for a legitimate interpretation of nature (Skogstad 2001; Spriggs and Isaac 2001). A rational environmental understanding of nature lies at the bottom of this system, in which science is given the authority to know and decide when nationally protective measures may be justified. Thereby the natural part of food is held at bay (at least this is what is attempted), preventing it from 'polluting' the commodity status of foods.

As in the case of the nature field discussed above, public authorities have different roles, and follow various goals in accordance with the commodity field. Regulatory competition politics ensure that products do not escape its commodity character and, hence, the transparency of the market. National economic policies, with or without the 'help' of the international supporters just mentioned, are based on the belief that the collective utility of a society will be optimized if products and services are made comparable through markets. Standardization, harmonization of regulations across national borders, deregulation of monopolies, and the dismantling of restrictions on import and trade, are important tools in this respect. Industrial politics, on the other hand, have often been given an opposite task: to help private entrepreneurs in the making of unique products and services. For instance, national and regional authorities in most countries have actively promoted different kinds of generic labeling, such as geographic-origin labeling, in order to promote national or regional economic interests (Tregear 2003).

The more food is understood as a commodity, the more a restricted time perspective tends to be implied. As a commodity food is a fungible, fundamentally comparable to other products and to the most universal commodity of all – money (Kopytoff 1986). Hence, food products as commodities are defined by their context, either the context of their production (Marx 1976) or the context of their exchange (Simmel 1990). According to a Marxist perspective, commodities in capitalistic societies are produced for barter and the production of surplus value or, in the case of farming, ground rent.[2] Marxist theory points to the production of surplus value as the basis for power and dominance in society. Standard economic theory claims power to be in the hands of consumers. Given that products are comparable and somewhat exchangeable, consumers are supposed to exercise choices, thereby optimizing utility along a price-volume dimension. Other parameters, like taste, visual aesthetics and 'image', should then, by definition, be irrelevant or reflected in the price.

Several scholars have claimed that society in general (Hirsch 1977; Kopytoff 1986) and food more specifically (Ritzer 1994) has become more and more commoditized. Referring to Marx's thesis on capital's subsumption of value and/or Weber's thesis on the rationalization of society, they argue that society has been progressively commoditized, standardized and rationalized. Critics point to the fact that there also are movements away from the sphere of commodities (for example Zelizer 1985 and 1988; Appadurai 1986; Parry and Bloch 1989) and that local identities and cultural expressions emerge countering these standardizing processes (see for example Smart 1999; Beck 2000). This applies to food as well, as exemplified by the Slow Food Movement, which has emerged as a direct reaction to McDonald's and Kentucky Fried Chicken (KFC) (Miele and Murdoch 2003).

Moreover, a transformation will always take place through appropriation, as consumers prepare and incorporate food into their daily lives and bodies. Food products purchased in the market have to be decommodified in order to function as food. This means that they have to be redefined in accordance with the other tropes, such as nature or culture. According to Arjun Appadurai (1986), things in general move in and out of commodity contexts, and we employ different kinds of ritual in order to accomplish this. Food and food products obviously make such shifts, and their movements seem swifter than many other kinds of product.

Food as Culture

Food is also frequently understood and promoted as culture. For instance, local food festivals are legion all over the Western world, demonstrating the frequently occurring connection of specific foods to specific places and identities. In festivals these connections are arranged, enacted and appropriated by enthusiasts, local businesses and authorities. In this way local food traditions are preserved, constructed and reconstructed, and the notion of food as culture is reconfirmed (Lewis 1997).

Taste and distinctions of taste are at the heart of such reconstructions. There may be a genetic predisposition for taste, but taste is mainly socialized and embodied in categorizations, likes and dislikes, forming aggregate patterns of family traditions, regional dishes or national cuisines (see Ben-Ze'ev, this volume). As Pierre Bourdieu (1984) points out, such patterns tend to be hierarchical-structured, reflecting power/impotence and dominance/marginality in society. Good taste tends to be defined by the middle classes with their high levels of cultural capital. But it is also a means for the execution of dominance, whereby the marginality of the working class is made manifest. This is also reflected in the public discourses on food, such as the prominence given to middle-class foods in newspapers and magazines and the corresponding ignorance or abhorrence of working-class tastes.

The hierarchical structuring of taste reflects food's genuinely social, symbolical and moral character (see for example Lévi-Strauss 1966; Douglas 1984; Murcott 1998). Food tends to point to some kind of socially and culturally differentiated community, and serves to draw up lines between an 'us' and a 'them' (Bourdieu

1984), between a present and a past. What you eat, how it is prepared and the context of the meal are thus socially and culturally regulated and sanctioned (Kjærnes 2001). It is the raw material of tradition and nostalgia, but may also serve as a bridge to other places and cultures, such as in the case of 'ethnic food'.

The cultural dimension of food is heavily exploited economically. Commercial actors (producers and retailers) try to give their products a particular identity. They attempt to hide or obscure the fungible character of their products by textual or iconographic reference to some unique property of the product. In the processing industry, packaging is used for brand building. Food from different areas (for example products in the French system of 'Appellation d'Orgine Contrôlée') or from specific producers is given a recognizable visual design indicating a specific quality, origin or social reference (Tregear 2003). This contrasts with the commodity aspects discussed above. Hence, in the market place a struggle between brands and producers for attention and trustworthiness is evident.

Food production is central to the regional policy of most countries. Hence, authorities tend to promote national or regional labeling. This is frequently part of a generic 'national brand building', in which national identities are reconstructed in order to suit a more globalized media reality (Tregear 2003). Cultural authorities are often active in these processes trying to preserve and refashion traditional collective identities linked to food and food production. Hence, museums and cookery courses are given public funding as a part of national or regional programs.

The relationship between the tropes of culture and nature is not without tensions. Food taboos are one of many examples of how humans try to distance themselves, not only from other humans, but also from other species (Douglas 1966). So called 'civilized societies' use cuisine, manners and etiquette to distinguish themselves from the 'savages' (see for example Elias 1998). In this way a felt need for distinction, and an evolutionary understanding of society and taste, serve to construct distance between food as nature and as culture (Lévi-Strauss 1966).

In Western societies, the notion of food as culture seems to be partly based on a romantic understanding of nature as wildlife and tradition. It is an idealized environmentalism, a conception of nature as the carrier of its own eternal values, that seems to dominate in kitchens, dining rooms and most of all in advertising and marketing (Mcnaghten and Urry 1998). It is certainly not the scientific, abstract, calculable nature promoted by nutritional education, such as in the Nordic countries of the 1930s.[3] Instead food is profiled by reference to farmers' traditional and 'natural' practices, wildlife as well as hunter's primeval instincts, the butcher's traditional professionalism and mother's cookery (based on grandmother's recipes). Moreover, even high cuisine – cookery as an art form – tends not to refer to science for its legitimacy, but rather to the chefs' creativity in unfolding nature's true and eternal values and aesthetics. In this way it is the uniqueness of the products that is emphasized, not their fungible properties. Hence, food as culture tends to be profiled in ways incompatible with its status as a commodity.

Trope – Actors and Interests

I have tried to indicate how different tropes serve in the construction of food as quite distinct social phenomena, each with its own set of interest constellations, moral universes, time perspectives and repertoires of action. In a somewhat simplified form, one may regard the different tropes as distinct games, with a high degree of overlap between the players, but where each game implies different goals, different rules and different sets of resources. It follows that the different actors will prefer games especially suited for their particular mix of economic, political and rhetorical resources. Hence, when new food-related questions arise in the public, actors will try to define them (and to get others to define them) in accordance with definitions favorable to their interests. For instance, in the description of media coverage of the BSE (Bovine Spongiform Encephalopathy) crisis in the UK, Adam (1998: chap 5) shows how swiftly the situation went from being a health crisis to being a beef crisis where the loss of jobs and export income dominated the national debate. Nerlich (this volume), on the other hand, shows how quickly the media debate around the 2001 food-and-mouth disease (FMD) outbreak in Great Britain evolved into a debate over cheap food.

Table 4.1 sums up some of the implications related to the three food-related connotative fields.

Several actors tend to present food as nature. However, there are competing notions of what this nature is, and how it interacts with human society. Notions of embodied nature, as experienced by traditional small-scale farmers and consumers, stands against more abstract notions of a single and universal Nature. In particular the role of science is contested. The food industry and governments tend to see science as the legitimate interpreter of Nature, a nature that is understood and treated as comprised of objects. Environmental NGOs and some consumers are more skeptical or even hostile to the role of science, and tend to see nature more as a subject in its own right. All of these notions of nature do, however, promote a long-term perspective on food, whether this encompasses individual lives, human generations or biological life on earth.

The presentation of food as a commodity is at the basis of retailing and in particular discount retailing, whereby retailers use their strategic power to impose a commodity understanding of food on society. Industrial farming and (transnational) large-scale manufacturers are also joining retailers in these commoditization efforts, for example through standardization and harmonization. They are backed by a system of international institutions for the promotion of free trade, with the WTO in front. A rational understanding of nature lies at the base of their

Table 4.1 Tropes of food – some implicit perspectives and practical implications

Trope	Actor or propagator	Time perspective	Relevant space	Rhetorical repertoire	Public regulators' role(s)
Food as nature	Environmental NGOs; Environmental bureaucrats; Nutritionists	Human life; generations; Evolution	Farm; Kitchen; The body; The Earth	Sustainable growth; Nature as subject of its own	Nature-management; Health and nutrition policies
Food as commodity	Retailers and large-scale manufacturers; WTO	Short term profits; life sustainability	Super-market; Industry	Utility; Cost-benefit; Fairness; Predictability; Science	Competition policy
Food as culture	Local and regional communities; Nation builders	Experiences of the moment; Nostalgia and tradition	Restaurants; Home; Festival	Aesthetics; Identity; Tradition; Uniqueness	Nation building; Industrial and regional policy

activities, where rational science is supposed to protect trade, and hence the commodity status of food, from being 'polluted' by nature and concerns for nature (human nature as well as the environment). On a national level, public authority seems split between competition-policy politics promoting the commoditizing of food, and industrial and regional politics, which often aims at protecting local entrepreneurs from competition.

References to food as culture are frequently applied in the brand marketing of specific food products, producers, regions or even nations. It is used as a vehicle to escape the commodity character of products, and hence, as an argument for higher prices. National and regional authorities are strongly involved in this, supporting the development of regional food industries and products. A romanticized conception of culture, as well as nature, seems currently to underpin these efforts.

Risk Society

In what scholars describe as the age of post- or late modernity (see for example Giddens 1990; Beck 1992), the commodification of food tends to dominate in the public domain. However, this is not total dominance, as advertising and marketing, for example, draw heavily on the natural as well as the cultural tropes. The prominence of the commodity trope follows partly from our private capitalistic economic system, and a situation where the intermediaries – processing industries and retailers – dominate in the distribution channels. In the private domain, on the other hand, food seems to be naturalized (Franklin 2002: 16) and 'culturalized' – embodied in shopping activities (Miller 1998) and eating practices (Kjærnes 2001).

The commodity dominance in the public domain is based on a realistic or instrumental environmental understanding of nature, in which science is understood as the only legitimate interpreter of nature (Macnaghten and Urry 1998). In this way science has contributed to concealing the hybrid character of food. In the aftermath of 'mad-cow' disease (BSE) and other food scandals, this particular understanding of nature and the nature–society divide has been heavily contested. Science and its different roles have been disputed and a reconstruction of the nature-society divide has taken place. The modernist conception of nature as manipulable and calculable through scientific methods and technology is challenged. Funtowicz and Ravetz (1993) describe this situation as 'postnormal science', where there is a high degree of systemic uncertainties – that is, scientific uncertainties – and where there are high decision-making stakes involved. The latter implies that people feel that important issues or questions are at stake. In such situations traditional mechanisms of scientific quality assessment may fail, as scientists openly disagree and policy choices involve values outside the domain of scientists and experts. If the authority of science fails in this way, it also implies a possible dismantling of the nature–society divide (Latour 1993). We become less able to distinguish them from each other; nature 'pollutes' society and society and humans become naturalized.

Disturbances in the construction of the nature–society divide seem to imply a reconstruction of all kinds of social relations in and around the food system. Social institutions and trust relationships have to be renegotiated, and relations of power and influence are changed. This also takes the form of adjustments in rhetorical strategies. This may be apparent in an increased prominence of the nature trope. As mentioned, food seems frequently to be 'naturalized' (Franklin 2002) – constructed, reconstructed and profiled as nature. If science no longer has the potential to legitimize food products and their production, actors may or must search elsewhere for justifications and markers of identity. The nature trope is here – and has probably always been here – and is readily available for these purposes. However, what nature this is, how new nature-claims should be justified, and the trustworthiness of such claims will be contested. Not only language, but also power, influence and economic interests are at stake.

Notes

1. There are obviously other tropes available, for example food as a gift. However, food as a gift belongs more to the private domain, such as in kin relations or

between friends, and does not have the same political potential as the three other tropes mentioned. However, it should be noted that producers often try to use advertising to present their products as gifts to the consumers.
2. Ground rent is based upon the fact that landowners may extract or manage a surplus from nature.
3. In Norway exemplified by The National Institute for Consumer Research (SIFO), the food package and the school breakfast, all instituted in that period (see for example Lyngø 2003).

References

Adam, B. (1998), *Timescapes of Modernity*, London: Routledge.

Appadurai, A. (1986),'Introduction: commodities and the politics of value', in A. Appadurai (ed.), *The Social Life of Things, Commodities in Cultural Perspective*, Cambridge: Cambridge University Press.

Bateson, G. (1972), *Steps to an Ecology of Mind*, New York: Ballantine.

Beck, U. (1992), *Risk Society*, London: Sage.

—— (2000), *What is Globalization?* Cambridge: Polity.

Bjørkhaug, H. and Flø, B. E. (1999), 'Production and Distribution of Organic food in Norway – from the Farmer's Point of View', Paper presented at the XVIII Congress of the European Society for Rural Sociology, Lund. Paper no. 5/99, Trondheim: Senter for bygdeforskning.

Bourdieu, P. (1984), *Distinction: A Social Critique of the Judgement of Taste*, Cambridge, MA: Harvard University Press.

Bråten, S. (1973), 'Modelmonopoly and Communication', *Acta Sociologica*, 16(2): 98–107.

Braun, B. and Castree, N. (1998), 'Introduction', in Bruce, Braun and Noel Castree, *Remaking Reality: Nature at the Millennium*, London: Routledge.

Brunsson, N. (2002), 'Organizations, Markets and Standardization', in N. Brunsson and B. Jacobsson (eds), *A World of Standards*, Oxford: Oxford University Press.

—— and Jacobsson, B. (2002), 'The Contemporary Expansion of Standardization', in N. Brunsson and B. Jacobsson (eds), *A World of Standards*, Oxford: Oxford University Press.

Chandler, D. (2002), *Semiotics: The Basics*, London: Routledge.

Condit, C. M., Bates, B. R., Galloway, R., Givens, S. B., Haynie, C. K., Jordan, J. W., Stables, G. and West, H. M. (2002): 'Recipes or Blueprints for Our Genes? How Contexts Selectively Activate the Multiple Meanings of Metaphors', *Quarterly Journal of Speech*, 88(3), August: 303–25.

Diplock, A. T., Aggett, P. J., Ashwell, M., Bornet, F., Fern, E. B. and Roberfroid, M. B. (1999), 'Scientific Concepts of Functional Foods in Europe: Consensus

Document', *British Journal of Nutrition*, 81, Supplement Number 1: S1–S27.

Douglas, M. (1966), *Purity and Danger: An Analysis of Concepts of Pollution and Taboo*, London: Routledge.

—— (1984), 'Standard Social Uses of Food: Introduction', in M. Douglas (ed.), *Food in the Social Order*, New York: Russel Sage Foundation, 1–40.

—— and Isherwood, B. (1979), *The World of Goods*, New York: Basic.

Elias, N. (1998), *Norbert Elias on Civilization, Power, and Knowledge: Selected Writings*, ed. and intro. by S. Mennell and J. Goudsblom, Chicago: University of Chicago Press.

Fernandez, J. W. (1974), 'Persuations and Performances: "Of the Beast in Every Body . . . And the Metaphors of Everyman"', in I. C. Geertz (ed.), *Myth, Symbol and Culture*, New York: WW Norton.

Fischler, C. (1988), 'Food, Self and Identity', *Anthropology of Food*, 27(2): 275–92.

Fiumara, G. C. (1995), *The Metaphoric Process: Connections between Language and Life*, London: Routledge.

Foucault, M. (1974), *The Archaeology of Knowledge*, London: Tavistock.

Franklin, A. (2002), *Nature and Social Theory*, London: Sage.

Funtowicz, S. O. and Ravetz, J. R. (1993), 'Science for the Post-Normal Age', *Futures*, September: 739–55.

Giddens, A. (1990), *The Consequences of Modernity*, Cambridge: Polity.

Heradsveit, D. (1992), *Political Rhetoric*, Norsk Utenrikspolitisk institutt, Notat nr. 457, April, Oslo: NUPI.

Hirsch, F. (1977), *Social Limits to Growth*, London: Routledge & Kegan Paul.

Kalland, A. (1993), 'Whale Politics and Green Legitimacy; A Critique of the Anti-whaling Campaign', *Anthropology Today*, 9(6): 3–7.

Kjærnes, U. (ed.) (2001), '*Eating Patterns: A Day in the Lives of Nordic Peoples*', Report nr. 7, Lysaker: National institute for consumer research.

Klein, N. (2000), *No-Logo: Taking Aim at the Brand Bullies*, Toronto: Alfred A. Knopf.

Kopytoff, I. (1986), 'The Cultural Biography of Things: Commoditization as Process', in A. Appadurai (ed.), *The Social Life of Things: Commodities in Cultural Perspective*, Cambridge: Cambridge University Press.

Lakoff, G. and Johnson, M. (1980), *Metaphors We Live By*, Chicago: University of Chicago Press.

Latour, B. (1993), *We Have Never Been Modern*, New York: Harvester Wheatsheaf.

Lévi-Strauss, Claude (1966), 'The Culinary Triangle', *Partisan Review*, 33: 686–95.

Lewis, G. H. (1997), 'Celebrating Asparagus: Community and the Rationally Constructed Food Festival', *Journal of American Culture*, 4: 73–8.

Lien, M. E. (1997), *Marketing and Modernity*, Oxford: Berg.

—— and Døving, R. (1996), *Grønnsaker som mat og handelsvare: Kvalitetsoppfatninger fra produsent til forbruker.* (Vegetables as Food and Commodities: Conceptions of Quality in the Trade and among Consumers.) Report nr. 2 – 1996, Lysaker: National Institute for Consumer Research.

Lyngø, I. J. (2003), 'Vitamins', Ph.D. Dissertation, University of Oslo, Department of Cultural Studies.

Macnaghten, P. and Urry, J. (1998), *Contested Natures*, London: Sage.

Marsden, T., Flynn, A. and Harrison, M. (2000), *Consuming Interests: The Social Provision of Foods*, London: UCL Press.

Marx, K. (1976), *Capital Volume III*, New York: Penguin.

Miele, M. and Murdoch, J. (2003), 'The Slow Food Movement in Italy', in R. Almås and G. Lawrence (eds) (2003): *Globalization, Localization and Sustainable Livelihoods*, London: Ashgate.

Miller, D. (1998), *A Theory of Shopping*, Cambridge: Polity.

Mol, A. (1999), 'Ontological Politics: A Word and some Questions', in J. Law and J. Hassard (eds), *Actor Network Theory and After*, Oxford: Blackwell/The Sociological Review.

Morgan, K. and Murdoch, J. (2000), 'Organic vs. Conventional Agriculture: Knowledge, Power and Innovation in the Food Chain', *Geoforum*, 31: 159–79.

Murcott, A. (ed.) (1998), *The Nation's Diet: The Social Science of Food Choice*, London: Longman.

Parry, J. and Bloch, M. (1989), 'Introduction: Money and the Morality of Exchange', in J. Parry and M. Bloch (eds), *Money and the Morality of Exchange*, Cambridge: Cambridge University Press.

Power, M. (1997), *The Audit Society: Rituals of Verification*, Oxford: Oxford University Press.

Ritzer, G. (1994), *The McDonaldization of Society*, Thousand Oaks: Pine Forge.

Simmel, G. (1990), *The Philosophy of Money*, London: Routledge.

Skogstad, G. (2001), 'The WTO and Food Safety Regulatory Policy Innovation in the European Union', *Journal of Common Market Studies*, 39(3): 485–505.

Smart, B. (ed.) (1999), *Resisting McDonaldization*, London: Sage.

Spriggs, J. and Isaac, G. (2001), *Food Safety and International Competitiveness: The Case of Beef*, Wallingford (UK): CABI Publishing.

Stern, J. (2000), *Metaphor in Context*, Cambridge, MA: MIT Press.

Tester, K. (1992), *Animals and Society: The Humanity of Animal Rights*, London: Routledge.

Tregear, A. (2003), 'From Stilton to Vimto: Using Food History to Re-think Typical Products in Rural Development', *Sociologica Ruralis*, 43(2): 91–107.

Vialles, N. (1994), *Animal to Edible*, Cambridge: Cambridge University Press.

White, H. (1979), 'Michel Foucault', in J. Sturrock (ed.), *Structuralism and Since:*

From Lévi-Strauss to Derrida, Oxford: Oxford University Press.

Zelizer, V. (1985), *Pricing the Priceless Child: The Changing Social Value of Children*, New Jersey: Princeton University Press.

—— (1988), 'Beyond the Polemics on the Market: A Theoretical and Empirical Agenda', *Sociological Forum*, 3, Fall: 614–34.

Part II
Nation and Nurture

–5–

Risky Science and Savoir-faire: Peasant Expertise in the French Debate over Genetically Modified Crops

Chaia Heller

The debate about agricultural biotechnology is not just about scientific risk. It is also a debate about agriculture: a debate about the production and consumption of food. In the French debate over genetically engineered food, there is a collision between two framings of 'risk' and 'agriculture' as farmers begin to reframe the issue into their own terms of expertise. When initially framed as a 'risk' issue, the French debate over agricultural biotechnology invokes scientific expertise for evaluating the environmental and health hazards associated with the technology. When it is defined as an agricultural issue of 'food quality', farmers shift the debate into the terms of peasant, or *paysan* expertise.

Based on ethnographic research on the genetically modified organisms (GMO) controversy in France during 1997–2000, this chapter explores two key frames that actors have used to bolster their claims about GMOs in France. First I analyze how an objectivist risk frame prevailed in the first phase of the French debate. Then I analyze how the CP (Confédération Paysanne – Peasants' Confederation) re-framed GMOs as a problem of food quality linked to productivist agriculture, cultural homogenization, and globalization.

This transformation of the French GMO debate is implicit. Actors promoting or undermining an objectivist risk discourse may be unaware that they are doing so – and thus may be unaware of the broader implications for debates about technoscience. Nevertheless the CP's discursive maneuvers have broadened understandings of what may count as expertise for technoscience practice and policy-making in the future.

Agricultural Biotechnology: An Initial Debate about Risk

In the first phase of the debate over agricultural biotechnology in France (1996–1998), the 'risk' frame and scientific expertise played a primary role in shaping public discussion, as risk regulation became the official procedure for evaluating GMOs (Roy and Joly 2000; Marris 2001a). Indeed, during this period, 'risk' was the common discourse of public debate; media, activists, and actors within powerful institutions focused almost exclusively on the environmental and health issues associated with genetically modified foods. Television newscasts featured images of science experts, micro-biologists arched over lab stations in spotless white coats, squeezing drops of mysterious substances from colorful pipettes, discussing the risks associated with the new technology.

Objectivist Risk Discourse
Objectivist risk discourse rests on two key assumptions, *universalistic* and *riskocentric*. While the universalistic assumption assumes risk to be inherently universal and value-free, the riskocentric assumption assumes risk as the exclusive and solely legitimate frame for evaluating technoscience practice generally. Due to the universalistic assumption, regulatory bodies tend to assume that they can objectively define their own problems – for instance by constructing particular 'risk objects' that constitute the target for network activity (Hilgartner 1992). For example, scientists working in both French laboratory and government settings have tended to define 'gene flow' as a primary problem for assessment and management; they foreground the question of 'gene flow', amid an unbounded field of other potential risk objects such as antibiotic-resistance markers or potential allergens associated with the technology. In so doing, they transform the idea of 'gene flow', one uncertainty among others, into a 'risk object'; they design safety protocols for laboratory and field tests to contain potentially 'wandering genes'. Despite the often subjective and conditional nature of the risk-construction process, actors tend to assume risk definition and management to be an objective endeavor, falling within the jurisdiction of risk experts, thus marginalizing 'non-experts' from the process of agenda setting.

The riskocentric assumption gives rise to a different set of beliefs and practices as actors assume the risk concept to be the primary and even exclusive frame for evaluating issues of technoscience. Assuming 'risk' as central, actors tend to exclude other, explicitly socio-cultural frames – such as food quality, farmer autonomy, or the ethics and political economy of life-patenting – as 'secondary' or as patently irrelevant. Likewise the risk frame excludes the associated forms of expertise.

In this analysis of the French debate, 'objectivist risk discourse' denotes both the universalistic and riskocentric assumptions. Sociologists of science have used empirical studies to problematize the universalistic risk assumption in the GMO debate; they explore the culture of regulatory bodies which take for granted whatever risk objects they construct (Levidow et al. 1996; Wynne 1995; Jasanoff 1990; Marris 2001a, 2001b). Complementing such analyses, this chapter focuses on the riskocentric assumption, or simply 'riskocentrism', by exploring the practices which reproduce or displace expert discourses of risk as the primary, natural frame for evaluating GMOs.

Riskocentrism emerges during the modern period as actors begin to recast 'natural' and institution-driven dangers as a set of statistically calculable, insurable harms assumed as a necessary price to pay for social progress (Heller and Escobar 2003; Ewalds 1991). For theorists such as François Ewalds and Robert Castells, risk constitutes a historical process through which powerful institutions such as the State or corporations regulate the potentially costly or liable behavior of populations – as well as the everyday processes through which individuals and organizations within modern populations come to regulate themselves and each other, voluntarily (and often unthinkingly) conforming to dominant expert discourses and practices by avoiding 'risky' or potentially dangerous employment, hobbies, and other practices (Ewalds 1991; Castells 1991). Riskocentrism is also the process through which actors are induced to voluntarily reproduce 'risk' as the central and natural way to talk about a variety of concerns – not solely matters commonly associated with technical or physical 'danger'. Indeed, through riskocentrism, actors come to regard risk as the most suitable frame for discussing arenas ranging from business investing and marital questions to career development and social work.

In the arena of technoscience, risk assumes a significant degree of centrality as the practices, evaluations, and images of science tend to orbit around the focal perspective of risk. As Wynne suggests, in the GMO debate, actors in regulatory bodies often trivialize 'non-risk' concerns, relegating the heterogeneous universe of intellectual and political claims to a secondary and monolithic category of 'ethical concerns' (Wynne 2001).

In the first phase of the French GMO debate, actors within a range of institutions tended to reproduce a riskocentric perspective, while showing little awareness that they were maintaining risk as the central frame. When asked open questions regarding 'the general stakes surrounding GMOs', nearly every actor interviewed, ranging from government and corporate officials to scientists and activists, would immediately deliver narratives regarding the potential risks surrounding the technology. Never did actors note the possibility that risk might be one frame among others for talking about technoscience issues. Nor did they appear to be conscious of, or troubled by, the prominence of risk in the debate and the corresponding muting of other related concerns such as food quality, the ethics of life-patenting, and so on. Actors appeared unable to *think about* their own voluntary conformity to risk as the central frame for talking about the technology.

When questioned about the relative absence of 'non-risk' frames for GMOs in public debate, actors in both powerful and activist institutions would often mention, off the record, that they did have 'personal' concerns regarding GMOs, but that they would never articulate such opinions in public because they fell outside the realm of 'what the media wanted to hear' or of 'what the public can understand.'

Leaders in consumer and ecology associations such as the Union Fédérale des Consommateurs and Greenpeace France, for instance, expressed what appeared to be genuine concerns about environmental and health risks associated with GMOs, always ending the interview on a more 'personal' note by talking about concerns regarding 'aggressive multinationals imposing GMOs on the world' or about 'a loss of a quality of life due to the globalization of food and culture'. Again, when asked why their organizations never expressed such concerns in public forums or in organizational literature, actors delivered the same response: 'To be taken seriously, you have to talk about science. You have to talk about the risks.'

I never had the impression, however, that actors consciously or intentionally compartmentalized their discourse. Rather, objectivist risk narratives seemed to reflect taken-for-granted understandings about science, society, and about 'risk' as a universal frame for evaluating science practice. Yet while standing in a shadowy zone between articulable and unarticulable understandings about science, actors were often aware of institutional constraints that limited what they could say publicly about GMOs: leaders of ecology and consumer groups, directors of research at public and private science bodies, as well as corporate executives, at times mentioned institutional expectations to reproduce their institution's official position on GMOs, focusing on risk. As one executive at a major food industry put it: 'Sometimes your personal political opinion doesn't match the company's opinion, and you better shut up.'

Not all actors, however, were conscious of such constraints – sometimes with deleterious results. One day in the Fall of 1998, a scandal broke at a key national public agricultural research facility when a television crew from a major French network arrived to interview two biologists conducting research on transgenic plants. After a general discussion about risks, the interview shifted in tone as one of the biologists, 'Cécile', articulated concerns regarding biological patents and the potential impacts of agricultural biotechnology on rural economies of third-world countries. The morning after the program aired on national television, the laboratory's director was barraged by phone calls from government officials and senior scientists both within and outside of the institution, expressing outrage at Cécile's audacity in sharing her 'personal opinion' in public. The remarks of one senior research director captured the sentiment expressed by many:

We were all shocked by what she said . . . no one ever thought she would behave that way, no one thought she would have such bad judgment, to just give her opinion like that, to just say whatever entered her head. You just don't do that. When you talk to the public, you have to talk about science. I guess she doesn't care about her career . . .

When interviewed several months after the incident, Cécile still appeared traumatized, describing a climate of ongoing alienation from colleagues who gossiped about her, avoided sitting with her at the center's cafeteria, and ceased to invite her to social gatherings both within and outside the laboratory. 'I don't know how I can tolerate it, to continue to work here,' she said, reflecting on her situation, 'they are making it impossible . . . and all because I said what I really thought . . . no one ever told me not to do so . . .' In the months following the incident , the director of communications at the research facility set up a series of 'trainings' for scientists to 'teach them how to speak to journalists, to know what to say and what not to say in public.'

The 'Cécile' incident illustrates an unspoken rule of hegemony: What must *not* be said, does not *have* to be said. Not only were Cécile's colleagues shocked that she had dared to step outside the bounds of 'acceptable' public science discourse, but they appeared shocked that she did not know that she should not have done so. When questioned, however, Cécile's colleagues appeared equally unable to explain exactly what Cécile had done wrong. No one could 'think' to say that she had spoken about issues other than risk. They just expressed disgust that she had spoken 'unscientifically'.

Adherence to a riskocentric perspective, however, does not guarantee that actors' claims will be regarded as legitimate. Actors within powerful institutions tend to portray anti-GMO scientists or activists who make risk claims as 'manipulators' of an otherwise unbiased and 'science based' debate about risk. In 1999, when a group of ecology and farmers' groups put forth and won an appeal to the French Supreme Court regarding the risks associated with antibiotic resistance markers (which ultimately led to a temporary moratorium on several varieties of GM corn), government, science, and industry officials portrayed Greenpeace as using the real debate over GMO risk as a proxy in order to promote their own political agendas. Notions of 'real risk versus political motives' express taken-for-granted understandings about 'science' and 'society' as two discrete realms. While 'political' claims may cunningly masquerade as 'science' claims, they will always *really* be about 'society' rather than science.

Agricultural Biotechnology: A Later Debate about Agriculture

If the first phase of the French debate promoted a hegemonic frame of scientific risk expertise, the second was greatly informed by *paysan* expertise surrounding questions of food quality and culture. Placing the terms of the debate within the discursive domain of peasant-identified family farmers, CP members established themselves as legitimate national experts on French food and culture as well as international experts on peasant survival, capitalist science, sustainable development, and other related questions of globalization. In so doing, they challenged the hegemony of risk in the GMO debate, opening the way for a broader set of terms and knowledges to be integrated into the general landscape of technoscience debate.

During the second phase of the debate, the CP shifted the site of expertise away from the GMO risk network. Through this shift, the CP established their own network of self-identified peasant farmers as a key site within a wider French anti-globalization network, and within the broader international anti-globalization network whose constituents range from trade unions and anti-GMO activists to environmental and indigenous NGOs.

The CP's formation in 1987 represents the culmination of a decade-long struggle to create an autonomous voice for family farmers in a milieu largely dominated by France's number one union of industrial farmers, the National Federated Union of Agricultural Enterprises (FNSEA). Since its inception, the CP has struggled (and after 1999, succeeded partly) to become a contending counter-power to the FNSEA, representing a network of socialist-leaning family farmers contesting the industrialized agricultural policy that intensified during France's postwar period. Reclaiming what had become in France a pejorative or 'backward' term *paysan*, the CP identifies with, and plays a key role in, an international network of peasants movements such as the European Peasant Coordination and Via Campesina. Engaged in the struggle for cultural, economic, and agricultural identity and survival, these NGOs are tightly integrated into the wider international anti-globalization movement.

Already linked to the French and international anti-globalization network through peasant movements, the CP widened its sphere of alliances when it launched its own anti-GMO campaign in 1997, presenting an anti-globalization message that defended the rights of peasants, workers, and indigenous peoples against agricultural biotechnology. Yet the CP was not the first to put forth a 'post-risk' anti-globalization critique of GMOs in France or internationally. Since the 1980s, international environmental NGOs associated with such publications as the Indian-based magazine *Third World Resurgence* and the British journal *The Ecologist* had been developing a cultural and political economy critique of GMOs. Between the 1992 Earth Summit in Rio de Janeiro, and the 1999 anti-WTO demonstrations in Seattle, these cultural and political-economy perspectives on North/South relations, international peasant movements, and 'sustainable development' expanded to become what could be called an 'anti-globalization critique' associated with the international anti-globalization network.

In France, national branches of international NGOs such as Greenpeace or Ecoropa had been developing their own anti-globalization critiques of GMOs for several years before the CP launched its campaign. However, as environmental groups lack wide public support in a French political milieu largely dominated by political parties and unions, they were unable to sufficiently popularize the anti-globalization critique, relying, often unknowingly, on hegemonic risk-based arguments. Again, while not the first to introduce an anti-globalization perspective into the GMO debate, the CP played a central role in *popularizing* the perspective, adding its own trade unionist and *paysan* discourses into the mix. As I will discuss later, after 1999, the CP was able to cultivate more cultural clout than environmental NGOs, by developing an anti-GMO/anti-globalization perspective cast in cultural terms that resonated with the French public.

The Trial of the GMOs

It was the radical sector of the CP, headed up by activist duo José Bové and Réné Riesel, that succeeded in organizing their first major anti-GMO event in 1998. On 8 January, Bové, Riesel and about one hundred CP farmers received international attention for destroying three tons of Novartis transgenic corn in a storage plant in the southern town of Nérac by spraying it with fire hoses. When Bové and Riesel were arrested and put on trial, they decided to transform their own trial into a 'trial of the GMOs', contesting the legal and moral status of agricultural biotechnology itself (Heller 2002).

It was during this week-long trial that Bové and Riesel set in motion a discourse and an activist strategy that would later counter the risk hegemony of the French GMO debate. In addition to inviting consumer and environmental activists, Riesel and Bové summoned the expertise of key scientists – such as Gilles-Eric Seralini (National Center for Scientific Research), biologist Jacques Testard (National Institute for Agronomic Research), and Richard Lacey (British professor and specialist in mad-cow disease) – who testified about GMO-related risk. However, alongside science expertise, they invoked their own expertise as *paysans* and as union workers uniquely situated to speak about food quality, farmers' duties to protect and develop French seeds, and the implications of industrialized agriculture on rural peoples and cultures.

As the trial illustrates, the CP's hybrid identity as *paysans* and as *workers* allows CP discourse to operate on both international and national levels. While new particular forms of political identity such as *paysan* have been steadily emerging in post-industrial France, they have not replaced universalist forms of identification such as class. Rather, groups such as the CP have begun to weave together seamlessly the particular and the universalistic, creating synthetic identities such as peasant-worker, or *paysan-travailleur* (the previous name of the union) that locate the culturally rooted *paysan* within a wider international struggle against worker exploitation. As CP literature states, 'for us, the land is a tool that we work, just as the worker has his machine' (Confédération Paysanne 1997)).

On the international level, the CP's hybrid identity of *paysan* and *travailleur* allows members to enroll themselves into the anti-globalization network, becoming a key bridge between both northern and southern NGOs seeking a symbolic intermediary that represents both North and South: a symbol of the pre-industrial peasant that is both located within, yet disenfranchised from, powerful sites of capitalist accumulation. Through an alliance with Étienne Vernet (of the French branch of the European NGO, Ecoropa), the CP was able to concretize its new, more central position within the anti-globalization network by linking the CP to key spokesperson of the anti-globalization network, Indian scientist-activist Vandanna Shiva. On behalf of the CP, it was Vernet who invited Shiva to the trial to testify on behalf of 'The Third World'.

The CP's potency as a credible spokesperson at the trial and within the national anti-globalization movement is tied to its ability to 'silently' translate a debate about scientific risk into the CP's own terms of expertise. In particular, the CP translates underlying notions of 'nature' associated with agricultural science and risk expertise into discourses of 'nature' associated with *paysan* expertise. The CPs discourse on 'nature', however, is quite distinct from the 'environmental' discourse that dominates European (and much of Northern) opposition to techno-science. Rather than promoting an 'environmental' notion of nature as a distinct category from that of culture, the CP promotes a French understanding of nature *as* culture.

Contemporary environmental and ecological discourses predominant in the US and throughout much of Western Europe emerge out of nineteenth-century Germanic nature romanticism which understands nature as pristine, 'wild' or pre-social wilderness (Heller 1999). In contrast, what might be called a 'French nature' is predicated on romantic notions of *social* rural life. These include discourses on the soil and savoir-faire that produce the wine, cheese, and pâtés that are emblems of French culture and history (Fischler 1993).

By invoking notions of rurality at the trial, the CP established the *paysan* as cultural expert and spokesperson for French nature, symbolizing France's rural past, a popular topic within French discussions of globalization and cultural homogenization. The CP frequently appealed to the plight of the small farmer saving heirloom seeds cultivated for many generations, along with its popular anti-GMO slogans, 'the world is not merchandise', and 'the earth is not for sale'. These appeals built upon societal anxieties about the ongoing effects of modernity on France's rural past. They drew in turn upon a widely shared collective sense of regret shared by many French about the continued dispossession of the peasant farmer that has intensified in the postwar period; this regret endowed the *paysan* with a status analogous to that of the American Indian in the French popular imagination.

In addition to drawing on expert *paysan* discourses of nature, the CP draws from trade-unionist discourses of the *travailleur* as well. Again, the CP articulates a worked nature, a socialized nature whose value is not only historical, cultural, or aesthetic, but also *economic*, providing *paysans* with a viable and productive way of life. The CP's key slogan, printed on its pamphlets, T-shirts, and posters, reads, '*To Produce, To Employ, To Preserve*'. The idea of 'preservation' portrayed here is distinct from environmentalist understandings of preserving or conserving nature by protecting it from human activity. For the CP, the *paysan* preserves nature by knowing and caring for *le paysage*: by working and transforming the earth into a productive and meaningful landscape.

By invoking the identity of the French *travailleur*, struggling to survive in an increasingly competitive and exploitive national and international agricultural economy, the CP is able to win support for its struggle. By challenging multinationals' roles in investing in and shaping public agricultural science research and development – a science they regard as disenfranchising small farmers – the CP makes salient links between questions of global capital, science, and labor.

From GMOs to McDo: The Anti-Globalization Perspective

While the trial brought the CP modest attention in the French and international media, it was not until 1999 that the union began to play a central role in shaping the French GM debate. Indeed, it was a series of events that occurred between 1999 and 2001 that brought the CP national and international notoriety as anti-GMO activists, a series of events sparked off by an anti-McDonald's action. As I will illustrate, it was an anti-McDonald's action that serendipitously allowed the CP to enter the national spotlight, creating a clear link in popular consciousness between GMOs and globalization that would indirectly challenge the hegemony of objectivist risk.

In the summer of 1999 (despite the moderate success of the trial in 1998), the anti-globalization perspective promoted by the CP and other groups still lacked a sufficiently meaningful and potent frame of cultural reference. But that was soon to change. At the end of the summer, while Riesel was attending a PGA (People's Global Action) meeting in India, Bové planned what had become a routine demonstration against a McDonald's in his region. Having for several years demonstrated against '*McDo*' (French slang for McDonald's) as 'a symbol of globalization', Bové and 100 other local sheep farmers, as well as friends and families, symbolically dismantled a McDonald's construction site in the town of Millau by painting slogans in Occitane (the local ancient dialect) on the half-built roof, prying off a few tiles along the bare walls. For CP activists, the event represented a symbolic retaliation for Clinton's sanctions against Europe that had resulted in an extra tariff placed on French exports such as Roquefort cheese – Europe's punishment for refusing to import US hormone-treated beef.

According to Bové, for a young local judge in Millau, the *McDo* incident was a kind of last straw after the summer of 1999, a period during which the CP spearheaded a series of GM crop pulls in southern France. Determined to punish Bové for the anti-GMO actions, the judge ordered Bové and the six others arrested an unusually high bail and charge, uncharacteristic for trade union-related crimes of that nature and scale (Bové 1999). Unknowingly, the judge's actions set in motion a surprising chain of events that forever transformed the French GMO debate, thus putting Bové and the CP on the international map along the way.

At the time the bail orders were served, Bové and his family were vacationing in southern France. Upon his return a week later, Bové learned that he would have to wait for up to one week in the local prison for his bail hearing. Finally informed of the $25,000 bail, Bové decided to remain in jail to await his second hearing (a hearing to determine charges) instead of asking the CP to pay the fee. As Bové reflects, 'I figured I'd already spent a week there, I might as well wait another two for the charge hearing . . . besides, I'd realized that we were getting pretty good media by my being in there' (1999). News of Bové's three-week imprisonment, in addition to his elevated bail, captured national attention, hitting a cultural nerve that within weeks catapulted Bové to the status of national martyr and hero in the international anti-globalization movement. According to Bové, 'the French don't like to see a farmer or a union man put in jail like that for such a small thing. They saw the high bail and charges as being more like the American system. They say, "that's how Americans do it, and we're not Americans"' (1999).

Suddenly renowned for the *McDo*, rather than the GMO issue, Bové seized the opportunity to advance both causes. While Bové did not explicitly attempt to counter the hegemony of risk, he did discuss his intention to illustrate the links between GMOs and globalization. As Bové explains, 'In every interview after *McDo*, I would talk about GMOs . . . it was an opportunity to make that link clear in people's minds, that GMOs and *McDo* were really two aspects of the same problem . . . that multinationals, that capitalism, are controlling everything from culture to food . . . (1999).' Drawing on both *paysan* and anti-globalization discourses, Bové has continued to reframe GMOs and *McDo* as examples of 'globalization and a decline in quality of food and life both in France and throughout the world' (Bové 1999).

The success of the *McDo* action in bringing the CP to national attention led the CP, on an organizational level, to more publicly endorse and promote the anti-GMO campaign first spearheaded by Bové and Riesel. Bové's public endorsement by the CP and by the key French anti-globalization group ATTAC! also marked the beginning of the end of the Bové-Riesel duo. Upon his return from India a week after the *McDo* incident, Riesel was dismayed by what he perceived as 'a serious change in the strategy and discourse' which the two had been developing for the two years previous (Riesel 1999). After the *McDo* action, Riesel publicly resigned from the CP, distanced himself from Bové, wrote an open letter to Bové during his imprisonment, and later published a book that sharply criticized Bové for 'selling over the anti-GMO campaign to the moderates at the CP and to the reformist anti-globalizationists as well' (Riesel 1999).

As Riesel receded from the public GMO controversy, Bové rose to become the central figure in France associated with the anti-GMO and anti-globalization movements and has largely succeeded in reshaping the debate. While risk still remains a key topic of controversy, increasingly the media, activist groups, public researchers, and even government officials have broadened their discourse, including in their GMO narratives questions ranging from biological patents and the fate of the small farmers in France and internationally, to the homogenization of cultures by multinational capitalism.

Bové has indeed become a cultural folk hero in France and internationally, symbolizing French resistance to perceived processes of Americanization in domains of food, language, music, and business. However, the French and international media have challenged Bové's folksy cultural image, often patently questioning his status as a 'real' *paysan*. Bové's postmodern identity indeed defies static and romantic notions of pre-modern French peasantry. Son of bourgeois scientists in genetic research at INRA, Bové spent several years of his youth living in Berkeley, California where his parents were working as visiting researchers at the University there. Not until his late teens did Bové enter farm life: hiding as a draft-resister and anti-war activist, he worked on a small dairy farm in a village near Avignon.

A few years later, Bové fell upon a movement in which he would integrate his experience as an activist and farmer. In the mid-1970s, Bové joined the now infamous struggle known as '*Le Larzac*', a Ghandian-influenced non-violent movement named after an arid plateau in Roquefort country in southern France. In this movement, Roquefort-producing sheep farmers and young anti-war activists protested together against the expansion of a military base. Bové and one hundred other youths took over several abandoned farms on the would-be base, farmed the land, and continued the struggle until the late 1980s, when President Mitterand's socialist government agreed to forgo the expansion plan, instead allowing the squatters to farm the land collectively.

For the past several decades, Bové has remained in Le Larzac, producing sheep's milk for Roquefort, co-founding the CP, and engaging in national and international peasant movements. Since his rise to stardom, Bové has become a key figure in the international anti-globalization network, spending a good part of the year touring, speaking, and organizing in countries from Mexico to Brazil, while spending the other part tending his farm at home. Despite Bové's hybrid identity, he has enjoyed tremendous acceptance by the French public.

La Malbouffe

Bové's rise to stardom has allowed him to popularize a unique anti-GMO discourse that has strengthened his position as key spokesperson for national and international anti-GMO and anti-globalization networks. The centerpiece of Bové's discourse is the symbol, *la malbouffe*, which literally means 'bad food', which he equates with GMOs, *McDo*, and all products of globalized culture and agriculture. *La malbouffe* is a slang term created by an author of a little-known book in the mid-1990s, bemoaning the fate of French culture and cuisine. Translated imperfectly into 'bad chow', or 'junk food', *la malbouffe* symbolizes for Bové everything distasteful about globalization ranging from the cultural homogenization associated with McDonald's fast food to the industrialized agriculture associated with hormone-treated beef.

To uncover the more subtle meanings of *la malbouffe*, we must first understand the meaning of '*la bouffe*' itself, an affectionate colloquial term referring to 'grub', or food in general, from which the English term 'buffet' is most likely derived. *La bouffe*, though, really has no translation in English, bringing together notions of pleasure, tradition, and French cuisine, synonymous with French culture itself. To be 'cultured' in France, is to be 'cultivated', or to have good 'taste'.

The meaning of 'taste' here is twofold, as both food and people may be understood as cultivated or tasteful. While a food is well cultivated when produced according to regional agricultural traditions, an individual is considered cultivated when capable of recognizing, and taking pleasure in, well-cultured, good-tasting food, or *la bouffe*. Within this cultural-culinary universe, *la malbouffe*, represents the antithesis of cultural pleasure and cultivation. It signals that which is not traditionally cultivated, that which lacks cultural expertise and history – and thus, that which has no 'taste' (literally and figuratively). By pronouncing *McDo*, GMOs, and hormone-treated beef as incidents of *la malbouffe*, Bové creates a salient symbolic synthesis of the cultural and agricultural features of globalization.

In referring to *la malbouffe*, Bové invokes and solidifies his agricultural authority and cultural expertise. As a producer of sheep's milk for Roquefort cheese, Bové is linked to a particularly potent cultural symbol (pun intended). As the first French product to achieve *controlled origin* status in 1921, Roquefort embodies notions of *le terroir*, the distinctive geography of a French region that, when combined with the traditional savoir-faire of the French *paysan* and artisan, renders products of French high culture such as wines, cheese, or pâtés (Hervieu 1996). To receive controlled origin status, a Champagne can only be produced in Champagne, Bourgogne in Bourgogne; and Roquefort can only be produced in one particular arid zone in southern France.

Integrating notions of biology, geography, and cultural expertise or savoir-faire, *le terroir* embraces all parts of the production process from the bacterial cultures utilized in cheese or wine production to the historical cultures of local farmers. Reflecting upon the evocative power of *le terroir* and of Roquefort in particular, Bové asserted wryly, 'Clinton made a big mistake when he chose to mess with Roquefort. He didn't know what he was dealing with. It means something to French people' (Bové 1999).

By proclaiming GMOs '*la malbouffe*', Bové translates a debate about technical risk into an overtly socio-cultural debate about food quality, *paysan* survival, and globalization. In so doing, he shifts the site of discursive authority from the objective and scientific-risk expert standing outside of culture and history to the intensely engaged *paysan* expert standing *for* culture and history.

Operation Roquefort: The CP Challenges the WTO

In November 1999, a few months after the *McDo* incident, the CP sent a delegation of farmers to the now infamous Seattle WTO negotiations as legal observers of official forums and as key participants in NGO meetings dealing with issues of international agricultural policy. Through local fund-raising and monies from the union itself, the Seattle delegation consisted of Bové, CP officials and members – as well as the author, who went along as Bové's translator (and ethnographer).

Capitalizing on Bové's increasing national popularity as a media figure, the voyage promised (and indeed delivered) a big media event, providing French audiences with weeks of television and print media coverage before, during, and after Bové's journey. Bové was also continually surrounded by an entourage of about thirty French and international television and newschapter journalists, along with Bové's biographer, Gilles Marchaud, who had begun following Bové since that August. His book, *Le monde n'est pas une merchandise*, eventually became a French best-seller the following March and was soon published in English (Bové and Dufour 2001).

A seasoned non-violent activist, Bové arrived in Seattle fortified with a strategic supply of symbolic capital. Shipped illegally over the boarder by the Papillon Roquefort company (at Bové's prodding), two hundred kilos of cheese made its way to Seattle, circumventing Clinton's extra tariff that had raised the price of Roquefort almost three-fold. During that week, Roquefort continued its career as a potent non-human actor in the anti-globalization network. As a symbol of French culture and resistance to US imperialism, it had first incited crowds to dismantle a *McDo* in Millau. Now, in Seattle, Roquefort continued its mission, enticing or repelling activists and reporters with its pungent aroma, invoking notions of French cultural expertise and agriculture.

The Roquefort circulated through the streets and press conferences all that week, toted around in duffle bags by Bové and the other farmers in its sparkling black and gold foil. The Roquefort's charisma moved NGO leaders to assist the farmers set up tables and platters full of thick bread and cheese. Creating an ambiance of sharing and cultural awe, it inspired reporters to run out to local markets to buy wine as accompaniment. Riddled with blue pockets of bacterial culture, Roquefort was a visual and olfactory reminder of the stakes that had brought activists to confront globalization in both Millau and Seattle: Roquefort stood for culture against transnational capital.

Despite US media portrayals of Bové as an anti-American French nationalist, Bové and the Roquefort consistently delivered a clear international message, standing in solidarity with remaining peasant societies throughout the world, which, for Bové, includes US family farmers. During his five-day stay in Seattle, Bové strategically appeared in press conferences side by side with Bill Christison, president of the National Coalition of Family Farmers (who was invited to add his Wisconsin cheese to Roquefort platters), and was photographed walking arm in arm in the main labor march with Indian and Mexican farmers from Via Campesina. In media interviews, Bové stated repeatedly that he didn't see GMOs or McDonald's as 'American', but as products of international capital imposed on *all* cultures throughout the world (Bové 1999).

McDo and the Boston Tea Party

Bové's international message culminated in a demonstration the day before the now infamous days of direct action in Seattle began. Learning from Internet networks that Bové would be in Seattle for the WTO events, a group of US activists from the NGO Public Citizen sought to plan an anti-McDonald's demonstration in Bové's honor. Initially, Bové was reluctant, concerned about reinforcing the 'anti-American' image constructed by US media. Assured that the event would be a small, non-violent demonstration with an international message, Bové consented. The CP delegation decided to meet at noon in front of the McDonald's to give a short speech and to distribute Roquefort and bread to passersby. On the way to the McDonald's, Bové spotted pasted to a bus-stop a large poster advertising the demonstration whose headline read:

> Famed French Farmer José Bové to Warn Consumers of Biotechnology, WTO at Seattle McDonald's. José Bové, Jailed in France for Destroying a McDonald's, to Speak at Peaceful Press Conference with Farmers from Asia, Africa, Latin America, U.S. and Europe. Speakers to Condemn McDonald's 'Frankenfoods' Bio-engineered French Fries, Beef Treated with Hormones and Antibiotics. Bové to Serve his High Quality Roquefort – Cheese Was Heavily Taxed by U.S. in Retaliation For European Ban on U.S. Hormone Beef.

When Bové and the other *paysans* in the delegation arrived, a crowd of a nearly a thousand demonstrators gave uproarious cheers as they recognized Bové by his now iconic handle-bar moustache and pipe they had seen in the media and on the Web. With microphone provided by the Public Citizen activists, Bové gave a speech about globalization, local food security, and GMOs. Dotted throughout the crowd were black-clad anarchists, anti-GMO activists dressed in what has become the emblematic anti-GMO garb, the orange and black monarch butterfly costume. Bové waved the Roquefort and bread over his head, shouting:

> I am a sheep farmer from France and we bring you good Roquefort cheese . . . we don't want to eat hormone beef and GMO, it is not normal that Americans must be punished because of Clinton and the WTO. Americans, too, have a right to good food. They should not be forced to only eat GMO, McDonald, and hormone-treated beef . . . Together we must fight for no more GMO! And tomorrow, we will do this non-violently . . . [In response the crowd repeatedly cheered, 'hey hey, ho ho, GMOs have got to go!'). (Bové 1999)

By the time the crowd had risen to about 4,000 organizers from Public Citizen realized that the original plan of holding a press conference in front of the McDonald's was no longer a logistical possibility. Almost out of nowhere, a large white van materialized at the crowded intersection before the McDonald's golden arches. Out from a sky-light on the van's roof climbed a string of international farmer activists including Professor Swami from India (of the KRRS and representing Via Campesina), Bill Christison and John Kinsmen of the National Family Farm Coalition. In the frenzy, the CP delegation surrounded Bové, assisting him as he made his way through the raucous crowd to join the other farmers on the van's roof. When Bové climbed through the sky-light, the crowd went wild, banging on the windows of the McDonald's across the street, chanting and cheering. It was clear that Bové was the star of the show.

Standing on top of the van, pipe in hand, Bové broke bread with the other farmers, holding wedges of Roquefort up toward the sky as the crowd roared below, spreading out for blocks. He then gave a short speech comparing his sabotage of McDonald's and GMOs to the Boston Tea Party, referring to the non-violent direct action Americans took to free themselves from British imperialism centuries ago. This tea-party reference, that appeared in nearly all Bové's US interviews that week, served multiple functions: invoking US revolutionary history, it expressed solidarity with US activists demonstrating against global imperialism today. In addition, the Boston Tea Party serves as a symbol of US hypocrisy, casting Clinton into the ironic role of imperial power, this time punishing a *Europe* struggling to rid itself of *US* tyranny.

Images of revolutionaries tossing boxes of tea and of peasants sabotaging transgenic fields, green-houses and McDonald's are worlds away from scenes of serene and careful lab scientists manipulating pipettes on news spots about GMOs. The image of GMO debate displayed that day in Seattle, one that satellited its way back to France and across the world, was indeed undergoing a dramatic transformation. Without a scientist in sight to be consulted about 'risk', Bové stood on the van's rooftop, between US and Indian farmers, symbolizing a new hybrid identity of cultural expert, family farmer, and international worker, speaking for local cultures and international worker solidarity in an age of transnational capital and free trade. As we now move further into what many now herald as post-Seattle era, farmers such as José Bové are catalysing anti-globalization networks; they are becoming a crucial new international symbol of cultural expertise, identity, and international resistance to global capital.

Conclusion: Counter-hegemonic Expertise

The French debate over GMOs is about more than the practice of a new genetic technology. It is also a collision between competing frames, stakes, and forms of expertise among a wide range of actors and networks. This collision illustrates how hegemony is maintained and disrupted.

The French case provides insights into the ways in which framings such as 'risk' gain ascendancy and are displaced. When initially framed as an objectivist risk issue, the GMO debate invoked scientific expertise for evaluating the environmental and health hazards associated with the technology. When later reframed as a 'food-quality' issue, the GMO debate shifted to *paysan* expertise, which linked issues of food quality with productivist agriculture, cultural homogenization, and globalization.

This transformation of the French GMO debate was implicit. Anti-GMO activists did not appear aware that their anti-globalization critique and *paysan* expertise displaced dominant-risk frames. So it may be misleading to say that the CP challenged the hegemony of objectivist risk, since the term 'challenge' implies conscious, intentional acts. Perhaps it is more meaningful to say that the CP, with great intention and intelligence, developed a discursive strategy that unwittingly decentered hegemonic ideas of risk. Such ideas demarcate what can be said from what can not be said, thought and not be thought, at a particular time and place in history.

The CP's discursive journey exemplifies both the resilience and vulnerability of objectivist-risk hegemony, as well as the potency of discourses and symbols which counter it. For the first two years of the CP's anti-GMO campaign, the *paysan* frame lacked sufficient cultural potency to capture the imagination of the French public. When the CP became renowned both nationally and internationally for challenging McDonald's as a *cultural* symbol against globalization, they were able to popularize an anti-globalization critique of GMOs.

By framing *McDo* and GMOs as two examples of cultural homogenization, Bové was able to transfer negative popular sentiment from the former to the latter.

GMOs were thus reborn as a cultural symbol of the multinational against the local, of *la malbouffe* against good food and culture, and of global capital gone awry. Ultimately, Bové popularized the idea of GMOs as a cultural problem which *paysan* experts could oppose –on behalf of not only French history and tradition, but also of worldwide cultural survival.

The French case could influence the GMO debate internationally. As various actors and publics in France become increasingly able to talk about GMOs in broader terms – in relation to life-patenting, or food quality, for example – a post-risk anti-globalization perspective is emerging. Indeed, activists around the world are increasingly popularizing the connection between such issues as free trade, agriculture, and intellectual property, and cultural homogenization.

As this counter-hegemonic process continues to unfold, actors may consciously challenge the objectivist-risk frames. Actors may develop the self-reflexivity necessary to be conscious and critical of the expert knowledges that continue to define the boundaries around 'legitimate' debates about technoscience in an age of globalization. Thus they may open the way to establish new norms and criteria for what constitutes a legitimate debate – not just about GMOs, but also about other aspects of technoscience.

As the CP promotes *paysan* savoir-faire as a body of expert knowledges legitimate for evaluating GMOs, they are not only broadening the terms of a debate about a particular genetic technology. Even more, they are transforming beliefs that have kept the terms and practices of science and expertise in the hands of the few, while excluding the many. Thus the many are beginning to have their say, breaking bread together and speaking into the microphones of the world – in their own terms.

Acknowledgements

Thanks to the journal *Science as Culture* in which an earlier version of this chapter appeared (Heller 2002). I would like also to thank Les Levidow, Claire Marris, Arturo Escobar, and Alan Goodman for their invaluable comments and discussions, which informed and helped develop my thinking on this chapter. Special thanks goes to the National Science Foundation, which made possible my research in France during 1998–2000. Many thanks also to Bruno Latour and Michel Callon at the Centre de Sociologie de l'Innovation for a wonderful and important year of intellectual support and guidance.

References

Bové, J. (1999), Personal Interview.

Bové, J. and Dufour, F. (2001), *The World is Not for Sale: Farmers Against Junk*

Food, London: Verso; translated from *Le monde n'est pas une marchandise*, 2000.

Callon, M. (1986), 'The Sociology of an Actor-network: The Case of the Electric Vehicle', in M. Callon, J. Law and A. Rip (eds), *Mapping the Dynamics of Science and Technology*, London: Macmillan.

Castells, R. (1991), 'From Dangerousness to Risk', in G. Burchell, C. Gordon and P. Miller (eds), *The Foucault Effect: Studies in Governmentality*. Chicago: University of Chicago Press.

Comaroff, J. and Comaroff, J. (1991), *Of Revelation and Revolution: Christianity, Colonialism, and Consciousness in South Africa*, Chicago: University of Chicago Press.

Confédération Paysanne (1997), *Technologies génétiques: pour un moratoire sur la mise en culture et la commercialisation pour l'application du principe de précaution'*, Paris: Confédération Paysanne.

Ewalds, F. (1991), 'Insurance and Risk', in G. Burchell, C. Gordon, and P. Miller (eds), *The Foucault Effect: Studies in Governmentality*, Chicago: University of Chicago Press.

Fischler, C. (1993), *L'homnivore*, Paris: Éditions Odile Jacob.

Genovese, E. D. (1971), *In Red and Black: Marxian Explorations in Southern and Afro-American History*, New York: Pantheon.

Hall, S. (1986), 'The Toad in the Garden: Thatcherism among the Theorists', in C. Nelson and L. Grossberg (eds), *Marxism and the Interpretation of Culture*, Urbana and Chicago: University of Illinois Press.

Hebdige, D. (1988), *Hiding in the Light: On Images and Things*, London and New York: Routledge.

Heller, C. (1999), *The Ecology of Everyday Life: Rethinking the Desire for Nature*, Montreal: Black Rose.

—— (2002), 'Scientific Risk to Paysan Savoir-Faire: Peasant and Expertise in the French and Global Debate over GM Crops', *Science as Culture*, 11: 5–39.

—— and Escobar, A. (2003), 'From Pure Genes to GMOs: Transnationalized Gene Landscapes in the Biodiveristy and Transgenic Food Networks', in A. Goodman, S. Lindy and D. Heath (eds), *Genetic Natures/Cultures: Anthropology and Science Beyond the Two Culture Divide*, Berkeley: University of California Press.

Hervieu, B. (1996), *Au Bonheur des Campagnes*, Paris: Éditions de l'Aube.

Hess, J. (1997), 'If You're Thinking of Living in STS: A Guide for the Perplexed', in G. Downey and J. Dumit (eds), *Cyborgs and Citadels: Anthropological Interventions in Emerging Sciences and Technologies*, Santa Fe NM: School of American Research Press.

Hilgartner, S. (1992), 'The Social Construction of Risk Objects: or, How to Pry Open Networks of Risk', in J. Short and L. Clarke (eds), *Organizations,*

Uncertainties, and Risk, Boulder, CO: Westview.

Jasanoff, S. (1987), 'Contested Boundaries in Policy-relevant Science', *Social Studies of Science*, 17: 195–230.

—— (1990), *The Fifth Branch: Science Advisors as Policy Makers*, Cambridge MA: Harvard University Press.

Latour, B. (1987), *Science in Action: How to Follow Scientists and Engineers Through Society*, Cambridge MA: Harvard University Press.

Levidow, L. (2000), 'Which Sustainability? Policy Dilemmas over GM Crops', plenary talk at POSTI conference, 'Policy Agendas for Sustainable Technological Innovation', December, University of East London, http://www.esst.uio.no/posti/workshops/levidow.html

—— and Carr, S. (1997), 'How Biotechnology Regulation Sets a Risk/Ethics Boundary', *Agriculture and Human Values*, 14: 29–43.

—— Carr, S., Von Schomberg and Wield, D. (1996), 'Regulating Agricultural Biotechnology in Europe: Harmonization Difficulties, Opportunities, Dilemmas', *Science and Public Policy*, 23(3): 135–57.

Marris, C. (2001a), 'Swings and Roundabouts: French Public Policy on Agricultural GMOs since 1996', *Politeia*, 60: 22–37.

—— (2001b), 'Public Perceptions of Transgenic Products: The Influence of the Behaviour of Laboratory Scientists', in J.-P. Toutant and E. Balàzs (eds), *Molecular Farming: Proceedings of the OECD Workshop held in La Grande Motte (France), 3–6 September 2000*, Versailles: INRA Editions (collection Science Update).

Morrell, J.-B. (1999), Personal Interview.

Riesel, R. (1999), Personal Interview.

Roy, A. and Joly, P. B. (2000), 'France: Broadening Precautionary Expertise?' *Journal of Risk Research*, 3(3): 247–54, http://www.tandf.co.uk/journals/authors/r-authors/jrrspecialissue.html

Wynne, B. (1995), 'Technology Assessment and Reflexive Social Learning: Observations from the Risk Field', in A. Rip, T. J. Misa and J. Schot (eds), *Managing Technology in Society*, London: Pinter.

Wynne, B. (2001), 'Creating Public Alienation: Expert Cultures of Risk and Ethics on GMOs', *Science as Culture*, 10(4): 445–81.

–6–

Enjoyment and Choice in an Age of Risk: The Case of BSE in the Czech Republic

Haldis Haukanes

How Food Risks Become Real

The last decade has seen an increased focus on the negative consequences of industrial food production, and the possibly damaging effects on human health that these consequences imply. The food scandals that have hit Europe over the last few years both exemplify and reinforce this tendency to see food as potentially dangerous: dioxin in Belgian chickens, foot-and-mouth disease in British livestock (see Nerlich, this volume), and of course BSE or Bovine Spongiform Encephalopathy (a cattle disease that *can* be transmitted to humans and can cause vCJD or variant Creutzfeldt-Jakob Disease, a debilitating brain disease). All of these incidents have attracted wide media attention and have heightened public awareness of possible food-related risks. But how does this increased attention paid to risks in food affect people – the consumers of dubious meat and other dangerous things – in their everyday food practices? What do people actually do when they are confronted with information about food-related risks, and in particular when they are faced with scandals such as the outbreak of BSE?

According to Ulrich Beck (1999: 135) risks do not refer to damages incurred. Risk is a peculiar state between security and destruction, a period when the worst can happen but has not yet occurred. To understand the social materialization of risks, their *becoming real* for people, we have to think of them in terms of a *virtual reality* which is itself defined by the way that risks are mediated in science, politics or popular culture. This process of 'virtualization' is particularly important in cases such as the BSE situation, where the risk is invisible and cannot be detected by the sensory apparatus of humans. The media may explain the disease for us, for example by electronically representing the workings of prions, which are thought to transmit BSE from animals to humans (ibid.: 136). In this way images are created in our minds and present us with two options: to buy beef or not. 'CJD is no longer exclusively a hazard, as a strain has been identified that can be linked to BSE' (ibid.). This does not mean that vCJD has become real in the sense that it has affected someone that we know, but it has become something of which we are aware and which we – both as national communities and as individuals – have to deal with politically, emotionally and practically.

We can thus think of *becoming real* as a staged process mediating between two extremes: on the one hand there is total unawareness and on the other there is a feeling of total catastrophe. Between these two poles we find several intermediate stages ranging from:

1. Knowing vaguely about the risk (we have heard about BSE but we do not really know what it implies).
2. Getting informed about BSE and its relation to vCJD through the media, including images of actual but unknown persons hit by the disease.
3. Experiencing the brutal consequences of BSE – that is, seeing someone we know die from vCJD.

This chapter will focus mainly on the transition from stage one to stage two; i.e. the period of time when 'virtualization' in terms of media-conveyed information is massive. As I will try to argue, the process of *becoming real* is more than the simple mediatization – or 'virtualization' – of risk in terms of scientific images delivered through the media. It is a process that is deeply political in character, involving politics at different levels, ranging from international and national institutional policy-making to power relations within the family. This chapter will mainly focus on the micro-political level – that is, the level of individual adjustments, attitudes and interpretations. I want to understand the social and cultural dimensions of risk handling; how negotiations about dietary changes are made in individual families; and how the choices people make are connected to culturally defined traditions and roles, including gender relations. I will also consider the microprocesses of *becoming real* in relation to the *becoming real* of BSE at the level of the Czech nation: I will relate people's understandings and strategies to the way that (uncertain) knowledge is communicated to them via the media; how awareness is created out of unawareness. I will also briefly examine some of the international and national food policies with regard to the disease, which reflect, among other things, the Czech Republic's relation to the wider European community.

The first case of BSE in Czech cattle was discovered in June 2001. In August of the same year two additional cases were found. My analysis builds on material from two periods of fieldwork undertaken in a rural and an urban setting, shortly after the first case had been discovered (June/July and October/November 2001).

This fieldwork is part of a wider research project called 'Food, Gender and Environmental Risks' (see Haukanes 1999a, 1999b and 2001). The core material used in this chapter is a set of in-depth interviews with twenty-four women, which dealt with issues of food, health, and women's reaction to BSE.

The first section of this article focuses on BSE in the wider society. It examines how it came to the country and how it was discussed in the media and among people. The next part of the article is based upon a detailed analysis of the interview material and examines the individual strategies that were adopted to deal with the threat of vCJD linked to the consumption of meat that might be infected with BSE. These two main parts are preceded by a short overview of the socio-historical context within which my study took place.

The Czech Republic after Communism – Food and Gender

The empirical setting for the study is the post-communist Czech Republic, a society that has gone through enormous change since 1989. Electoral multiparty democracy has been established, EU membership is right around the corner and privatization of the economy has reached all sectors, including the food industry and agriculture. Foreign trade, which used to be exclusively directed toward other Comecon[1] countries, is now focused on Western Europe and the EU. The development of a capitalist and consumer-driven economy has enormously increased the selection of consumer goods – including foodstuffs. Economic differences between rich and poor have increased, although the society as a whole has not been thrown into poverty. Family patterns have changed: the average age at first marriage has increased, while the birthrate has declined (Heitlingerová and Trnková 2001).

Although there have been great changes, continuities can also be found in many areas of society. In agricultural production, the structure developed during communism has been largely retained. Most commercial production still takes place within large industrial complexes, on the sites and – to a large extent – with the equipment of former cooperatives and state farms (Zelená Zprava 2000). Private, family-based farming, which disappeared during communism, has not been revived as a major sector of the economy, although some private farms have re-emerged. Intensive subsistence production, which emerged within the communist economy of scarcity, has continued, particulary in villages (Haukanes 1999a).

Continuities can also be detected with regard to gender relations and the gendered division of labor. During communism work was compulsory for all citizens, and women could not choose to stay at home unless they had very small children. In spite of this, traditional gender roles for domestic work were preserved, often embedded in a discourse of biological determinism (Heitlingerová 1995). The double burden women had to carry was therefore excessive, in particular considering the amount of work needed to supply a family with basic goods (Castle-Canerová 1992; Haukanes 2001). Since 1989, work is no longer compulsory. However, for a number of reasons – including financial ones – women still choose to remain employed and they value their participation in the work force (Kuchařová 1999, Hutton Rabe 1999). And yet, they continue to perform the majority of household tasks, including most of the food preparation (Križková 1999; Friedlanderová and Tuček 2001).

How BSE came to the Czechs

BSE – Bovine Spongiform Encephalopathy – better known as 'mad-cow' disease – was discovered in the United Kingdom in 1986. It was later identified as a so-called prion disease, a fatal nerve disease causing brain cells to degenerate.

For a long time scientists considered the risk that the disease could potentially jump species and be transmitted to humans via the consumption of bovine products to be merely hypothetical. However, in 1996 a connection was discovered between BSE and vCJD and suddenly BSE became a major news item. In 1996 ten new and atypical cases of vCJD were discovered and linked to the consumption of BSE-infected meat. Now BSE became real in a big way, as the disease was 'virtualized' by the media showing photos of actual infected people (Reilly and Miller 1997: 234 ff; Ridley and Baker 1998). As mentioned above, the fact that BSE could spread to humans had been regarded as a possibility at a much earlier stage, and some measures to prevent this transmission had already been implemented after 1989.[2] However, this risk was considered to be very remote, and had been completely under-communicated by the British authorities. As a result many producers failed to take the ban seriously, which probably allowed BSE to spread to other European countries (Bradley 2001, Klint Jensen 2001; *New Scientist*, 10 February 2001).

However, after 1996, the EU announced a new range of security measures. Some measures were implemented all across the EU, others were more country-specific, depending on how widely BSE had spread. These measures helped to bring a major epidemic to a halt (Bradley 2001). With this achieved, increased worries were expressed inside the EU about the control of meat imports to the union. Of particular concern were imports from accession states in Eastern and East Central Europe – including the Czech Republic – which were considered to have insufficient control of their bovine products (*New Scientist*, 5 April 2001).[3]

From February 2001 onward the Czech Republic, along with the other accession states, was forced by the EU to introduce a new method for animal testing.[4] The Czech veterinary authorities had already implemented a series of precautionary measures to avoid the spread of the disease to the Czech Republic, including a ban on the import of bovine products from Britain in 1994. The ban was extended during the 1990s to include other 'risk countries'. This new demand from the EU was just one among many of the amendments of its own laws and regulations that the country had to make as a candidate for membership to the EU (Kubát 2001). But this time the amendment had immediate results, as the first Czech case of BSE was discovered only a few months after the new rules had been implemented.

When laboratory tests confirmed BSE in the Czech Republic on 8 June, there was massive 'virtualization' in terms of media attention. Front pages in all of the major newspapers presented what had happened as an evil breach of the nation's border and headlines, such as 'Mad-cow disease also in the Czech Republic', 'Mad-cow disease is here' could be found everywhere. This was quite new as BSE had never been a major issue, neither for the media nor for the consumers, before June 2001. In 1995, when I spent six months in the Moravian countryside interviewing agrarian experts and farmers, mad cows or fear of bovine meat had never been mentioned. 'The becoming real' had not yet happened on a large scale.

During the weeks following 8 June 2001, numerous articles in the Czech press were devoted to BSE. Specialists were interviewed and expert advice was given on how best to avoid the risk of catching vCJD through contaminated bovine products. People were informed that pure bovine meat (infected material had not yet been found in muscular cells,[5] such as steaks) posed the least risks to human health, whereas bones, intestines and brain and products based on such cuts carried the most risks, as they may contain nervous tissues infected by BSE. Some newspapers provided lists of specific products that should be avoided. The widely read daily *Mladá Fronta Dnes* warned people that sausages, salamis and pâtés are made from 'cut-offs' from bones and should therefore be regarded as particularly risky (MFD 9 June), while other newspapers included jelly and children's sweets among the things to be avoided.

In the first days after 8 June, the newspapers mostly published reports that had shock value. In the weeks that followed, more analytical articles started to appear, examining for example the possible effect of the disease on Czech agriculture and on consumers' behavior. Compared with the way in which foot-and-mouth disease was handled by the British media, discussed by Nerlich (this volume), there was no attempt to find 'deeper' causes for the disease – that is, to blame it on industrial agriculture and its ethically questionable methods of raising animals in an eager attempt to satisfy consumers' demand for cheap food.

My general impression is that few Czech newspapers criticized the government's handling of the case.[6] Nor did they criticize the scientific knowledge made available to them by experts. When presenting such knowledge, the inherent uncertainty was not very deeply elaborated. The new security measures taken by the government were reported in all newspapers and other media,[7] but they were not criticized for being insufficient. Leading bureaucrats in the field of food safety were interviewed, and were allowed to reassure people. The head of the State Veterinary Services was quoted in several of the newspapers, assuring readers that this was not the top of an iceberg. 'More important than the fact that BSE emerged here, is that we discovered it. It shows that tested meat is safe', he said (*Zemské Noviny*, 9 June 2001). The chief of hygienic control in Prague tried to normalize the situation by comparing the Czech Republic to the rest of Europe: 'Everywhere in Europe the disease is found, and it could be expected [to appear] here too'. Seen in its totality, the message conveyed to people by the media was that BSE is a dangerous disease, but that the measures taken to detect BSE before it entered the food chain were working. As an employee at the State Veterinary Services, whom I interviewed in November 2001, stated: 'It has never been as safe to eat beef as it is now, so why stop buying it?'

Popular discourse, as I came across it in the South Bohemian countryside a few weeks after 8 June, was more critical than the media discourse. One point of criticism focused on the way in which the disease had been discovered. As indicated above, the responsible political authorities held that they should be given credit for the implementation of new security measures. These measures, and Czech food control in general, were said to be up to a Western and 'civilized standard', much higher than those of other post-socialist countries (implying that this was the reason why BSE had not been discovered in the countries further to the east). However, the press made it clear that the first case of BSE had been discovered in a private slaughterhouse that had independently implemented EU standards in its handling of bovine products long before the Czech state had done so. In local discourse this contradiction was picked up and used widely to ridicule the government's self-righteousness. Local discourse also focused on the origins of the disease. On 21 June the Agricultural Newspaper (*Zemské Noviny*) informed people that BSE had entered the country via fat in substitute milk for calves imported from the West, most likely from Germany, France or the Netherlands. Among some people in the village this 'coming from the West' became a conspiracy theory. The slaughterhouse where the first case was discovered was partly German-owned. Some villagers said that the positive test had been 'planted' by representatives of the German food industry, in order to place Czech meat at a disadvantage in EU markets. 'The Germans already have the disease in their livestock and they want us to have it too, so that people do not ask for Czech meat instead of German', the argument went.

After the fall of communism, the East–West dichotomy has become an extremely important trope in political life all over Eastern Europe. The Czech Republic, being geographically close to the EU and at the same time having managed to establish a comparatively successful market economy and stable democracy, has actively pursued a closer association with the West (Haukanes 1999a). On the other hand, there is great ambivalence toward the West, and toward Germany in particular, in Czech society.

Food, Risk and the Consumption of Meat

Since I first visited the Czech countryside in 1990 I have been fascinated by the importance of food in everyday life – as a time-consuming activity, as a favored topic of conversation and as a measure of a woman's dignity (Haukanes 1992, 2001). One reason for food gaining such an important place in village life is the rather extensive subsistence farming practiced by most villagers, making them, if not self-sufficient, at least very well supplied with fresh meat and vegetables that are locally produced. This production involves a great deal of work, but also produces a lot of enjoyment and pride. *Domácí výrobky* – home [grown] products – are normally preferred to bought ones, as they are considered to be better, more tasty and healthier than industrially produced food (Haukanes 1999, 2001; Dvořáková 1999). The distinction between home-produced and industrially produced food is thus a significant one in Czech (village) society. In fact, it was people's preoccupation with this distinction that led me to formulate research questions about food and risk, as I found that the distinction was linked to powerful ideas about purity and pollution in food.

I probed more deeply into matters of food and risk through research undertaken during fieldwork in the summer and fall of 2001. The first and longest period was spent in rural South Bohemia (Strakonice district) – an area to which I have returned continually since my first fieldwork there (1990/1991) and which I know well. In addition to participant observation I conducted semistructured interviews with thirteen women, all of whom were responsible for the preparation of food for their families. The interviews were supplemented by a simple questionnaire. For comparative purposes I chose to repeat this investigation – interviews and questionnaires – in an urban setting, the city of Plzeň[8]

I arrived in South Bohemia only ten days after the discovery of BSE had been made public. Going around to say hello to old friends and acquaintances, I had the impression that BSE was definitely on people's minds. Many people took it as an opportunity to criticize the government or the EU or to express their worries about the future of Czech agriculture. Others coped with the issue through humor: 'Mad cows? – Well, I guess we'll all become mad now', or 'We do not have to worry about mad cows. We are already as mad as can be.'

The connections made in these jokes (which I also heard in Plzeň a couple of months later) between animals and humans are significant. Meat is not only a high-status food; it is also ambiguous food, not only because of its capacity to transmit diseases, but also because a life has to be sacrificed to turn the animal into food (Guzman and Kjærnes 1998). The jokes draw attention to the otherwise concealed similarities between humans as consumers and the substances (the meat) that they consume, similarities that are normally rendered invisible through modern procedures of slaughtering (Vialles 1994) and modern methods of marketing (Fiddes

1997). As will be demonstrated below, such 'substantial' connections are crucial to understanding how people deal with BSE with regard to their own consumption of bovine meat and other bovine-based products.

Bovine Meat in the Czech Diet

The Czech diet is a meat-centered one, although the yearly consumption falls a little bit below the Western European average (Zelená Zprava 2000: 55). The main meal of the day (*oběd* = lunch) is consumed at midday, and often consists of soup followed by a main course. The soups are normally bouillon-based (frequently made of bovine broth), with vegetables and sometimes meat- or liverballs added, and thickened with eggs, pearl barley or noodles. The main course has almost always meat as one of the ingredients. Favored meat-based dishes are roast chicken or schnitzels, which are served with potatoes or potato salad, or the 'national dish' of the Czechs – *vepřo-knedlo-zelo* – which consists of roasted pork with dumplings and sauerkraut. Another typical way to serve meat is with dumplings in thick gravy, tomato-based, with dill, mushrooms or the classic *svíčková* (a complicated gravy made of minced vegetables with cream). Most of these gravy-and-dumpling meals should be served with bovine meat; at least that is what is stated in cookbooks. Beef as such – that is, fried entrecotes or filets – is less commonly prepared in homes, although commonly offered in restaurants.

While lunch is often consumed at work or at school, supper, which is the second substantial meal of the day, is prepared at home. Supper can be cold or hot, and will often include a piece of meat; leftovers from lunch, a piece of cold meat loaf, sausages, or salami/pâté with bread. Both salamis and sausages are favored, and there is a variety to choose from. Bovine meat is found in many of these products. Moreover, bovine bonemeal is used (or was, until the outbreak of BSE) to make gelatine for jelly, puddings, children's sweets, etc.

The last decade has seen a significant change in the types of meat consumed in the country. Even before the outbreak of BSE there has been a decline in consumption of beef, from 18.8 kg per capita a year in 1995 to 12.5 kg in 2000, a trend that can also be observed in other European countries (Lien, Bjørkum and Bye 1998). Pork is still the preferred meat, although its consumption has declined from 46.5 kg in 1995 to 40.9 kg in 2000, while the consumption of poultry has risen from 13 to 22.3 kg in the same period.[9] In general, the Czech diet is becoming lighter and 'faster'. Soups as starters are in a slow decline and there is a tendency to eat more vegetables, particularly in the form of salads, although the Czechs on average still consume far fewer vegetables and less fruit than Western Europeans (Zelená Zprava 2000: 55).

From an urban perspective, villagers are thought to be more traditional when it comes to the food they serve (and consume) –with regard to both type of dish and amount of food served (heavy, rich and generous). In my material the difference is less between the rural and the urban than between generations. Several of the younger women I interviewed – both the urban and the rural – said that they seldom made gravy with dumplings, but rather used pasta, salads and poultry. Many younger people even regard the gravy-meat-and-dumpling dishes as old-fashioned, and not part of the new and more 'Western' lifestyle they aim for. In villages, by contrast to towns, more time is spent on the preparation of food, which also involves activities such as tinning and canning and other kinds of conserving work. Meat produced at home is mainly rabbit, poultry and pork, although the latter is less common now than it was only five to ten years ago. It is not common to keep oxen or cows, so bovine meat has to be bought by villagers and urban consumers alike.

Let me now turn to individual attitudes and interpretations I encountered when interviewing women in the countryside and in Plzeň. I was looking for answers to the following questions: has BSE changed individual families' eating habits, or has it changed the boundary between the edible and the non-edible? What – if any – actions do people take to protect themselves, and how should their strategies be interpreted and explained? To what extent do people relate to the images and understandings of BSE provided by the media, or consider the disease within a wider European context?

Attitudes and Actions

Indifference and Resistance to Change

Some of the women I talked to rejected the suggestion that they had been affected by the information about BSE and told me that they had made no attempts to change their diet after June 2001. One of them, Anna,[10] is a Plzeň woman in her early thirties who stays at home with two children. Her weekly menu is extremely complex and her cooking is done 'from the ground up' – very few ready-made products appear on her table. Every weekday she prepares two main courses in addition to soup – one for her husband, who is a bodybuilder and demands a special diet, and another for herself and the children. When I ask whether she follows news about pollution in food and mad-cow disease she answers yes – she reads articles about it, but she does not pay attention to the information provided. When mad-cow disease was discovered, other people she knew stopped buying bovine meat, but not her. Her feelings about eating beef have not changed at all, she says, and she has not stopped buying the meat: 'We even still enjoy a beef à la tartare', she says, as if to shock me, 'even though it contains both beef and raw eggs . . . We just believe that what *we* eat is a good thing'. But she would not give the beef à la tartare to her children, she admits, 'if there was something wrong in it the child's body would not manage to handle it'. 'I show concern for the children', she says. Looking at her weekly menu and listening to her talking about her feelings of disgust toward chemicals found in ready-made products, it is evident that she is concerned about and takes care of the health of her whole family. But this does not include worrying about the possibility of contracting vCJD from BSE-infected bovine products.

Jindra, a cook in her early forties who lives and works in a village, also claims to be untouched by the news of mad cows. Like Anna, she is very interested in the art of cooking, and extremely competent: I have had the pleasure eating her delicacies many times. She takes great pleasure in preparing nice food for other people, including her own family, and enjoys it a lot. Jindra proclaims that her ideal diet is a mixed and varied one. She is skeptical about the use of chemicals in food production and is very happy about their big garden, which supplies her and her family with an abundance of fruit and vegetables. She is not afraid of bovine meat, however; she has followed the news about the Czech case closely, but believes that the measures implemented to detect suspected cases of BSE in cattle are sufficient.

Like Anna and Jindra, most of the women I interviewed seemed to be well-informed about BSE; the media's 'virtualization' had made BSE real for them in the sense that they had taken an active stand on how to deal with it. Only one woman, a pensioner of sixty-seven, did not seem to know that the disease was impossible to detect by the eye. 'I know that they have advised us to stop buying some things, but I believe that that piece of meat, when it is well prepared, can not do any harm', she said, and prided herself on her own ability to distinguish between good and bad meat. All the others seemed to be informed about the main characteristics of the disease as well as the precautions taken by the government to avoid its spread. Like Jindra, the village cook, several expressed confidence in the control systems and said that they – on the basis of this trust – had made no changes in their diet. Some expressed a laissez-faire attitude, however: 'we cannot trust the experts and controls anyhow, so we just have to risk it'. When I asked Hana, an urban working-class woman in her early fifties, whether she follows news about pollution in food, she said: 'I will tell you one thing: I do not listen to these things . . . I hear it, but I pretend not to have heard it, I consciously do not let it into my head'. Hana feels that experts' opinions on what is healthy are changing all the time, making it impossible to follow all the advice. This is also the reason why she has continued to buy bovine meat. 'At one moment chicken have salmonella, the next time it is cows that are mad . . . if you think about it all the time, you could not eat anything!!' Moreover, she is one of the women who prepares a lot of the traditional gravies with beef. For her it seems impossible to avoid bovine meat and she will not let any stupid information destroy her enjoyment of it!

Ambivalences

The number of women indifferent to the disease were far outnumbered by those who, in some way or another, reacted to its coming to their country. The latter form two categories – those who expressed a greater ambivalence though not a real fear of meat, and those who had become frightened and/or had changed their diet after 8 June.

Milena is a young woman, a mother of two and living in a village. Milena and her family stick to a 'modern' kind of diet; on their weekly menu are pasta, vegetable salads and poultry, but no dumplings-and-gravy meals. Milena is also the only one of my village informants who does not consider home-grown food to be better than bought food. When I ask her the question, 'what do you consider to be healthy food or a healthy diet', she answers: 'vegetables, meat of chicken, rabbits, just a little of pork. But beef – not at all!' 'Before I would have said cooked beef, with vegetables,' she adds, 'but not now'. Milena denies that she has become afraid of bovine meat. At work she has eaten it several times even after the outbreak of BSE in the country. Her husband is afraid, though, so she has stopped buying it for home consumption.

Although she claims to be unafraid, Milena's conceptions of bovine products have changed; bovine meat has moved from the category of healthy to that of non-healthy food. Another informant who expresses a change in her feelings toward bovine products is Radka, a woman of about forty that lives with her husband and her two adolescent children in the same village as Milena. Radka is a well-educated woman who holds a position of responsibility in an adjacent town. She commutes to work and she often does not return home until 7 o'clock in the evening. Despite this she still cooks a hot supper for her family – often two hot suppers, one around 7 p.m. and the other around 10 o'clock, as both her husband and son demand lots of food. Unlike Milena, Radka is very fond of home-produced food, both meat and vegetables. She expresses a skeptical attitude toward industrially produced vegetables – in particular she is afraid of genetic modification. When she sees tomatoes that are all the same size, she refuses to buy them, because she suspects that they have been genetically modified. She only buys beef rarely, because the children do not like it. For herself, she finds that it is drier than other meat and takes too long to prepare (a common complaint among Czech women). When making the classic gravy-and-dumpling dishes, she normally uses pork instead of beef. The news of BSE coming to the Czech Republic has made her feel what she calls a kind of 'inner resistance' toward bovine products. When doing her shopping, she has started to look for labels on these products, be they meat, sausages or salamis, confirming that they have been made from tested meat. She also admits, smiling, that the day when she first heard about the outbreak of BSE in her country, she had planned to buy a piece of salami. She did buy it, but came home with a smaller piece than she had planned to get.

The time factor is of course important when trying to understand how people relate to BSE. Radka's immediate feelings on 8 June developed into an inner resistance, which has made her more careful about what she eats. From having been totally unaware of the possible risks hidden in beef products, she now looks for a label saying that the product is OK. Other women recount reactions that are *only* of a temporary character. Jarka, for example, is an urban woman in her late thirties whom I interviewed in November 2001. She has two boys and a husband to cook for, and she says that she knows of many people who have come to be afraid of bovine meat and who now refuse to buy it or eat it. 'In the beginning I stopped buying it too, I did not have confidence in it either' Jarka says. But now she has returned to her original diet, and bovine meat is back on the menu.

Fear and Change of Practice

Some of the women express a greater fear, and tell about deliberate attempts to remove bovine meat from their diet. One of them is the young village woman Petra, a mother of two pre-school children, who is extremely interested in food and highly competent in the art of cooking. During our conversation she demonstrates a great interest in ecological questions and in food safety in particular. We discuss genetic modification of vegetables, the whiteness of rice and similar issues. As for bovine meat, she admits that she has reacted negatively to the information, and tells of a day when she wanted to buy minced meat. She studied the contents, and found out it contained beef, so she put it back and went to pick up some pork instead. Even at work she has chosen to avoid the dishes made from bovine meat. When I ask her whether she used to cook bovine meat previously, she confirms that she did. Since the outbreak of BSE, when cooking typically bovine-based dishes, she uses pork or rabbit instead. She has not avoided it completely, though, as she admits to having bought some sausages for barbecue – a much-favored summer activity among younger village couples.

I found the same 'selective avoidance' among quite a few of the women. Jana, a young urban woman of Petra's age, who stays at home with her two pre-school children and who cooks every day both for them and for her husband, is another who has made permanent but not systematic changes in her diet. In contrast to her village peers, she is not particularly fond of cooking, and has a limited number of recipes to choose from when preparing lunch for her family. 'To be honest, I know about ten dishes, between which I alternate', she says. One of the dishes that she used to make was tomato-gravy with beef. The discovery of BSE in Czech meat has scared her off from buying bovine meat for this classic dish. She admits feeling afraid of the epidemic and feels disgusted by bovine meat in general. Like Pavla, she does not try to avoid all bovine products: she still makes minced steak for her children, as they are really fond of this dish and it is one of the few dishes that she knows how to prepare.

One of the few women with a more systematic attitude is Helena, a retired Plzeň woman who cooks for her husband and her grandson. Like the other three she admits that the outbreak of the disease had frightened her, not so much for her own health as for that of her grandchildren. She has therefore decided to try to avoid all processed products made of bovine meat (salamis, sausages, minced meat and pâtés). She still buys 'pure' bovine meat though, as she knows that this is considered to be the least dangerous for consumption.

A final category of women who have made changes in their diet because of BSE are those who have done so not because of their own fear, but because their husbands demanded it. One of them is Milena in the example above. The young bricklayer to whom she is married became frightened a long time ago, even before BSE came to the Czech Republic, and refuses to eat bovine meat, soups made of bovine bouillon and salamis. Three other women, all of them from villages, told the same story: they cannot serve bovine meat anymore, because their husbands refuse to eat it. Marie, a woman in her mid-forties, has not made any bovine-based meals since 1994, the year when the Czech Republic stopped importing bovine meat from Britain and when there probably was some of fuss about the disease in Czech newspapers.

Enjoyment, Disgust and Risk

Trust, Control and Substitutability

Comparing the interviewees' comments on BSE to the comments I overheard in various public places in the villages, it became evident that the former are less critical and less focused on macropolitics than the latter. I explicitly tried to address macropolitical issues during the interviews, by asking what they thought the food scandals in Western Europe had done to people's perception of foreign food. Very few had anything to say about this. The tendency was for the interviewees to 'concretize' my questions and answer them in terms of examples from their own family. Trust or mistrust in state authorities were, however, issues discussed in many of the conversations. Some interviewees were skeptical and complained that the controls promised by both retailers and the state could not be trusted. However, quite a few of the women interviewed expressed trust in the control systems established by the state, and in what was done to avoid a spread of the disease (although they might have made some dietary changes in any case). Although a few admitted that it was difficult to be sure of what actually might lie behind a label saying that meat had been checked, many, like Radka in the example above, were reassured by the sight of such a label. Their confidence may, in part at least, be explained by the rather reassuring way that the Czech media first dealt with BSE.

As regards the actions taken to protect themselves against the health threats posed by BSE, interesting contrasts appear between the rural and the urban informants: fewer urban than rural women claim to have changed their diet. My material is too limited to generalize this point, but on the basis of my long experiences in the 'rural field', I will nevertheless suggest an explanation.

In 'modern' societies, trust in food means trust in abstract knowledge and control systems (Guzman and Kjærnes 1998). Many of us do not even want to know what is going on when a living animal is transformed into beef, pork or salami (Vialles 1994). The access to home-grown products – vegetables and meat alike – that Czech villagers have gives them a feeling of control which most people do not have. The control aspect is, I will argue, exactly what makes the home-grown foodstuffs so valuable: 'We know what we have put into it, so therefore our own food is better, more healthy and trustworthy than the food we buy in the shops'. Home-grown food is also regarded as reliable and wholesome because it is social food, produced through cooperation within intimate social relations. The feeling of control makes rural women firmer in their decisions concerning bovine products – that is, in their rejection of it. Moreover, rural women are more used to replacing bovine meat, even in the classic bovine-based dishes, with their home-produced meat, be it pork, rabbit or chicken. Urban women seem to display a greater dependency on recipes; if it says 'beef goes with tomato sauce', then it has to be beef.

Expert Advice, Substance and Enjoyment

Most of those who claim to have made changes in their diet, admit that these changes have not been systematic: in fact almost all of them say that they have stopped cooking pure meat while retaining salami, sausages and pâtés on their menu. With one exception (Milena's husband), I have heard of no cases where a chicken-based bouillon has been used instead of a beef-based one, nor have I heard of anyone who has stopped making, for example, jelly cakes (typical summer cakes made of sponge cake with fresh fruit in jelly on the top), because they fear being infected with vCJD. A few women concede that they are aware of the potential dangers inherent in gelatine; but, nevertheless, it is clear that they would not dream of giving it up.

There are some interesting paradoxes in the ways in which people confront expert advice: what is considered to be the least dangerous by the experts – pure meat – is what is cut from the menu. This has a practical explanation, as the women simply cut out that which is easiest to sacrifice. As I mentioned earlier, the consumption of bovine meat is in decline. This is a tendency reflected in the consumption patterns of many of my informants; bovine meat is not their favored meat and they rarely cook bovine-based dishes anyhow. Therefore it is not such a big sacrifice to cut this meat from the diet. Moreover, some of the traditional gravy-meat-and-dumpling dishes are going out of fashion among young people. To abandon beef dishes should therefore be seen as a way of handling the feelings of disgust created by BSE, rather than an attempt to deal systematically with the risk of contamination.

Another explanation for people's sacrifice of the least dangerous bovine products can be found when we examine their attitudes toward the *substance* or texture of beef products. When my informants express their ambivalent feelings for bovine meat, they often do so in terms of its substance: it is dry, fibrous and difficult to process into the ideal meat – which in Czech cuisine means a really well-cooked meat. BSE just adds a new dimension to this 'substantial disgust', I believe. Furthermore, meat in general is ambiguous food, not least in terms of associations to the life that it may evoke. When people go to the butcher's and see 'bloody' beef exhibited on his shelves, they easily associate this with the animal and hence with the disease itself. In semiotic terms one may argue that the fresh meat comes to stand metonymically for the whole animal, including the infections that it may carry. This semiotic connection between the animal and the meat is much less evident in salamis and sausages and is therefore a much weaker one. Some women are very explicit about this: a 37-year-old Plzeň woman for example mentioned that she would not dream of putting raw beef into her mouth after BSE, although she still consumes the meat when it is 'hidden' in other products. By contrast, Jindra in the example above demonstrates her total lack of fear of mad-cow disease by mentioning her preferences for beef à la tartare – bovine meat in its purest and rawest form.

Enjoyment and taste play an important role in this picture: the food you favor is of course much more difficult to renounce than the food you are indifferent to. A young village woman says, for example, that she has never really cooked much beef in the form of the classic beef-with-gravy dishes. But from the moment BSE came into the country she would not even think of cooking such food, she proclaims, her obvious disgust showing all over her face. She still buys salamis though, and quite often, too: 'those we really like', she adds. It takes more than a few mad cows to make most people stop eating what they really like.

Negotiations and Power Relations in the Family

As many studies have shown, food is central to family life in most parts of the world (Henson et al. 1998: 183ff; Guzmán, Bjørkum and Kjærnes 2000). There is also evidence that women, although they are in charge of food-related work in daily life, demonstrate a considerable will to adapt to the tastes of their family members in their food choices, and make a great effort to satisfy the various demands of those for whom they cook (McIntosh and Zay 1998). Both these tendencies are evident in my material. All of the interviewees are, as most Czech women, responsible for most of the housework in their families, including planning, preparing and cooking food (Friedlanderová and Tuček 2001: 104; Haukanes 2001). They all have an extremely detailed knowledge of the likes and dislikes of each family member, and try to fulfill their wishes. 'He does not like this' . . . 'she loves that' . . . – such comments were constantly popping up during the interviews. It was also evident that the women often renounced their own likes (and dislikes) in favor of those of their families. In particular the women often expressed a desire to have more vegetables on the menu than they actually had, but found it was difficult because their husbands demanded 'proper food' in the form of substantial portions of meat. One Plzeň woman, who admitted that she had become skeptical about bovine products, said: 'Now I really just use it for *svíčková* and *guláš*, that is, food that the boys [her husband and adolescent son] want and which cannot be made without bovine meat'. In cases such as those of Milena and Marie, where the husbands had become afraid of bovine products, the wives adjusted to this situation and stopped cooking them. In other respects Milena and Marie belong to quite different generations, and are quite different in their ways of performing the role of a spouse: while Milena, the younger woman, is a person who leads quite a 'wild' and independent life, Marie is a more typical middle-aged, family-oriented person, who rarely challenges established conceptions about the proper way in which to be a wife. However, when it comes to cooking both do their best to accommodate to the desires and needs of their spouses.

Concluding Remarks

The becoming real of BSE and vCDJ is a gradual process, occurring at different times and at unequal paces at different levels of society. The disease is transnational, both in its spread and in the way it is dealt with politically. At the level of the Czech state, BSE had been recognized as dangerous as early as the beginning of the 1990s, just a few years after it became publicly known in Europe. Among the vast majority of consumers, it seems that BSE becomes real only when it breaches national boundaries. A study from Norway on consumers' reaction to media reports about BSE reflects the same tendency: the fact that the newspapers wrote about the disease elsewhere in the world did not make people more worried; on the contrary, they felt confident that Norwegian meat was the best and therefore safe (Storstad 2001). 'BSE is here' on the front pages of all newspapers brings a new kind of uncertainty to people and forces them to take an active stand – should patterns of consumption be changed or not?

As I have tried to show, the process of bringing BSE to the Czech Republic was in itself far from innocent or something that 'just happened' of its own accord. It came about through a combination of new technologies and political measures. The process of accommodation to the European Union forced the Czech authorities to implement new technologies of testing, which in turn lead to BSE being 'discovered' – or should we say 'created' – in the country. The head of marketing at the slaughterhouse where the first case was discovered expressed it well: 'From the moment we started to do these tests, we had to expect that some piece would be positive' (*Lidové Noviny*, 13 July 2001).

The becoming real of BSE in Czech society at large is definitely related to the great media attention that was paid to it. As I have argued above, the way in which the media dealt with the case was a significant factor in peoples' retaining a certain trust in the controlling systems. The media's *concrete* 'virtualization' of the disease – its explanations, illustrations and advice – did not directly influence people's response to the disease in their daily food practices, however. The expert advice given to people through the media was not really heeded. Culturally developed tastes and preferences, practical concerns, and not the least the 'substantial' qualities of the meat itself – which makes the meat 'speak back' – were more important in influencing people's everyday strategies.

In issues of risk it is important to ask: who is the risk-taking unit? To what extent do decisions about risk-handling strategies in late modern society involve more than individuals confronted with global threats? As is evident from my material as well as from other studies (Henson et al. 1998; Kemmer et al. 1998), food choice is not only an individual choice. It seems that, in the course of time, families develop a common taste or repertoire, which manifests itself in their diet – a kind of medium of the various members' likes and dislikes. The smallest consumption unit is thus a collective of family members rather than isolated individuals. But the repertoire developed within each family is not stable; it is constantly changing, and it is negotiated over and over again. When confronted with information about new food-related risks, renegotiations must take place. As was demonstrated above, husbands seem to have a strong say here – if the man of the family does not want bovine meat anymore, it may disappear from the menu altogether.

Notes

1. 'Council for Mutual Economic Aid' – organization founded in 1949 by the socialist countries of Eastern Europe to promote economic cooperation between and industrial development in its member states. Later it came to include also Mongolia, Cuba and Vietnam.
2. Among other things the use of certain specified bovine offal for human consumption was banned (Bradley 2001).
3. In the year 2001 more than 50 per cent of the total Czech export of bovine meat went to the European Union (Report from the Ministry of Agriculture, May 2002).
4. Among other things to introduce the so-called blot method of testing animals (prionic check).
5. It has by now, 1 December 2002, see http://society.guardian.co.uk/publichealth/story/0,11098,852064,00.html
6. I only came across one really critical article (*Respekt* from 18 to 24 June 2001).
7. The measures included rules that all slaughtered animals older than thirty months should be tested for BSE before they enter the market (later this limit

was lowered to twenty-four months), and that risk material from now on should be sent to one specific place to be destroyed under controlled circumstances.

8. All except one of the interviewees – both the rural and the urban- were married. All had children, grown up/independent or small. The youngest woman interviewed was twenty-five, the oldest sixty-seven. Socio-economically, most of the informants belonged to the working class or lower middle class; they were manual workers such as cooks or agricultural workers, or women with secondary education employed in shops or as secretaries. Only two of the women had university education. All the interviews were carried out by me, in the Czech language.

9. Source: a report on bovine meat from the Czech Ministry of agriculture from May 2002.

10. The names of the interviewees are pseudonyms.

References

Beck, U. (1999), *World Risk Society*, Cambridge: Polity.

Bradley, R. (2001), 'Bovine Spongiform Encephalopathy and Its Relationship to the New Variant form of Creutzfeldt-Jakob Disease', in H. F. Rabenau, J. Cinatl and H. W. Doerr (eds), *Prions: A Challenge for Science, Medicine and Public Health System*, London: Karger.

Castle-Canerová, M. (1992), 'The Culture of Strong Women in the Making?', in Chris Corrin (ed.), *Superwomen and the Double Burden: Women's Experience of Change in Central and Eastern Europe and the Former Soviet Union*, London: Scarlet Press.

Dvořáková, V. (1999), *Lidé a jídlo* (People and Food), Prague: ISV.

Fiddes, N. (1997), 'Declining Meat, Past, Present . . . and Future Imperfect?' in P. Caplan (ed.), *Food, Health and Identity*, London: Routledge.

Friedlanderová, H. and M. Tuček (2001), *Češi na prahu nového tisíciletí*. (Czechs on the Doorstep of a New Millennium), Prague: SLON.

Guzmán, M. and Kjærnes, U. (1998), *Menneske og dyr: En kvalitativ studie av holdninger til kjøtt*. (Human Beings and Animals: A Qualitative Study of Attitudes to Meat), Oslo: SIFO, report no. 6.

Guzmán, M., Bjørkum, E. and Kjærnes, U. (2000), 'Ungdommers måltider: En studie av livssituasjon, mat og kjønn' (*Youth Meals: A Study of Food, Gender and Everyday Life*), Sifo report 6, Oslo.

Haukanes, H. (1992), 'Pohled norské studentky na život české vesnice' (A Norwegian Student's View on life in a Czech Village), *Sociologické Aktuality*, 1.

—— (1999a), 'Grand Dramas – Ordinary lives. State, Locality and Person in Post Communist Czech Society', Unpublished doctoral thesis, Department of Social

Anthropology, University of Bergen.

—— (1999b), 'Jord og identitet i Tsjekkia' (Land and Identity in the Czech Republic), *Nordisk Øst-forum* 3/13: 41–54.

—— (2001), 'Women as Nurturers: Food, Risk and Ideals of Care in the Czech Republic', in H. Haukanes, *Women after Communism: Ideal Images, Real Lives*, Bergen: Centre for Women's and Gender Research, vol. 12: 67–80.

Heitlingerová, A. (1995), 'Women's Equality, Work and Family in the Czech Republic', in B. Lobodzinska (ed.), *Family, Women and Employment in Central-Eastern Europe*, London: Greenwood.

—— and Trnková, Z. (2001), *Život mladých pražských žen.* (The Life of Young Prague Women), Prague: SLON.

Henson, S., Gregory, S., Hamilton, M. and Walker, A. (1998), 'Food Choice and Diet within the Family Setting', in A. Murcott (ed.), *The Nation's Diet: The Social Science of Food Choice*, London: Longman.

Hutton Rabe, P. (1999), 'Women and Gender in the Czech Republic and Cross-National Comparisons', *Czech Sociological Review*, 2(7): 223–230.

Kemmer, D., Anderson, A. and Marshall, D. (1998), 'The "Marriage Menu": Life, Food and Diet in Transition', in A. Murcott, *The Nation's Diet: The Social Science of Food Choice*, London: Longman.

Klint-Jensen, K. (2001), 'Kogalskap i England – katastrofal risikokommunikasjon' (Mad-cow Disease in England: Catastrophic Risk-communication), Paper given at the conference *Etter kugalskap – ingen tillit?* (After Mad-cow disease – No Confidence?) Oslo: Norwegian Research Council.

Křižková, A. (1999), 'The Division of Labour in Czech Households in the 1990s', *Czech Sociological Review*, 2(7): 205–14.

Kubát, M. (ed.) (2001), *Východní rozšiření Evropské unie* (Eastern Enlargement of the European Union), Brno: Masaryk University.

Kuchařová, V. (1999), 'Women and Employment', *Czech Sociological Review*, 2(7): 179–94.

Lien, M., Bjørkum, E. and Bye, E. (1998), *Kjøtt, holdninger og endring* (Meat, changes in attitudes and consumption), SIFO report no. 4, Oslo.

McIntosh, A. and Zay, M. (1998), 'Women as Gatekeepers of Food Consumption: A Sociological Critique', in C. M. Counihan and S. L. Kaplan (eds), *Food and Gender: Identity and Power*, Amsterdam: Harwood Academic Publishers.

Reilly, J. and Miller, D. (1997), 'Scaremonger or Scapegoat: The Role of Media in the Emergence of Food as a Social Issue', in P. Caplan (ed.), *Food, Health and Identity*, London: Routledge.

Ridley, R. M. and Baker, H. (1998), *Fatal Protein: The Story of CJD, BSE and Other Prion Diseases*, Oxford: Oxford University Press.

Storstad, O. (2001), *Kugalskap i media: Effekter på forbrukertillit* (Mad-cow Disease in the Media: Effects on Consumers' Confidence), Paper no. 1,

Trondheim: Centre for Rural Research.

Vialles, N. (1994), *Animal to Edible*, Cambridge: Cambridge University Press.

Newspapers

Lidové Noviny, 13 July 2001. 'Testy na BSE si zvolili dobrovolně' (They Chose the BSE Tests Voluntarily).

Mlada Fronta Dnes, 9 June 2001, 'Párky a paštiky se vyrábjí rizikovým škrábáním kostí' (Sausages and Pâtés are Made from Risky Cut-offs from Bones).

New Scientist.com, 10 February 2001, 'Tomorrow the World. Have Contaminated Feed Exports Spread BSE across the Globe?'

Respekt, 18–24 June 2001, 'Nejezte jahodové knedlíky' (Do not Eat Strawberry Dumplings).

Zemské Noviny, 9 June 2001, 'Nemoc šílených krav i v Česku' (Mad-cow Disease also in Czechia).

Zemské Noviny, 21 June 2001, 'BSE přenesl tuk v krmivu' (BSE Came with Fat in Fodder).

Reports

2002, May: *SKOT- Hovězí maso* (Report from the Czech Ministry of Agriculture on Bovine Meat), Prague: Czech Ministry of Agriculture.

Zelená Zprava (2000), *Zpráva o stavu zemědělství R za rok 1999* (Green News: Report on the State of Czech Agriculture for the year 1999).

−7−

Western Food and the Making of the Japanese Nation-state

Katarzyna J. Cwiertka

Introduction

On 4 November 1871, distinguished foreign officials residing in Japan gathered for a dinner party organized by the Japanese Foreign Ministry and commemorating the emperor's birthday. The party took place at the Hotel des Colonies (better known as Tsukiji Hoterukan or Hoterukan) – the only Western-style hotel in the city of Tokyo at the time, situated just outside the Tsukiji foreign settlement. The establishment entered the history books as the venue of the first Western-style state banquet for foreign diplomats (Muraoka 1984: 173–84).

The menu consisted of eight courses and followed the mid-nineteenth-century London fashion for French-style dining. Throughout the following century, French cuisine continued to dominate Japanese state dinners, while British and American cookery proved more influential in less formal settings. By the 1880s, dining Western-style was widely emulated by Japanese government officials and members of the imperial court. This is remarkable considering the fact that practically every aspect of Western-style dining revolutionized the existing Japanese conventions. Not only did the form and taste of the food differ greatly from the native fare, but also the eating utensils and dining furniture contradicted considerably the Japanese customs. Sitting on chairs and handling cutlery was already a torture for novice Japanese diners, not to mention the challenging taste of butter, beef and wine. On top of that, a Western-style banquet required its participants to be dressed Western-style, which at the time was in itself an adventure for many members of the Japanese upper class. In short, the introduction of Western food into the lives of the Japanese elite was much more complex than merely a change of the menu. The phenomenon is a fascinating example of 'eating the other',[1] but the emperor's birthday party denoted something far more significant. It marked the beginning of the carefully orchestrated process of nation-state making in Japan. It was one of the various measures undertaken by the new government with the aim of reconstituting the Japanese people into active subject-citizens.

As the future would show, Western food and Western nutritional knowledge were to play an important role in this development, their particular functions and notions changing along with the changing phases of Japanese politics. However, the tightening grip of the state[2] on the diet of its people reappeared as a consistent trend. It gradually expanded from the symbolism of Western-style banquets of the elite in the late nineteenth century to the totalitarian system of wartime food control encompassing the entire society. As was the case with other modernizing nations, the increasing influence of nutritional science on the food habits of the ever-growing share of the Japanese population did not liberate them from external control, but rather intensified the means of social regulation (Turner 1982: 23).

By identifying three stages in the involvement of the modern Japanese state in the matter of public nutrition, I will demonstrate the strengthening level of the state's control over its citizens between the late nineteenth and mid-twentieth centuries. First, I will document the use of Western food in the construction of the emperor as the central national symbol and in the formation of the nationally uniform, modern folklore. Next, I will describe the role that Western food and Western nutritional concepts played in the transformation of the Japanese military diet, and, finally analyse the enrollment of the Western-inspired notion of proper diet in the state's total control over the citizens' minds and bodies during the 1930s and 1940s.

As in Europe and the United States, the development of capitalist production and the introduction of general conscription made the Japanese state dependent on the bodies of its population as never before (Kamminga and Cunningham 1995: 2). This new dependence enhanced the government's interest in nutritional matters and strengthened its involvement in public nutrition. By the same token, however, it provided the regime with splendid new instruments of social control. I will demonstrate that the young Japanese state quickly learned how to utilize new control mechanisms that developed in the circumstances of extended power-relations of modern capitalist states. I will also argue that in some respects, it even surpassed the success of its Western mentors.

The Emperor's New Diet

No matter how democratically the members of the elite are chosen (usually not very) or how deeply divided among themselves they may be (usually much more than outsiders imagine), they justify their existence and order their actions in terms of a collection of stories, ceremonies, insignia, formalities, and appurtenances that they have either inherited or, in more revolutionary situations, invented. It is these – crowns and coronations, limousines and conferences – that mark the center as center and give what goes on there its aura of being not merely important but in some odd fashion connected with the way the world is built. (Geertz 1977: 152–3)

The first object of the state's dietary strategies in Japan was the emperor himself. As the symbol of the modernizing nation, Emperor Meiji (1852–1912) was to pave the way in embracing Western models. When in 1875, for example, the smallpox epidemic broke out, the fact that the imperial family was vaccinated was widely publicized in order to give Japanese, who might have otherwise feared an injection of foreign medicine, the courage to have themselves inoculated as well (Keene 2002: 254). The task of promoting Western-inspired innovations in Japan acquired a particular importance in view of the emperor's father having been well known for his hatred of foreigners and his wholehearted rejection of Western civilization (Keene 2002: xiii, 197). Every aspect of his son's life was utilized to prove the true devotion of Japan's new leadership to modernity and change.

Emperor Meiji's accession in 1868 came at the time of cataclysmic political circumstances in Japan. In 1854, the country's self-imposed isolationist policy that had lasted for more than two centuries was ended. In the following years, Japan was forced to sign a series of commercial treaties with Western powers, which included the standard nineteenth-century 'unequal treaty' clauses of extraterritoriality and mandatory tariffs that gave special privileges to Westerners, and de facto compromised Japan's sovereignty. The foreign pressure empowered the domestic opposition of a coalition of samurai leaders from the southwestern domains and court nobles, who called for the overthrow of the existing regime and the restoration of the imperial rule. It needs to be clarified at this point that the political status quo before 1868 rested upon a centuries-old complex structure of the warrior government detached from the imperial court, headed by the *shōgun* or military regent. Officially, the *shōgun* ruled under a reigning emperor, but in reality, the imperial office was reduced to a ritual and legitimizing role.

Confronted with the Western imperialist encroachment and domestic pressures, the *shōgun* agreed to surrender his office, and the oligarchy of middle-ranking samurai established a new political order modeled on constitutional monarchies of Europe. Along with introducing wide-ranging Westernization policies of 'Civilization and Enlightenment' (*bunmei kaika*), which were to reform the country through the incorporation of Western science and technology, the new government, commonly referred to as the Meiji Government, began its project of turning the young emperor into a modern monarch. Impressed by the political possibilities of the ceremonial activities, the new leaders revived, fabricated and encouraged emperor-centered rituals with unprecedented vigor (Fujitani 1996; see also Geertz 1977).

As Fujitani has shrewdly observed, the common people in nineteenth-century Japan had neither a strong sense of national identity nor a clear image of the emperor as the Japanese nation's central symbol (1996: 4). Customs, beliefs and practices of the population were localized and diverse, with little or no national uniformity. Imperial pageantry was to become the key strategy employed by the modern state in order to mould the inhabitants of the Japanese isles into one nation. In time, the Westernized, homogenized, official culture fostered by the state replaced the diverse, local traditions of pre-modern times.

The emperor paved the way in absorbing Western elements into the Japanese lifestyle. In 1872, his traditional clothes were replaced by what would become his most typical costume – a swallow-tail uniform fastened with hooks. The following year, his hair was cut and he grew a beard and moustache (Keene 2002: 213, 237). These changes were echoed by equipping the empress with a corset, a crinoline and a bonnet. Soon, similar alterations were undertaken by members of the court and by government officials. As a British contemporary pointedly observed, 'this revolution in clothes helped powerfully in the recognition by the whole world of Japan as an equal in the brotherhood of nations' (Keene 2002: 194). Around the same time when the emperor's appearance was being modernized, French cuisine was introduced to the imperial court and the new style of dining was imitated by the growing share of the Japanese elite (Harada 1989: 234–5).

The fact that Japan's confrontation with the Western nations took place at a time when they already controlled a considerable part of Asia made the power relations between Japan and the West very uneven. These circumstances inspired new political leaders to mimic Western civilization. Yet, cultural conformity with the West maintained by the upper classes was not merely a means to raising Japan's status in Western eyes. As I mentioned earlier, Western elements were utilized for the sake of constructing uniform, official culture of the state. By the same token, Westernized lifestyle came to be perceived as a marker of an upper-class status (Sugiyama Lebra 1993: 187–9) which, in political terms, denoted domestic authorization of power.

Based on the fashion theory of Kon Wajirō (1888–1973), Kumakura argues that in pre-modern times the creators of fashions in Japan were not those in power, but wealthy urbanites with no political functions. New aesthetic trends were created to express the free spirit of their creators, and their detachment from feudal relationships (Kumakura 1990: 483). In contrast, the ruling elite of Europe deliberately created new fashions as a means of social display – fashions trickled down from the top to the bottom of the social ladder, and by imitating them the wider society acknowledged the superiority of their creators (Elias 1994).

Through a deliberate adoption of Western-style dining, members of the Japanese elite converted themselves into creators of fashions, as consumption of Western food soon became a nationwide trend in Japan. Turning the new political elite into the propagators of a new, Westernized lifestyle was in line with the growing importance of cultural statecraft in modern politics. In the era of the nation-state, states gained a large part of their legitimacy through the promotion of distinctive culture and through the cultural construction of citizens (Hannerz 1996: 24). The example of beef eating pointedly illustrates the new situation.

The meat-eating taboo is one of the characteristic features of pre-modern Japanese diet. The first recorded decree against consumption of cattle, horses, dogs, monkeys and chickens was issued in 675, and similar decrees were repeatedly issued during the following centuries. Resting upon the Buddhist prohibition of killing, the decrees were in line with the political and cultural orientation of the imperial court, which at the time was the center of power in Japan. However, the strength of the taboo was considerably bolstered when meat eating began to be considered defilement also according to Shintō – Japan's aboriginal religion (Ishige 2000: 1176). From the seventeenth century onward, the meat-eating taboo had begun to spread nationwide (Harada 1993: 257), but it is not entirely clear whether religious prejudice can be held primarily responsible for its diffusion. According to Hanley, it was the concern to maintain and increase agricultural production, rather than religious considerations, which inspired the authorities of the *shōgun* to issue in 1612 a decree banning the killing of cattle (1997: 65–6).

Historical evidence suggests that meat was widely consumed despite the existing taboo. Throughout the eighteenth and nineteenth centuries, the *shōgun* himself, as well as other members of the political elite, regularly received gifts of beef (Ishikawa 1996: 25–6), and restaurants specializing in game were thriving (Hanley 1997: 66). Nevertheless, an aura of pollution surrounded the practice of meat eating. Reports make it clear that eating meat was something fairly unusual, and euphemisms, such as *botan* (peony), *sakura* (cherry) and *momiji* (maple) were used when referring respectively to the meat of wild boar, horsemeat and venison.

The 675 edict prohibiting meat eating remained in power until it was announced in 1872 that the Emperor Meiji himself consumed animal flesh (Ishige 1986: 71). By this single deed, or rather its official proclamation, meat eating was transformed from a practice which had long been tolerated but kept low-profile into the symbol of Japan's transformation into a modern nation. During the following decade, the consumption of meat, and in particular beef, was glorified to such a degree that refraining from its consumption came to be regarded as a sign of backwardness. In 1875, for example, a local newspaper reported that 'nowadays, even a maiden from a remote and secluded place in the mountains does not think of someone not eating beef as a human being' (Saitō 1983: 73). Beef-eating fashion translated politics into a language that could easily be understood by the common man.

It needs to be pointed out that the nineteenth-century Western science of nutrition regarded beef as an ideal food essential to human growth. Refraining from its consumption was generally perceived in the West as a disadvantage in terms of physical, intellectual and even moral strength (Finlay 1995: 48). Thus it seems hardly surprising that the Japanese government undertook measures in order to turn its people into meat eaters. The public consumption of beef by the emperor not only helped to abolish a superstitious taboo, which did not fit into the image of a modern nation, but also enhanced the emperor's position as a progressive ruler who leads his people toward 'Civilization and Enlightenment'.

The Navy too Sails on its Stomach

> Armies travel on their stomachs; generals – and now economists and nutritionists – decide what to put in them. They must do so while depending upon the national economy and those who run it to supply them with what they prescribe or, rather, they prescribe what they are told they can rely upon having. (Mintz 1996: 25)

Once Japan officially paved the way toward modernization by abolishing the feudal regime and establishing the Meiji government in 1868, its general policy was conveyed by the slogan 'Rich country, strong army' (*fukoku kyōhei*). Within this policy, two aims were evident – industrialization and the establishment of modern armed forces – and measures to achieve them were undertaken without delay. Already in 1869, the Military Affairs Ministry was set up, and the Conscription Law promulgated merely four years later. By 1878, ten years after the overthrow of the old regime, the new government had constructed a single, highly centralized organizational model for both the Army and Navy (Westney 1986: 176).

From the very beginning of their existence, modern Japanese armed forces were separated from the normal social context. Modeled after armies and navies of Western powers, Japanese military men wore Western-style uniforms, slept in beds, smoked cigarettes and consumed food that was unfamiliar to the most of their fellow countrymen. Along with the emperor and the elites, Japanese armed forces played a crucial role in the construction of the Westernized, uniform national culture. General conscription, moreover, was a perfect channel for its dissemination. By the 1930s, not only did the ratio of men with the conscription experience considerably increase, but the military also began to enjoy extreme popularity among the population. Due to political instability of the country throughout the 1920s and the world-wide economic depression following 1929, it was increasingly to the military that the people looked for the solutions they hoped would bring them a better future (Waswo 1996: 88–9). These circumstances formed favorable grounds for the popularization throughout the country of the Westernized, uniform culture of the military.

Contrary to the complex incentives for the adoption of Western food in the upper-class circles, as described earlier, Westernization of military diet was motivated strictly by efficiency – most nutritious food at least possible cost.[3] With the nineteenth-century Western nutritional knowledge, which stressed the importance of protein intake, playing an increasingly significant role in the considerations of Japanese military authorities, reforms in military diet became inevitable. The inconsistency between the ideal diet and what was made available under budgetary constraints was responsible for the development of an eclectic Japanese-Western mixture. The case of the navy reveals the dilemma of the authorities, and how they tried to find a middle ground between the scientific requirements of nutritional science and restraints of economy.

From its outset, the Japanese navy was much more Westernized than the army. It is by no means surprising, considering the fact that Japan had practically no maritime experience before the establishment of the Naval Training Institute in Nagasaki in 1855. As the Dutch Royal Navy served as the example for the Japanese at the time, food rations aboard were designed to resemble those of Dutch sailors (Sema 1985: 15). Only a few years later, however, costly Western-style diet had to be abandoned, and the Japanese marines returned to the home fare centered on rice. The outbreak of a beriberi epidemic, which by 1883 surpassed the alarming ratio of 120 cases per thousand sailors, was directly responsible for the implementation in 1890 of a new, Westernized diet.

Beriberi has long been known in Japan as 'Edo disease', because it broke out mainly in big cities, such as Edo (Tokyo), where white, polished rice was a conventional staple (Hagiwara 1960: 16). The disease is caused by vitamin B1 deficiency, or, more precisely, a deficiency of thiamine, of which rice bran is a rich source. Because white rice – the samurai staple – constituted the bulk of food rations in the modern Japanese armed forces, beriberi became a major problem of the Japanese military authorities throughout the late nineteenth and early twentieth centuries.

By 1883, the health conditions in the navy were so alarming that the Beriberi Research Committee of physicians was established in order to fight the disease (Kikuchi 1930: 24). One of the individuals involved in the work of the committee was the director of the Tokyo Naval Hospital and the Head of the Bureau of Medical Affairs of the Navy, Takagi Kanehiro[4] (1849–1920). Takagi, who had studied anatomy and clinical medicine at St Thomas Hospital Medical College in London, turned attention to the fact that beriberi was a typically 'Asian' disease, rarely occurring among Westerners. As the concept of vitamins had not yet been discovered, Takagi was not able to determine precisely the cause of the disease, but he was correct to link it with nutrition. Presuming that the illness was a result of a very low protein intake, Takagi suggested that a diet comparable to that of the Western navies might be a remedy. Despite the fact that Takagi's assumption of the link between beriberi and protein intake was incorrect, his measures proved effective and convinced the leadership of the Japanese navy to immediately order all units to switch to a Western-style diet (Sema 1985: 16–22).

Takagi's reforms not only marked the reintroduction of a Western-style diet in the Japanese navy, but also, more importantly, indicated the inauguration of the system of central food control. From 1890 onward, provisions were distributed centrally by the Munitions Bureau of the Naval Ministry, and the bureau determined in detail the kinds and amounts of foodstuffs that were to be consumed by each Japanese sailor, as is shown below.

Daily Rations in the Japanese Navy under the 1890 Regulation
(Sema 1985: 50)

Mondays and Fridays:	337.5 g ship's biscuits[5]
	150 g canned meat
	150 g preserved fish
	dried beans or dried fruit
Remaining days of the week:	450 g bread and 187 g rice
	225 g fresh bone meat
	150 g fresh fish
	450 g fresh vegetables

From accounting records it is evident that other Western foods, such as butter, condensed milk, jam, canned vegetables, coffee, brandy, gin, or rum were also rationed in the navy. These luxuries were not supposed to be consumed on a daily basis, but to sustain weak or ill bodies (Sema 1985: 9–10, 50). Even without them, however, the Westernized diet proved far too costly for the navy's budget. Moreover, young men hitherto accustomed only to boiled rice, millet, or barley as a staple and suddenly forced to switch to bread-and-biscuit-based diet expressed considerable resistance, and even organized food strikes (Sema 1985: 61–2). In the meantime, experiments in the army showed that a rice-barley mixture proved to be an effective and cheap measure against beriberi. In March 1895, the navy authorities ordered the replacing of white rice rations by a rice-and-barley mixture, and a few years later resolved to gradually abandon bread-and-ship's-biscuit-based meals. The new 1898 regulations assigned one bread meal and two rice meals daily. From 1924 onward, rice was served three times a day five days a week (Sema 1985: 65, 80). However, the navy diet did retain its Westernized character, as the dishes that accompanied rice were often Japanese-Western hybrids, as illustrated in the 1936 menu compilation below.

Western-style dishes served in the Imperial Japanese Navy (Kaigun shukeika 1936)

Karē meshi (Curried Rice): The mixture of rice, barley and sweet potatoes in pieces, boiled in a sauce made of minced beef, carrots, onions fried in butter or lard with curry powder, salt and pepper.

Makaroni biifu (Macaroni with Beef): Macaroni, pieces of beef, potatoes, carrots and onions boiled in white sauce seasoned with salt and pepper.

Hikiniku bōru shichū (Meatballs Stew): Stew made of potatoes, onions, carrots, radish, tomato sauce and minced meatballs. Thickened with lard with flour, and flavoured with salt and pepper.

Keiniku guratan (Chicken Gratin): Pieces of chicken, eggplant and onions boiled in béchamel sauce, seasoned with salt and pepper.

Poteto korokke (Potato Croquettes): Mashed potatoes mixed with yolk, shaped into small ovals, coated with breadcrumbs and deep-fried.

Mikkusudo sarada (Mixed Salad): Pieces of boiled chicken, cucumber and eggplant dressed in mayonnaise sauce.

Furai kanpan (Fried Ship's biscuits): Ship's biscuits deep-fried in sesame oil, served with sugar.

Next to Westernization, the 1890 reform of the navy diet introduced the revolutionary system of total dietary management over the bodies of its men. During the following decades, navy authorities determined precisely (at least in theory) when and what enlisted men on their fleet ate. Hereafter, all provisions were not acquired locally, but carried aboard, which made the navy less vulnerable to unexpected circumstances. The daily rations of calories, protein, fat, carbohydrates, etc. of all the marines remained the same regardless of the location. From the 1920s onward, the navy leadership also began to pay careful attention to the variety and the quality of sailors' diet (Cwiertka 2002: 10–15).

A tendency to devote increasing attention to the quality of nourishment could also be observed within the army authorities, in particular after the First World War (Cwiertka 2002). Adoption of high-in-calories Western dishes in the army and navy menus was not a result of ideological considerations, but was an expression of efficient solutions of the authorities in order to fulfill nutritional requirements within the provided budget. From the late 1930s onward, when the military concepts began to be extended by the state to encompass the civilian population, the emphasis on efficiency of nutrition – thus far characteristic for the military – became the key principle of civilian diet as well.

Managing the Nation's Diet

Ship's biscuits are rationalized portable food. They have always been an important military provision for the brave warriors of the Imperial Army in every location. Let's all together experience the real value of soldier's food. (from an advertisement in the magazine *Asahigurafu*, 1939 no. 10, back cover)

As Foucault has observed in *Discipline and Punish* (1977), the way in which power is exercised changed in modern times from being 'visible' to 'invisible'. While in ancient times power functioned through public executions observed by mass gatherings, modern forms of power do not work solely by punishing the body, but rather at the level of conscience – controlling the soul (Coveney 2000: 8–9, 14; Foucault 1977). In his later work, Foucault introduced the term 'governmentality' to express the rise of a concern for populations and the development of a range of techniques for managing populations through knowledge (Foucault 1991). The term 'management of populations' is employed here in the sense of strategies, techniques and aspirations of the state to shape beliefs and conduct of the people.

Coveney used Foucault's concept of governmentality to analyse the rise and spread of nutritional knowledge within the framework of the modern state (2000: 26–7). The application and dissemination of nutritional science through a range of state's institutions had, according to Coveney, the effect of making individuals objects of knowledge and power. It was not an oppressing and dominating power, but rather a kind of a government 'at a distance'. While the autonomy of individuals was preserved, they were controlled through the establishment of rules and by shared expert knowledge and shared conceptual frameworks (2000: 89).

The adoption and implementation of the modern science of nutrition in Japan exposes these intricate connections between power, welfare and knowledge within the workings of the nation-state. The entire process is more transparent, and perhaps more spectacular than in the case of Western societies, due to the fact that nutritional science was a knowledge that originated in the West and had to be adapted to the Japanese context. In fact, the application of scientific nutritional concepts within the Japanese daily practices often required the adoption of Western food into the Japanese diet as well.

The first step in the importation of Western nutritional knowledge in Japan was the establishment in the 1880s of the Tokyo Hygienic Laboratory. It was funded by the Home Ministry in lines with the official policy of 'Civilization and Enlightenment' that aimed at furthering the country's progress through the importation of Western science and technology. It took several decades, however, before the government realized the importance of nutrition as a means of 'managing the population'.

As we have observed in the previous section, the Imperial Japanese Army and Navy were deeply concerned with the issue of 'proper diet', as they were directly confronted with the consequences of malnutrition. The direct involvement of the Japanese government in public nutrition developed slowly, and was stimulated, as in Europe, by the outbreak of the First World War. The economic recession and inflation, caused by the war, confronted the government with a series of popular disturbances that were unparalleled in modern Japanese history in their magnitude, diffusion and violent intensity. The so-called Rice Riots (1918) – sparked by sharply inflated rice prices – brought about a collapse of the current cabinet, and prompted the new leaders to pay more attention to the issue of nutrition and food supply. The initiatives of the League of Nations and other organizations toward overcoming hunger and malnutrition in Europe at the time undoubtedly sustained the new trend in Japan. The rise of Newer Knowledge of Nutrition,[6] with its emphasis on 'proper' nutrition as preventive measures for health improvement, also caught the attention of the Japanese policy-makers. All these developments formed a favorable ground for private initiative of the concerned professionals and organizations to receive state support for their activities.

One of the most influential individuals of the time, often referred to as the founding father of Japanese dietetics, was Saeki Tadasu (1876–1959). After receiving a PhD in dietetics from Yale University, Saeki established in 1915 his private Nutritional Laboratory – the first research institute in Japan to deal exclusively with the issue of human nutrition (Hagiwara 1960: 36). He was a generative power behind the establishment of the Imperial Government Institute for Nutrition, which was to operate under a direct control of the Home Ministry. The institute, founded in 1920, was very advanced even by Western standards, with the Vitamin Laboratory, the Laboratory for Economic Nutrition, the Laboratory for Metabolic Experiments, the Physiological and Bacteriological Laboratory. It was one of the first institutions of such a scale in the world devoted entirely to research on human nutrition and propagation of knowledge about healthy eating.[7]

Serious efforts were made by the institute to transform nutritional knowledge from a scientific domain of the specialists into a practical advice for the public. The so-called 'Economical and Nutritious Menus', which were to serve as a model of healthy and cheap diet, were published daily. Easy-to-follow instructions and recipes were propagated via cooking demonstrations, exhibitions and lectures. In the year 1933 alone the Imperial Government Institute for Nutrition carried out 275 lecturing tours all over the country. The institute was also involved in composing menus for cheap restaurants that were managed by the municipal government of Tokyo (Imperial Government Institute for Nutrition 1935; Ishikawa and Ehara 2002: 131).

From the 1920s onward, the support of the variety of state institutions for the dissemination of nutritional knowledge among the population grew remarkably.

This trend went hand in hand with the gradual extension of military concepts to encompass civilian society, as the new doctrine of 'total war' emphasized the importance of the home front and the necessity of total mobilization of the civilian population (Duus 1998: 210). Throughout the 1930s, the total mobilization of the Japanese population for the war effort became increasingly pronounced.[8] As the war progressed, and the country needed strong conscripts and workers more than ever, the grip of the state on the nutrition of its people tightened in a swift tempo.

Diet was singled out by the authorities as an important home-front weapon. As elsewhere (for example Bentley 1998), the Japanese state propaganda elevated efficient nourishment to the level of a patriotic virtue. The knowledge of how to eat healthily at the lowest possible cost became a matter of national security. The cry for the limitation of side dishes found its epitome in the patriotic dish called 'Rising Sun Lunch Box' (*hinomaru bentō*), that consisted only of plain boiled rice and Japanese apricot pickle (*umeboshi*) arranged together in a rectangular lunch box resembling the Japanese flag. However, with rice becoming a luxury item on the table, more efficient foods that contained more calories and were cheaper to produce, such as sweet potatoes and squash, were propagated. Special campaigns advocating methods to economize on rice through careful chewing, mixing it with vegetables and other grains, were carried out through posters, pamphlets and advertisements in popular magazines. In 1937, the year in which the war with China broke out, the state management of the nation's diet entered the ultimate stage, symbolically represented by the introduction of ship's biscuits (see note 5) to civilian consumers.

This maritime innovation had spread in Japan along with other Western artifacts, customs and ideas during the second half of the nineteenth century. While éclairs and chocolate won the hearts of the Japanese elites, ship's biscuits – known in Japanese under the name *kanpan* – attracted the attention of the new government's policy-makers responsible for the second half of the Meiji government's slogan 'Rich country, strong army'. By the 1920s, *kanpan* became an indispensable component of the navy and army diet, but remained practically unknown to civilians. As of 1937, when the public campaign propagating the consumption of ship's biscuits began, approximately 90 per cent of total biscuit production of Japan was constituted by products other than *kanpan*. Only seven years later the ratio became reversed (Kizara 1990: 582–3).

Kanpan was propagated as a substitute for rice, which became in increasingly short supply. Consumption of ready-to-eat biscuits instead of rice required neither fuel nor cooking equipment. The biscuits were also propagated as efficient in terms of nutrition, providing three times more energy than rice. Most importantly, however, ship's biscuits acquired a clear ideological connotation. *Kanpan* advertisements often carried scenes from the battlefield and patriotic texts like the following:

In order to let one soldier fight at the battlefield hands of eight people are required at the home front. The amount of food they need is enormous. Saving and storing rice – our staple – has become the necessity. Using foods made of flour as a substitute for rice can make a difference. Once we learned that kanpan next to being a staple of the front is also a defense food guaranteeing perfect preservation, we feel our duty to store it not only for the calamities of the peacetime, but also as an air defense at wartime. (from an advertisement in the magazine *Asahigurafu*, 1938 no. 15, back cover)

The *kanpan* propaganda proved successful not only owing to the persuasive power of the state, but first of all due to the rapidly deteriorating food supply. The enactment of the Food Management Law took place in 1942, de facto establishing a nation-wide staple food-rationing system, which included wheat, barley and pearl barley as well as rice. Later, sweet potatoes and white potatoes were classed as a staple food. Sugar, fats and oils, soy sauce, even salt gradually entered the ranks of rationed foods (Johnston 1953: 200–12).

The further Japan got involved in warfare, the less food became available for the civilian population. By 1944, the authorities had to rely increasingly on scientific solutions in their battle against food shortage. Various chemical devices were designed in order to diminish the loss of nutrients in the process of digestion of food and make the food intake as efficient as possible. Researchers were also assigned to look for new methods to keep the nation's body going without sufficient nutrition. Various food and vitamin supplements appeared on the market, along with pills for indigestion, constipation and other ailments brought about by wartime diet (Cwiertka 1998).

These desperate attempts to nourish the nation through the use of chemical supplements explicitly illustrate the increasing reliance of nation-state governments on scientific solutions in their 'management of populations'. As Turner has pointedly observed, scientific advances did not liberate the body from external control, but on the contrary, intensified the means of social regulation (1982: 23). However, one may wonder whether the 'control at a distance' really works in the circumstances of hunger and near-starvation. It is highly probable that through the dissemination of scientific advice on healthy nutrition the citizens developed trust in the solutions propagated by the state. We may presume that they even began to alter their eating habits in order to meet the recommended requirements. However, at the point when choice was no longer possible, a management of a half-starved population via nutritional regime seemed hardly plausible. The 'control at a distance' through nutritional advice makes sense only if a minimum level of dietary sustenance is achieved.

Concluding Remarks

The connection between food and politics is both universal and long-standing. However, the mutual interdependence between politics and food has never been as great as since the rise of the nation-state, when the pressure for the increased social control over bodies intensified (Turner 1982). From the late nineteenth century onward, when scientists proved that the health and the strength of one's body were closely related to diet, the issue of public nourishment began to weigh heavily in governmental agendas and the direct political impact on nutrition was initiated.

It became the citizen's duty to be fit and healthy in order to do physical labor and go to war in service of the state. In return, the state was to take responsibility for creating the conditions, under which its citizens could be helped, educated or even coerced to be fit (Kamminga and Cunningham 1995: 2). It was only during the First World War that this mutual dependency came to be fully understood by the governing bodies of the European states (Barnett 1985; Davis 2000). As this chapter has demonstrated, the Japanese authorities did not lag behind in their comprehension of the importance of nutrition in the 'management of populations'. This is quite remarkable, considering the fact that the country began to modernize relatively late, and that nutritional science itself was an utterly foreign concept in Japan.

In this chapter, I have examined the involvement of the Japanese state in the matter of public nutrition during the late nineteenth and the first half of the twentieth centuries. I have focused on the adoption and popularization of Western food and Western nutritional knowledge, and their changing notions in the face of different phases of Japanese politics. I have identified three ways through which the authorities brought about change in the food habits of the population, their decisions motivated each time by different considerations.

At first, Western food was utilized in order to create a civilized, modern image for Japan abroad and gain it recognition as an equal of Western nations. At the same time, the creation of fashion to eat Western-style became a means of confirming the position of the emperor as the progressive leader and the symbol of the nation. By deliberately influencing the food choices of the elite (and indirectly also the general public), this stage presaged the development of the state's 'control at a distance', which matured a few decades later.

The second strategy employed by the Japanese state for the sake of regulating the nation's diet involved a range of dietary reforms in the armed forces. The leadership of the Imperial Army and Navy realized that nutrition became a critical component of modern warfare. In this respect, the Japanese military leaders did not differ from their counterparts in the West, who, at the same time, sought cheap food that would improve the physical condition and the endurance of the troops (see Finlay 1995: 53–4; Dusselier 2001: 36, 40).

As I have elaborated elsewhere (Cwiertka 2002), reforms in the armed forces did not concern merely the diet of enlisted men, but also indirectly affected food choices of the entire population. As the growing number of Japanese men underwent military training, they became accustomed to the taste of military menus. Once they returned home, they spread the lore of new Western-style dishes, perpetuating the uniform, official culture of the state and endorsing its 'control at a distance'.

The third and most powerful measure in the process of transforming the diet of the population was employed during the 1930s and 1940s, under the reign of the wartime totalitarian regime. The government fully realized that disability and disease in the male working-class population, which formed the bulk of the armed forces, constituted a serious threat to the state's military power. Moreover, in the circumstances of the 'total war', bolstering the health conditions of the labor force was perceived equally crucial for the country's survival as the performance in the battlefield. Consequently, the implementation of Western nutritional science, accompanied by the dissemination of Western food, continued uninterrupted throughout the war, regardless of the growing Japanese hostility toward the West.

The methods that were employed in order to accommodate Western food in the Japanese context ranged from strictly culinary means, such as adapting the flavoring of Western dishes to the Japanese taste preference or serving them with rice, to the more aesthetically-centered ones such as giving Western dishes poetic, Japanese names (Cwiertka 1999: 49–56). In many respects, the domestication of Western food in Japan resembled the processes of embedding of foreign food that took place elsewhere (see Davidson 1983; Levenstein 1985; Gabaccia 1998). Not only did the taste and form of Western food alter, but also the incentives for its popularity shifted along with the changing phases of the Japanese politics. Exclusive Western-style banquets of the upper classes, that in the late nineteenth century functioned as an instrument for expressing social prestige and political legitimacy, gradually transformed into nourishing and economical food for the nation.

By the 1930s, the popular notion of nutritional knowledge and Western-style food being a Western import largely faded. Instead, they acquired a clear connotation of the eclectic, uniform culture of modern Japan. Social engineers of the Meiji government would not have dreamed of better results, when they embarked on their project of nation-making by organizing the emperor's birthday party on 4 November 1871.

Notes

1. Consuming foreign, unfamiliar food in order to validate or elevate one's social status, out of a sense of adventure, or due to other reasons. See also Cwiertka 2003.

2. Throughout this chapter, I use the term 'state' as defined by Corrigan and Sayer (1985: 2–3) – a repertoire of activities and institutions that collectively shape and reproduce the dominant ideology or status quo (Robertson 1998: 219).

3. Similar strategies were employed in the second half of the nineteenth century in British workhouses. See for example Coveney 2000: 82–3.

4. Throughout this chapter, Japanese names are presented family name first, as this is an established practice in Japan.

5. Ship's biscuit is a baked mixture of flour and water. It could contain neither sugar, eggs, yeast, nor fat so that there were no ingredients which could putrefy. The baking had to be brief enough to avoid caramelization, which would also encourage deterioration, and was followed by prolonged, slow drying to remove any residual moisture (Swinburne 1997: 310).

6. The 'Newer Knowledge of Nutrition' was based on the recognition of the fact that an adequate diet also comprised substances other than proteins, carbohydrates, fats and salts. These substances, which were discovered due to investigations into deficiency diseases such as scurvy, beriberi and rickets, later came to be referred to as 'vitamins'. See also Teich 1995.

7. In Great Britain, for example, the first nutritional laboratory was the Institute of Animal Nutrition established within the School of Agriculture in Cambridge in 1914. In 1927, another laboratory was founded by the Medical Research Council, known under the name Dunn Nutritional Laboratory (Weatherall 1997: 30–5).

8. Historians disagree whether the outbreak of the Manchurian Incident in 1931, or the Marco Polo Bridge Incident of 1937, should be regarded as the starting point of the Second World War in the Far East. To the Western public both dates are probably unfamiliar, as the attack on Pearl Harbor in 1941 is generally regarded as the beginning of the war in the Pacific.

References

Barnett, L. M. (1985), *British Food Policy During the First World War*, Boston: Allen & Unwin.

Bentley, A. (1998), *Eating for Victory: Food Rationing and the Politics of Domesticity*, Urbana/Chicago: University of Illinois Press.

Corrigan, P. and Sayer, D. (1985), *The Great Arch: English State Formation as Cultural Revolution*, Oxford: Blackwell.

Coveney, J. (2000), *Food, Morals and Meaning: The Pleasure and Anxiety of Eating*, London: Routledge.

Cwiertka, K. J. (1998), 'Spirit versus Matter: Nutritional Policies in Wartime Japan'. Paper presented at the First International Convention for Asian Scholars (ICAS), Noordwijkerhout, the Netherlands.

—— (1999), *The Making of Modern Culinary Tradition in Japan*. Ph.D. dissertation, Leiden University, the Netherlands.

—— (2002), 'Popularizing Military Diet in Wartime and Postwar Japan', *Asian Anthropology*, 1: 1–30.

—— (2003), 'Eating the World: Restaurant Culture in Early Twentieth Century Japan', *European Journal of East Asian Studies*, 1: 89–116.

Daini Kantai Shukeika (1935), *Kenkyū Kondate Shū*. Internal publication of the Imperial Japanese Navy.

Davidson, A. (1983), *Food in Motion: The Migration of Foodstuffs and Cookery Techniques*, Leeds: Prospect Books.

Davis, B. J. (2000), *Home Fires Burning: Food, Politics, and Everyday Life in World War I Berlin*, Chapel Hill: University of North Carolina Press.

Dusselier, J. (2001), 'Bonbons, Lemon Drops, and Oh Henry! Bars: Candy, Consumer Culture and the Construction of Gender, 1895–1920', in S. A. Innes (ed.), *Kitchen Culture in America: Popular Representations of Food, Gender, and Race*, Philadelphia: University of Pennsylvania Press.

Duus, P. (1998), *Modern Japan*, Boston: Houghton Mifflin.

Elias, N. (1994 [1939]), *The Civilizing Process: The History of Manners and State Formation and Civilization*, Oxford: Basil Blackwell.

Finlay, M. R. (1995), 'Early Marketing of the Theory of Nutrition: The Science and Culture of Liebig's Extract of Meat', in H. Kamminga and A. Cunningham (eds), *The Science and Culture of Nutrition, 1840–1940*, Amsterdam/Atlanta: Rodopi.

Foucault, M. (1977 [1975]), *Discipline and Punish: The Birth of the Prison*, New York: Pantheon.

—— (1991), 'Governmentality', in G. Burchel, C. Gordon and P. Miller (eds), *The Foucault Effect: Studies in Governmentality*, Sydney: Harvester/Wheatsheaf.

Fujitani, T. (1996), *Splendid Monarchy: Power and Pageantry in Modern Japan*, Berkeley: University of California Press.

Gabaccia, D. R. (1998), *We Are What We Eat: Ethnic Food and the Making of Americans*, Cambridge MA: Harvard University Press.

Geertz, C. (1977), 'Centers, Kings, and Charisma: Reflections on the Symbolics of Power', in J. Ben-David and T. N. Clark (eds), *Culture and its Creators: Essays in Honor of Edward Shils*, Chicago/London: University of Chicago Press.

Hagiwara, H. (1960), *Nihon Eiyōgaku Shi*, Tokyo: Kokumin Eiyō Kyōkai.

Hanley, S. (1997), *Everyday Things in Premodern Japan: The Hidden Legacy of Material Culture*, Berkeley: University of California Press.

Hannerz, U. (1996), *Transnational Connections: Culture, People, Places*, London: Routledge.

Harada, N. (1989), *Edo no Ryōri Shi: Ryōrihon to Ryōri Bunka*, Tokyo: Chūō Kōronsha.

—— (1993), *Rekishi no naka no Kome to Niku*, Tokyo: Heibonsha.

Imperial Government Institute for Nutrition (1935), *The Imperial Government Institute for Nutrition and Nutrition Experts*, Tokyo: The Imperial Government Institute for Nutrition.

Ishige, N. (1986), 'Shokutaku no Fūkei no Henbō', in Nihon Art Centre (ed.), *Nihon Kodai Shi 5*, Tokyo: Shōeisha.

—— (2000), 'Japan', in K. F. Kiple and K. C. Ornelas (eds), *The Cambridge World History of Food*, Cambridge: Cambridge University Press.

Ishikawa, H. (1996), 'Nihon ni okeru Sesshō Kinrei to Nikushoku no Kiseki', *Vesta*, 24: 20–7.

—— and Ehara, A. (eds), (2002), *Kingendai no Shokubunka*, Tokyo: Kōgaku shuppan.

Johnston, B. F. (1953), *Japanese Food Management in World War II*, Stanford: Stanford University Press.

Kamminga, H. and Cunningham, A. (1995), 'Introduction: The Science and Culture of Nutrition, 1840–1940', in H. Kamminga and A. Cunningham (eds), *The Science and Culture of Nutrition, 1840–1940*, Amsterdam/Atlanta: Rodopi.

Keene, D. (2002), *Emperor of Japan: Meiji and his World, 1852–1912*, New York: Columbia University Press.

Kikuchi, M. (1930), 'Kaigun Heishoku ni tsuite', *Ryōyū*, 5: 24–6.

Kisara, S. (1990), 'Bisuketto', in Nihon Shokuryō Shinbunsha (ed.), *Shōwa no shokuhin sangyōshi*, Tokyo: Nihon Shokuryō Shinbunsha.

Kumakura, I. (1990), 'Kaisetsu (2)', in S. Ogi, I. Kumakura and C. Ueno, *Nihon kindai shisō taikei 23: Fūzoku, Sei*, Tokyo: Iwanami Shoten.

Levenstein, H. A. (1985), 'The American Response to Italian Food, 1880–1930', *Food and Foodways*, 1: 1–24.

Mintz, S. W. (1996), *Tasting Food, Tasting Freedom: Excursions into Eating, Culture and the Past*, Boston: Beacon.

Muraoka, M. (1984), *Nihonjin to Seiyōshoku*, Tokyo: Shunjūsha.

Robertson, J. (1998), *Takarazuka: Sexual Politics and Popular Culture in Modern Japan*, Berkeley: University of California Press.

Saitō, T. (1983), *Nihon Shokuseikatsushi Nenpyō*, Tokyo: Gakuyu Shobō.

Sema, T. (1985), *Nihon Kaigun Shokuseikatsu Shiwa*, Tokyo: Kai'ensha.

Swinburne, L. (1997), 'Dancing with the Mermaids: Ship's Biscuit and Portable Soup', in H. Walker (ed.), *Food on the Move: Proceedings of the Oxford Symposium on Food and Cookery 1996*, Devon: Prospect.

Sugiyama Lebra, T. (1993), *Above the Clouds: Status Culture of the Modern Japanese Nobility*, Berkeley: University of California Press.

Teich, M. (1995), 'Science and Food during the Great War: Britain and Germany', in H. Kamminga and A. Cunningham (eds), *The Science and Culture of Nutrition, 1840–1940*, Amsterdam/Atlanta: Rodopi.

Turner, B. S. (1982), 'The Discourse of Diet', *Theory, Culture & Society*, 1: 23–32.

Waswo, A. (1996), *Modern Japanese Society*, 1868–1994, Oxford: Oxford University Press.

Weatherall, M. W. (1997), 'The Foundation and Early Years of the Dunn Nutritional Laboratory', in D. Smith (ed.), *Nutrition in Britain: Science, Scientists and Politics in the Twentieth Century*, London: Routledge.

Westney, E. D. (1986), 'The Military', in M. B. Jansen and G. Rozman (eds), *Japan in Transition from Tokugawa to Meiji*, Princeton: Princeton University Press.

–8–

The Politics of Taste and Smell:
Palestinian Rites of Return

Efrat Ben-Ze'ev

Our arms and legs are full of sleeping memories of the past.

Marcel Proust, *The Past Recaptured*

In 1948, roughly 400 Arab Palestinian villages and towns were depopulated and appropriated by the State of Israel. Since then Palestinian refugees have continued visiting the sites of their obliterated villages. These visits are condensed experiences, momentarily erasing the time that has passed and mediating between people's current lives and their pre-dispersion lives. The return visit is characterized by a set of practices and acts carried out to (re)discover places and objects and to stimulate the senses. During the visit the 'returnees' pay special attention to the fruit and herbs that grow at the site.

In this chapter, I shall argue that these plants act as mnemonic devices and memory containers, enabling a temporary (re)creation of the past and a reflection on pre-1948 life. Yet beyond their role as triggers of autobiographic recollection, the village plants are part of a collective reconstruction of the past. Their symbolism is aimed at others, mainly family members, village-folk and Palestinians at large. Through these plants, and the way they are distributed and discussed, Palestinians negotiate among themselves the image of Palestine.

Palestinian memory, it should be emphasized, is highly politicized because of the ongoing Palestinian-Israeli conflict and the Palestinian aspirations to return to their land. The Israeli policy has generally been to obliterate, transform and cover Palestinian 'signs' such as Palestinian villages and towns with their old stone houses, mountain terraces and fruit trees. On top of those, new Jewish neighborhoods and settlements, industrial areas, agricultural enterprises and roads were and still are being constructed. Hebrew has replaced one-time Arabic names on road signs and maps. Hence, the seemingly naive Palestinian act of visiting the obliterated village site becomes a political and subversive statement indicating that beneath the Jewish landscape lies a Palestinian one.

The Palestinian case should be seen in light of a small, yet growing body of literature that explores the links between the senses, the body, the consumption of food and remembrance (see Connerton 1989; Feldman 1991; Seremetakis 1994; Stoller 1989, 1997; Sutton 2001). As most of the writers focus their attention on the process of recall rather than on the content of memory, remembrance seems to be the more accurate term. In Paul Connerton's book *How Societies Remember*, bodily practices are a major focus. Echoing an approach previously popular among French scholars, such as the classic work of Maurice Halbwachs and the contemporary work of Pierre Nora, Connerton argues that the past is sedimented or amassed in the body (1989: 72). Hence, through the analysis of bodily practices one can decode social pasts. More recently, writing on food and memory on the Greek island of Kalymnos, David Sutton makes a related argument, noting that 'if "we are what we eat", then "we are what we ate"' (2001: 7–8). Sutton further comments that within this wide field of research, little attention has been dedicated to the historical consciousness and the understanding of people's subjective perceptions of their past. By examining the Palestinian handling of village plants, I seek to explore the historical consciousness and intersubjectivity of contemporary Palestine.

Two main types of source are used here. The primary sources are my first-hand observations made during visits to obliterated Palestinian villages in the late 1990s and the oral accounts of these visits as retold afterward by the former inhabitants of the villages.[1] Secondary sources used in this chapter are Internet sites commemorating the ruined villages and towns, as well as fine literature dealing with Palestinian return visits and remembrance. The primary sources, especially the oral accounts by members of the older generation who remember the village, reveal a 'Proustian' type of recall, namely the overwhelming sensual and emotional effect. In contrast, the secondary sources, such as the Internet and the novels, reflect and circulate the imagery that is taking root in collective commemoration. Whereas the larger bulk of this chapter is dedicated to the older generation's recollections and the practices associated with the actual rites of return, the latter part will move on to the emergence of commemoration enterprises through which various components of the rites of return are turned into symbols.

Re-(in)sist, Re-member, Re-enact and Re-embody

The 1948 War shattered and disintegrated Arab Palestinian society, forcing roughly 800,000 people – well over half the population – into exile.[2] Despite, or possibly because of the dispersal, the majority of Palestinians strive to maintain traditional kinship patterns and the prominent role of the extended family. In this context, the community from one's place of origin in Palestine – the village, the town, the locality – is a salient feature. In refugee camps in particular, the Palestinian landscape is recreated by a residence pattern that imitates that of the place of origin and by the naming of quarters after demolished villages (Farah 2000). Second and third generations of refugees are encouraged to marry into families from the same ex-village or ex-locality, and ex-village communities, and sometimes large extended families establish guesthouses (*madafeh, diwan*) where shared ceremonies take place (Slyomovics 1998: 137–68). On a daily basis, people tend to use the services of those originally from their ex-village or locality – such as a grocery store, a garage, or a restaurant.

All these practices reconstruct the memory of the village from a distance. In addition, some Palestinians also try to arrange pilgrim-like visits to their villages. Those who manage to reach the obliterated sites can be divided into three main categories. One is that of the 'internally displaced' who were uprooted in 1948 but remained within Israel's borders.[3] As their current places of residence are often located near their villages of origin, they have been able to visit regularly.[4] The second category is comprised of the vast majority of Palestinian refugees who live outside of Israel, mainly in the surrounding Arab states. Some were granted temporary permission to enter Israel after 1967, following the occupation of the West Bank and the opening of bridges as passageways between Jordan and Israel. These 'visitors' would come mainly from the Occupied Territories of the West Bank and Gaza and from Jordan, as well as from other Arab states if they obtained Jordanian documents. The Palestinians from 'outside' (*min al-kharij*) would be accompanied by family members who were internal refugees (*min ad-dakhil*). Their visits were relatively rare and for them exceptionally memorable. Due to long closures of the West Bank during the 1990s and the escalation of the conflict since September 2000, visits of this second category are almost non-existent at the present time. The third category includes Palestinians who have acquired citizenship mainly in European and American states and come to Israel as such.

For the members of all three categories, the return visit, be it a one-time occasion or a weekly habit, is quite ceremonial. At the village site Palestinians perform a set of mini-rituals, though not necessarily the whole set and not necessarily in a certain order. These consist of searching for remains, uncovering them, touching them and resting alongside them; bringing little prayer mats and praying near the ruins; attending the graves of family members and reciting there the first *sura* of the Koran (*al-fatiha)*. The rituals also include picking herbs, winter greens, mushrooms and summer fruit (from the pre-1948 trees) both to be eaten on the spot and be taken back home, preserved and shared. Moreover, when there are Jewish-Israeli settlements above or near the Palestinian sites, as is often the case, tense encounters occur between the old (Arab) and the new (Jewish) inhabitants.

Prominent among the practices carried out at the site is the picking of local wild plants and fruit from indigenous shrubs and trees planted before 1948. In winter,

Palestinians come to collect edible greens such as *'elet* (winter greens) (*'aqoub* (tumble thistle) and *fuq'a* (mushrooms), in spring the new leaves of perennial bushes such as *maramiyyeh* (sage) and *za'atar* (hyssop), and in summer and autumn fruit such as *sabr* (prickly pear), *tin* (figs), *'enab* (grapes) and *zaitun* (olives).

During my fieldwork, stories of such visits were often told, and many interlocutors tied the visit with picking fruit and gathering plants. 'Aisheh, born in 1959 to Qasem of at-Tireh and to a mother from the city of Haifa, recalled the fruit while talking of her visits to the village. We met at her parents' home, located near Haifa's beach, only a few kilometers west of the ruins of at-Tireh. 'Aisheh noted that 'almost every week, twice or three times, we would go to the village . . . to the place where my father used to live. There were figs and almonds there, and pomegranates and olives. We would always go and fetch some.'[5] Her father, Qasem, born in 1931, also talked of these visits. There was one specific visit that clearly left its imprint on him, as he told me the following story on two separate occasions. It happened sometime in the 1960s and demonstrates Qasem's small act of resistance. The date is significant since until 1966 the Arabs in Israel were under military control and even later were under strong surveillance.

> *Qasem*: We used to own some olive trees at the entrance to at-Tireh . . . I would go there every year to collect the olives . . . There was an Iraqi man [a Jew]. He saw my children picking olives and thought that the children were alone. [He passed them with his car and then] reversed and came back to them. I was up on the tree. I came down and he said to me: 'Oh, it's you.' I said: 'Yes, it's me.'
> 'Are you the owner here that you come every year and pick olives?'
> I said: 'These are my father's olives. My grandfather planted them and we pick them every year.' He said: 'No, it used to be yours. It's not any more.' I said to him: 'You came from Baghdad yesterday and now it is yours and my grandfather planted it here and it isn't mine. I want to come every year to pick the olives, and you do as you please.'

Here, the visit becomes a minor act of political opposition, re-insisting and resisting, when Qasem confronts the new Jewish inhabitants. The fact that olives were debated makes the event even more significant as olives are the most treasured fruit for Palestinians, grown from the Mountainous area of the Upper Galilee in the north to the Southern Hebron Hills. The harvesting of olives in autumn is a family occasion with countrywide traditions – children and the elderly lend a hand, people sing while working and shared meals are laid out at the olive grove. Olive trees, especially since 1948, loom as a national symbol in Palestinian stories and poems.[6]

Qasem's visit turned into an act of resistance, though he did not necessarily plan it as such. What attracts his generation to visit the sites of their obliterated villages is not necessarily this act of resistance. Rather, it stems from a universal kind of longing for one's place of origin and for the tastes and the smells that one has left behind. Marcel Proust's famous description of the 'petite Madeleine' epitomizes the overwhelming effect and the lingering relevance of a familiar taste. In a century characterized by masses of people forced to migrate, whether as a consequence of war and persecution, or simply in search of a better life, the petite Madeleine encapsulates the possibility of temporarily recreating 'things past'. For those uprooted, this means not only reaching back in time, but recreating the features of a place to which one cannot return. Proust further wished to demonstrate that this type of recollection brings about a strong emotional reaction and some consolation: '. . . at once, the vicissitudes of life had become indifferent to me, its disasters innocuous, its brevity illusory – this new sensation having had on me the effect which love has of filling me with a precious essence; or rather this essence was not in me, it *was* me' (Proust, 1982 [1913]: 48). It is this Proustian recall that transpires when Palestinian refugees visit their demolished villages: although facing the destroyed village may be devastating, there is also consolation in the temporary return.

One event marked for me a rare chance to grasp the close link between daily life, the consumption of plants from the lost village and the return visit. At the end of October 1997, I visited Saleh, born in 1938 at at-Tireh and today a resident of a Druze village farther east.[7] As Saleh, his family and I were eating *za'arur*[8] on their balcony, Saleh recounted how he had picked the fruit a few days before, when he went on his own to visit the ruins of at-Tireh. Although he was pressed for time, he suggested we go right then to the *za'arur* tree. Soon we were on our way, joined by his youngest daughter, a teacher in her mid-twenties.[9] Although Saleh was almost sixty years old, he was quickly up between the tree's branches, shaking them vigorously to drop the fruit to the ground. He encouraged his daughter and me to be diligent in collecting the fruit. As Saleh and his family had to attend a wedding that evening, his daughter urged him to leave. Saleh, all-immersed in stripping the fruit from the tree, refused to stop. This embodiment of his pre-1948 world was not confined only to picking; the fruit was taken home, consumed and distributed to family and friends, encapsulating and circulating the story of the place in which it has been picked.

Another bodily expression of attachment to the homeland is expressed in the story of Saleh's reunification with his brother, whom he had not seen for almost fifty years. In 1998 Saleh traveled to Jordan with his son Muhammad, who recounted to me the following events.[10] The objective of the trip was to meet Samer, Saleh's brother, whose permanent place of exile is Syria. When the two brothers met, one of the first things Samer said to Saleh was: 'Come, I wish to smell you and see if you have the aroma of at-Tireh, the fragrance of the village.' For Samer, Saleh embodied the village. Muhammad further attested to the strange relationship that developed between the two brothers during their stay in Jordan.

He said that it seemed as if time had stood still for fifty years and both were behaving as if they were still children.

Samer had hoped that he could continue traveling from Jordan to Palestine/Israel and had asked Saleh if he could arrange a visiting permit for him. Since this was impossible, they decided to drive along the Jordanian/Israeli border. Muhammad described how near Bakura they stopped in an orchard and his uncle faced Palestine taking deep breaths:

> He was crying there. He had tears. He said, 'I do not know if I shall live another day to see this again, to go back there.' He stood and wept. It wasn't very nice. Bakura wasn't nice. He said, 'Look at the absurdity. I am just a few meters away here . . . I can almost grab it with my hand yet it is so far.'

Muhammad commented that as they were observing Palestine, an Israeli army jeep stopped on the opposite side of the border and a soldier watched them with binoculars. The incident epitomized the conflictual state of affairs and added to the discomfort.

The air, smell and taste of the village were topics of the utmost importance. This was evident both in the practice of visiting the village and picking and consuming specific plants, as well as in the discourse on the village. Older women were exceptionally lucid in the tangible way they remembered the village. Majda, born in 1928 at the village of 'Ain Hawd and currently living in the Jenin refugee camp (West Bank), recalled the small agricultural plot that each family had near the house, where one would grow for home consumption vegetables such as *lubia* (a type of bean), *batinjan* (eggplants) or *mulukhiyyeh* (*Corchorus olitorius*: a thick liquid dish is made of this green herb). The leaves of the famous dish of *waraq dawali* (stuffed vine leaves), noted Majda, were substituted in the winter with two types of wild green leaves – *al-Saine* and *za'amatot*. While talking of the long path to the spring of al-Mashariyyeh, Majda mentioned that the girls would pick *'ulleq* (raspberries) and while talking of honey, Majda mentioned that the bees were exceptionally fond of *qandul* (*Aspalathus*) and *zarzarok*. Her son, an educated man in his thirties, was listening all along attentively. At one point (just after Majda spoke about the plants on the way to the spring) he interrupted and asked: 'Ya ma, everything you describe is from nature?' 'Natural (*tabi'iyyeh*)', she answered. The names of plants were like a secret code, known to those who had lived in the village but alien to the generations born in exile.

The Plant Syntax

The plants in Majda's stories symbolized her world, whether as a young girl fetching water or as a youth learning from her mother how to cook. Naturally, Palestinian men were more ignorant of plants for cooking because they do not cook. Hence, even among the members of the older generation who used plants to remember the past and communicate with each other, there were internal divisions based or gender or place of origin, as became apparent during a conversation with Kamal and Jamil at the latter's apartment in Irbid (Jordan). Jamil, born in 1937 in the small Palestinian village of 'Ain Hawd and today a university professor, introduced me to Kamal, a businessman born in 1938 in at-Tireh. As mentioned earlier, since 'Ain Hawd and at-Tireh were neighboring villages before their destruction in 1948, refugees from these villages in the Diaspora tend to know each other, especially in a city like Irbid, most of whose residents are ex-Palestinians. As the three of us were talking, Jamil recounted a scene from a documentary he had recently seen on television. It was the second time that he mentioned this specific scene, in which Hisham Sharabi, a notable American University professor originally from Palestine, was filmed while visiting Israel/Palestine. The film shows that when Sharabi reaches his old home in Jaffa, he strokes the wall and says, 'A jasmine used to grow here'. Kamal reacted to Jamil's description by recollecting the mulberry tree that still stands near his uncle's house in at-Tireh and that he had visited recently. For Jamil, the film episode aroused certain personal recollections and emotions but also served as a case study; it enabled self-reflection on the process of recollection. He followed the jasmine story by developing the theme, arguing that the suffering and the consequences of exile 'exlarged memories', a phrase he invented on the spot. He emphasized a bond between objects, be they real or imagined, and the 'exlargement' of memories.

The signifiers (a jasmine vine, a mulberry tree) create not only homogeneity in the form of remembering but also mark differences through the content and context that they represent. Each locality, each village and each family have their own significant set of plants: jasmine characterizes wealthy urban neighborhoods, oranges – the coastal plain, olives – the mountainous and hilly areas. Moreover, each Palestinian constructs Palestine through his/her own home's plants. When interviewing Zaqiyyeh and Halimeh (two older women originally from the depopulated village of Ijzim, who now live in another village in Israel), a long discussion revolved around pre-1948 food, attracting many other family members. Everyone was eager to contribute his/her own knowledge and specimens were brought in from the kitchen to display certain foods such as a pumpkin jam and a special kind of bread – *ftir*. Zaqiyyeh noted that she recently sent a dish of winter greens ('*elet*) to her relatives in Syria (via Jordan) because the '*elet* from Ijzim is considered by its people to be superior to all others. In the same vein, Palestinian writer 'Ali Qleibo notes: 'Each mountain village has its own olives and oil and villagers claim that each has a distinctive taste. Each Palestinian insists that his oil is the best kind of olive oil' (2000: 75).

Beyond indicating divisions of locality, plants can be markers for social class and social background. Fruit trees for the *fallahin* (the peasants) signify their land, be it the garden surrounding home (*al-hakura*) or the trees of one's distant plots. In contrast, for the urban Palestinians fruit and herbs are associated with the market place and the peasant women who came to sell their produce. Hala Sakakini, daughter of the prominent Jerusalemite educator Khalil Sakakini, describes in her book *Jerusalem and I* her mental map of the villages that surrounded Jerusalem:

> When I think of Battir I recall the peasant women with straight backs that used to stop at our house in the early morning in summer carrying on their heads round, flat, dark-brown baskets heaped high with those purple, longish eggplants of Battir, carefully arranged in tiers. The names of Walajeh and al-Khader bring back to my mind the sweet 'Jandaly' grape which was our favourite as children. From Beit Safafa a kindly, round-faced elderly woman used to bring us freshly-picked young marrows [namely, zucchini], cool and moist with dew, their yellow flowers still attached to them. In spring, a tall, lean woman from Malha used to get us (among other things) those large, velvety, green almonds, deliciously sour and tender, called 'Abu Farweh' (1987: 106)

Through the plants, then, Sakakini recreates the wider context. Sakakini begins her book with a detailed description of her return visit immediately after the 1967 war to her family home in Qatamon, from which they had been forced out in 1948. Throughout her book, Jerusalem is remembered and recreated by recalling plants as well as savory and sweet dishes that she and her family bought, made and consumed. In his phenomenological study of odors, Almagor distinguishes a social type of scent that he defines as 'a scent of the homeland', rarely noticed unless people leave their home and return to it. This smell is in fact a combination of different smells – 'cooking, spices, vegetation, patterns of sanitation, patterns of production, physical objects, humidity, evaporation and temperature' (1990a: 257–8). Moreover, Almagor argues that there is a lack of olfactory classifications because odors carry 'on their back' a string of associations:

> ...[T]he socially-held concept of odours is that they are not independent entities, but derive from something. It means that giving meaning to an odour (already associated with a context) when evoked in another context becomes a problematic issue of interpretation (i.e., 'out of context,' 'too blatant,' 'inappropriate,' etc.). Odours are thus highly contextualized concepts and any consideration of classifying odours must also encompass their contexts as well (1990b: 190).

These traits may explain why odors play such a prominent role for Palestinians in exile: Tastes, smells, plants and food are anchors of memory, invoking a much wider context. Refugees carry with them an 'internal Palestinian map' of tastes and smells which also represents local patriotisms. Plants, be they wild or farmed, are signifiers of their contexts – the house, the village and the region. While I was having lunch with Hajj Lutfi and his family, originally from 'Ain Hawd and today of the village of Tamra in the Galilee, his wife prepared special salads from wild plants such as *khubeizeh* (palmated mallow, *Malva aegyptdia*) and *za'atar* (hyssop). When I asked about the latter, Hajj Lutfi noted that he had uprooted the thyme plant from the land of his village of origin and replanted it in his garden.

Arjun Appadurai, writing on gastropolitics in Hindu South Asia, calls the social choices transmitted through food 'culinary syntax'. The advantage of such syntax, he notes, is its implicitness. In the Palestinian context, where plants and food are signifiers of a besieged nation, overt internal competition would be inappropriate. We therefore encounter subtle messages of fragmentation, more appropriate for the representation of the difficult conditions of Palestinian nation-building. In a second article Appadurai considers the recent appearance of a national Indian cuisine via cookbooks, in contrast to the regional cuisines that existed previously. One of his conclusions is that internal divisions are an integral part of emergent nations:

> The idea of an Indian cuisine has emerged because of, rather than despite, the increasing articulation of regional and ethnic cuisines. As in other modalities of identity and ideology in emergent nations, cosmopolitan and parochial expressions enrich and sharpen each other by a dialectical interaction. Especially in culinary matters, the melting pot is a myth (1988: 21–2).

Appadurai's reading of Indian cookbooks is relevant to the Palestinian context as well. On the one hand, edible plants, food and dishes are expected to mark Palestinian boundaries despite the fact that, traditionally, Palestinian food has been part of the cuisine of Greater Syria and the Middle East (Zubaida and Tapper 1994). On the other hand, the content of Palestinian plants and food is negotiated from within, a subtle yet necessary part of the process of molding a shared identity. A national discourse emerges from the multiplicity of memories and localities and their dialectic interaction. This is the thickening of the national story and the blending of private localized memories into public commemoration. The transition is, in many respects, a generational shift – from the generation that remembers Palestine before the Nakba (meaning 'the catastrophe') of 1948 (often nicknamed 'the Nakba generation') to the generations that were born later. The imagery that dominated the stories of the Nakba generation, such as the architecture, trees and plants, springs and wells, is adopted by the succeeding generations. However, as this landscape is unknown to those living in exile and fragmented even for those who live within Israel, it has to be charged with a less personal and more theoretical meaning. Palestine becomes an abstract entity, much like Jerusalem had been to the Jews during their years of exile. In this situation, the images of Palestine that are expressed through food also take the form of commodities. This commodification is literally expressed in the Market place in Irbid (the Jordanian town where a majority of ex-Palestinians now live), when dealers declare their merchandise shouting 'Jaffa oranges', 'Jericho dates', 'Nablus olives', although the fruit is from within Jordan. Using these place names adds aura to the fruit.

At a Palestinian-owned fruit-juice shop in Irbid the owner displayed two containers on the shelf. One contained the earth that he had collected at at-Tireh, his village of origin, and the other, the sole of his shoe. On the latter he wrote in a poetic manner (in literary Arabic) that with this shoe he once trod on Palestinian soil – on the land of his beloved village – and the precious earth that clung to the sole must not be allowed to fall back to the ground.[11] Through the objects, the visit was transformed into an artifact that became a public exhibit.

Under the current political conditions Palestinian museums, as sites to exhibit national objects, are almost non-existent.[12] Possibly in light of this absence, almost every Palestinian home and business becomes a mini-museum, displaying on the wall artifacts from the pre-1948 past, such as old keys, land deeds and fraying photographs. In his seminal work on 'sites of memory' the sociologist Pierre Nora notes that 'memory takes root in the concrete, in spaces, gestures, images, and objects' (1989: 9). Indeed, plants should be understood as another concrete element that carries memory.

The Scent of Palestine

The two containers exhibited on the shelf of the fruit-juice shop exemplify how the private experience becomes part of a public arena. Whereas the rite of return and its narrative are usually confined to the context of family and friends, we should ask in what circumstances the personal experience becomes part of the collective memory of a community. How is the personal narrative transformed into a story of a nation?

One such domain is the Internet, where the village can be resurrected through a pictorial and recorded recreation of the community. The Internet is exceptionally salient for a diasporic nation under severe restrictions of movement, as it becomes a valuable substitute for face-to-face interaction. In a recent ethnography of the use of this late twentieth-century invention, Miller and Slater (2000) demonstrate its prominent role for the Trinidadians, who are, like the Palestinians, a scattered nation. The Internet, they argue, is not singular but rather operates on multiple channels of communication (such as e-mail, ICQ, religious instruction face-to-face, e-commerce), each serving a different need. Hence, specific Internet channels are utilized according to one's needs. In the Palestinian case, the Internet provides a meeting place for those who cannot cross actual borders and a site for Anderson's 'imagined community' (Anderson 1991).

Miller and Slater's more general argument is that the Internet is far from being a virtual social arena, set apart from 'real life'; 'we need to treat Internet media', they write, 'as continuous with and embedded in other social spaces' (2000: 5). This argument is certainly applicable to Palestinians who seek ways to expand social solidarity beyond existing forms of communication which, due to political circumstances, are relatively limited. One implication of the Palestinian usage of the Internet is that the content and images used in daily life permeate the Internet media and circulate way beyond the close social circles.

Palestinian websites, mostly financed by public bodies, are growing fast both in volume and in number. One impressive site is Palestine Remembered (www. palestineremembered.com), built up of separate niches for every one of the 400 Palestinian uprooted villages and towns. On each of these interactive village-niches, one can find 'scientific' data on the village (such as population figures, land-ownership details, circumstances of uprooting), a place to insert ex-villagers' e-mail addresses, a guest book (serving ex-villagers for public communication) and the option to post pictures (mostly used to record the village site). Even on these websites, the village plants maintain a salient role, appearing in the photos of the visit and in people's recorded recollections. One case in hand is that of the large sycamore (*joumeizeh, Ficus sycomorus*) that stood on the path to at-Tireh's spring. After having heard of it in many interviews with people of at-Tireh, I also found it mentioned on at-Tireh's website by Fadi al-Batal, a Palestinian currently based in Canada:[13]

> Me too, I'm from there, that place that I've always dreamed of, the description of my grandfather's house, the fields, the streets, the school, the spring (*ras el-'ein*) and the *joumeizeh* that my beloved grandmother, God have mercy on her soul, talked about so many times, raising the love of this land in our heart and printing the image of our homeland in our minds. This description is what I find in the pictures taken by Mouttaz [a set of photographs posted on the web site of Mouttaz's visit to at-Tireh], consolidating my will to go there as soon as I can to embrace its soil. (http://www.palestineremembered.com/Haifa/al-Tira/MessageBoard176.html)

Such Internet sites are multivocal, incorporating diverging individual narratives and manifesting Appadurai's 'dialectic interaction'. At times, the subtle negotiations over rank and status become more apparent, as in the following response posted on the message board of the village of Qaqun. In it, Farouk Abu Hantash responds to Mr. al-Hafi's glorifying description of his own clan. (Both are descendants of families from Qaqun.)

Posted by **Farouk Abu Hantash** on MARCH-5–2002

Dear Mr. Al Hafi,
First of all I'd like to thank you for what you have done on this web site for our Village Qaqun but I think that you have to put a lot of information and facts regarding the subject, like:

The clans that used to live there at that time, especially the famous ones who owned most [property] there, like the ABU HANTASH clan. On your web page you . . . mentioned that before the 1948 war Al-Hafi family owned roughly 35 per cent of Qaqun's lands. Although I'm 34 years old, and I didn't know or visit or live there at that time, I didn't hear from the oldest people that your clan owned more than around 6 to 7 houses . . .

P.S. I have a question: why don't you ask your father or any of those people who used to live at that time in Qaqun about who owns Qaqun lands, houses and what is the most famous clan who used to live and own Qaqun ????[14] (www.palestineremembered. com/Tulkarm/Qaqun/MessageBoard382.htm)

Abu Hantash suggests that the elderly have more authority and hold definitive truths. In fact, the elderly continue to argue over such details and their disagreements are carried on to next generations. At the same time, those Palestinians in exile open up a new type of dialogue: the separation from the old rural lifestyle leads to a slow process wherein the trees and plants of Palestine are abstracted, gradually becoming symbols of the homeland and of one's village, such as the sycamore of at-Tireh that is revered by people who have never seen it.

A tangential site of plant remembrance, where taste or merely the discourse about taste is associated with a collective belonging, is that of traditional dishes. In a workshop on the common heritage of Palestinians and Israelis, organized by the Palestinian al-Quds University and the Israeli Truman Institute in Jerusalem, chef Sufian al-Ahmadi contributed a paper entitled 'The Palestinian Kitchen' in which he interweaves food into a national agenda, as in the following passage:[15]

Msakhan is [a] golden split roasted chicken on taboon bread soaked in olive oil, spread with onion saute, sprinkled with roasted pine nuts and seasoned summac . . .

My family, as many others I am sure, always meets on a feast of Msakhan, no matter where or what the occasion. Msakhan has somehow become the barometer of how Palestinian one is. Being able to make Msakhan everywhere you go has become a way of remaining Palestinian. That is because Msakhan is not just delicious food but it is the atmosphere, the aroma, the taste, the memory of the olive tree and the taboon, the garden, the family and above all, home. (Al-Ahmadi 2001: 4–5).

Msakhan incorporates a set of symbols – olive oil, the taboon (a traditional outdoor mud oven), the Palestinian garden around the house, summac – (a red sour spice made from the fruit of a local tree) – to make a sensual, powerful commemorative statement. Al-Ahmadi overtly refers to the national symbolism of food. Indeed, although not always stated explicitly, food marks social boundaries.

In Israel, although Palestinians and Israelis share the same land and have access to the same foodstuffs, there are marked differences between the two groups' food consumption. When it comes to the consumption of village plants and herbs, a rather clear borderline is maintained; most Israeli Jews do not know the herbs that are picked by Palestinians, or how to use them. Even fruit, including olives, is not systematically picked by Israeli Jews, nor is it revered by them as it is by Palestinians.

However, the culinary divide is not merely a binary one; the variance of food among Jewish Israeli households is probably as significant as between Jewish Israeli and Palestinian Israeli ones. Moreover, a major trend within Jewish-Israeli food is fundamentally Middle Eastern because of the many Jews that emigrated from Arab states.

At the same time, just as borderlines are drawn through food, so are they blurred and penetrated through food. Many Palestinian dishes, such as *labaneh*, humus or eggplant salad, are now widely consumed by Jewish Israelis. One could argue that this is colonization through food. Yet at the same time it is also the permeation of Arabness into Israeli daily life. A recurring story told among Israeli Jews is that the Palestinian workers at restaurants urinate into the humus that they make. Such a conviction is exemplary of the tension surrounding even the consumption of Palestinian food by Jewish Israelis – they want to eat it, fear eating it, and think it necessary to have a Palestinian worker make it. However, these comments were merely a short detour into the Israeli – Palestinian conflict as manifested via food. Let us return to the topic of smell and memory by looking at the last genre to be discussed here – Palestinian literature.

I choose to focus on Elias Khoury's *Bab al-Shams*, a novel filled with odors. Khoury, a Lebanese leftist writer, sided with the Palestinians for many years and dedicated *Bab al-Shams* to the experience of the Galilee Palestinians who found refuge in Lebanon, The book is primarily about Yunis, a Palestinian activist and fighter based in Lebanon, and his relationship with his wife Nahila across the border in Israel, whom Yunis meets in a secret cave. Throughout the book the narrator Khalil (a Palestinian, a friend and admirer of Yunis) talks to Yunis though the latter is lying in a coma, on his deathbed. Early on in the book, Khalil says to Yunis:

> On that day you taught me how to smell nature. You put your tea-cup down, stood, inhaled, inflating your lungs with air and scent (*al-hawa wal-riha*). You captured the scent within your breast and your face turned red. When you returned to drinking your tea you spoke of thyme (*za'atar*) and jasmine (*yasmin*), of raspberry ('*uliq*) and wildflowers (*al-azhar al-barriyyah*). You said she resembled the seasons. In every season

she would come to your cave wrapped in a new smell. She would untie her long black hair and spread out the scents of flowers and herbs. You said you were fascinated by the new scents again and again, as if she transformed into a new woman each time. (1998: 26)

This description is an opening note to a world of smells – the penetrating smell of a Beirut hospital where Yunis is hospitalized (p. 35), the smell of old age (p. 44), the 'smell' of Khalil's father's photograph, drawn from the vase with basil or Damascene rose that always stood beneath it (pp. 298–9). The smell of the family of al-Awad that he describes as 'the smell of blood intermingled with scents of flowers and herbs' extracted into Grandma's hand-made pillow stuffed with dried leaves (pp. 311–12). It is through odors that Elias Khouri invokes experience and summons the past.

Khouri's usage of smell goes beyond the importance of remembering and commemorating. Rather, the message is that sensual memory should be mobilized to activate people and turn them into agents of change. This becomes apparent when Khalil, in exile in Lebanon, receives from Umm Hassan a branch with oranges, brought back from her secret visit to Palestine. Umm Hassan forbids him to eat the fruit under the pretext that the oranges are the homeland and one must not eat the homeland. Yunis, seeing the rotting oranges hanging on the wall, rebukes Khalil for not having eaten them, saying:

Umm Hassan is senile. You should've eaten the oranges. We must eat our homeland and not allow her to eat us. We must eat the oranges of Palestine, eat Palestine and the Galilee ... Shame on you. What are all these old women's tales (*Ya 'ib e-shum. Ma hadha al-khurafat alati taliq bil-'aja'iz*)? Instead of hanging your country on the wall, break the wall and go (*badal 'an ta'alaq biladuka 'al al-ha'et, aksar al-ha'et wa-idhhab*). We must eat all the oranges of the world without fear because a homeland is not an orange. The homeland is us. (1998: 29)

Yunis criticizes Umm Hassan and Khalil from his position in their eyes as a legendary freedom fighter. He is unhappy with passive reverie, arguing that remembrance should be transformed into political action. He wants to move from the plants to action.

Khouri's fascination with odors is not merely a literary resource but rather a reflection of a Palestinian world of olfactory imagery. One recurrent Palestinian way to relate to Palestine is to speak of its smell – *rihat al-watan* – the smell of the homeland. *Rih*, the root of the word for smell in Arabic, means also wind, and a closely related word, *ruh*, means spirit, soul, breath of life. All these meanings are tied together while recollecting Palestine. When Khouri describes the celebrations organized for a Palestinian prisoner released from an Israeli prison and returning to Lebanon, he echoes Salah's aforementioned meeting with his brother, writing:

'hug him [the released prisoner] and smell the scent of Palestine' (*u'butuhu washimu ra'ihat falastin*) (1998: 138). This very same image comes up again in a different context – in a recent interview with Palestinian national poet Mahmoud Darwish who describes his first meeting with Yasser Arafat: 'He embraced me. He was very warm. He said: "I can smell the fragrance of the homeland on you"' (2002: 74).

Conclusion

Because of this longing for what is defined as 'the smell of the homeland', Palestinians endeavor to hold pilgrim-like visits to the sites of their obliterated villages. These rites of return are sensual experiences, whereby taste and smell play a major role, assisting in the retrieval of memories through embodiment. There are multiple and sometimes conflicting strands to this type of remembrance: people recollect specific homes and localities while disregarding others; there are disagreements among villagers with regard to social structure and hierarchy; there are gaps of perception between those of rural versus urban origin and between women and men. While autobiographical memory can be defined as a first stage, the second stage is when the site, and specifically its plants, are recorded and turned into collective images. For instance, a return-visit is videotaped by Palestinians who regularly reside in Jordan and upon their return they screen it to family and friends. This mundane act signals a shift away from personal experience toward the circulating of images of the village. It marks a shift away from remembrance to commemoration and, indeed, commemoration enterprises are becoming more prevalent with the passing away of the older generation.

This process takes place in the absence of a permanent or influential Palestinian state. Had it existed, it would have taken on the role of constructing national symbols through school curricula, national holidays and ceremonies or through the forming and molding of a 'national landscape'. However, under the current conditions, there is much room for individuals to spread their own perceptions of Palestine. As a result, oral narratives of visits, memoirs, literature on Palestine, all come together in the process of consolidating a shared world of images of the past.

The salience of taste and smell in the lives of Palestinians should be understood as an outcome of more than one trajectory. Alan Dundes demonstrated in his classic article 'Seeing is Believing' (1972) the centrality of the visual for Americans. Indeed, much has been written on sight as a Western sense and on the 'gaze' as characterizing modernity. In contrast, 'smell is probably the most undervalued sense in the modern West', write the authors of *Aroma*, possibly because 'it is felt to threaten the abstract and impersonal regime of modernity by virtue of its radical interiority, its boundary-transgressing propensities and its emotional potency' (Classen et al. 1994: 5). Among Arabs, smell may have been retained as a leading sense in reaction to modernization and Westernization. Another possible explanation for the preservation of smell is the rural agricultural background of the majority of Palestinian refugees.[16] A third and last influence may be that 'Islam favors the use and appreciation of an intimate sensory experience, namely the olfactory', as argued by Aida Kanafani in her study of food and adornment rituals in the United Arab Emirates (1983: 3). Yet beyond all these possible effects, my argument in this chapter is that the unique Palestinian circumstances of uprooting and exile, combined with the wish to remember and commemorate, were catalysts for the preservation of the olfactory and savory senses. Taste and smell are vehicles of remembrance both in practice – during visits to the village site or in the commensality of shared eating – and in the creation of discourse and image.

In *Remembrance of Things Past*, Proust described in a literary manner what experiments in cognitive psychology and the anthropology of smell show: the olfactory sense is central in triggering and preserving memories, especially of early childhood, summoning a string of associations, creating a direct link between the past, smell and emotion.[17] Among his observations, he refers to the consolation derived from the rare and inadvertent moments of recall, such as the one that followed the taste of the 'petite Madeleine'. Toward the end of his monumental masterpiece, he adds another layer that explains this consoling effect, noting that '. . . memory, by bringing the past into the present unmodified, just as it appeared when it was itself the present, eliminates precisely that great dimension of Time, which governs the fullest realization of our lives' (1932 [1928]: 382). In our age of chronological, accelerating, despotic Time, Proust offers us an alternative perception in which the time between past and present collapses. Likewise, the plants, scents and tastes of Palestine that can appear in many guises – from the visits to the village to Palestinian cuisine and to fine literature – offer another perception of time that enables the Palestinians to contain the past within the present.

Acknowledgements

Many people contributed to this chapter, whether through discussions on the general phenomenon of the Rite of Return or of the specific role of plants, or by reading earlier versions of this manuscript. I would like to thank Uri Almagor, Eyal Ben-Ari, Paul Dresch, Udi Hrushovski, Edna Lomsky-Feder, Yoav Lossin, Michael Riordon, Ze'ev Rosenhek, Emmanuel Sivan, Vered Vinitsky-Seroussi, Jay Winter, Banan al-Sheikh and Elia Zureik. Also, I thank the Truman Institute in Jerusalem for its support and Lisa Perlman for editing. A special thank you for the comments by Marianne Lien and Brigitte Nerlich.

Notes

1. The material is mostly taken from my anthropological fieldwork conducted in Israel, Jordan and the Palestinian Territories of the West Bank between 1996 and 1998 toward a doctoral thesis. See Ben-Ze'ev 2000.

2. The number of the uprooted Palestinians in 1948 is controversial and ranges between 600,000 and 900,000 refugees. For a comprehensive table listing different estimates, see Zureik 1996: 17, table 3. Zureik, a leading authority on Palestinian refugees, tends to use 800,000 as a rough estimate.

3. On the internally displaced refugees, see Cohen 2000; Schechla 2001.

4. Until 1966, the internally displaced were under military governance and their freedom of movement was restricted. Freedom of movement was granted only on the Israeli Independence Day, ironically allowing Palestinian refugees to visit their obliterated villages then. The Palestinian film director Michel Khleifi documented one of these visits in his film *Ma'aloul Celebrates Its Destruction*, Sindibad Films, 1980. These visits remain an annual tradition for some refugees to this day. A recent film, Raanan Alexandrowitz' *Inner Tour* (Bellfilms Ltd 2001) presents a powerful visual representation of the return visit: In one of its final scenes an elderly Palestinian of 'Anabta walks through the remains of his village in the winter, picking green shrubs that grow near his father's grave, pulling off their thorns and handing the inner flesh to those who accompany him.

5. The interviews were conducted in Arabic, Hebrew and English. The above interview was originally in Hebrew.

6. In autumn 2002, Jewish settlers were violently trying to prevent Palestinians from harvesting their olives in the Occupied Territories of the West Bank. International solidarity activists and Jewish-Israeli leftists joined the Palestinians' harvest. One Palestinian was killed and some people were injured during the events.

7. Most of the Moslem villages of Mount Carmel were uprooted, whereas the two Druze villages atop the mountain remained intact because of earlier cooperation between the Jews and the Druze. Some Moslems found refuge in these villages, including Saleh and his father.

8. *Za'arur* is Spiny Hawthorn (*Crataegus aronia*), a round and firm fruit the size of a cherry that looks and tastes somewhat like an apple.

9. According to traditional Arab codes of behavior, it would be unacceptable for me as a woman to go alone with a man. Therefore, Saleh's daughter joined us.

10. I mention the fact that Muhammad was the source of information because there is a crucial difference between first- and second-hand observations. In her study of the memories of her extended family from Setif, Algier, Joelle Bahloul emphasized the mediators' role and its impact: 'Their recollections of these reunions are a discourse on narrative, a narrative of narrative, a narra-

tive molded in another narrative' (Bahloul 1996: 127). For Muhammad, this trip was his first encounter with his uncle and other family members who live outside of Palestine. During the trip he recorded information in a small notebook, much like an anthropologist's logbook.

11. In Arabic, there are two registers of language – colloquial (*'ammiyyeh*) and literary (*fus'ha*). The usage of literary Arabic signifies the intention to elevate the text.

12. Other than a museum on Jerusalem's holy mount (*al-Haram al-Sharif*), there are some private folklore collections. During the late 1990s the Palestinians were working on a national museum to be established in the village of 'Ain Sinia, near Ramallah. The current *intifada* put a halt to the project.

13. 'Palestine Remembered' is based in the United States. The site is probably one of the largest and technically advanced Palestinian websites recording the obliterated villages. In parallel, some Palestinian ex-villagers established independent sites for specific communities.

14. The text is originally in English. It was lightly edited and corrected in order to make it comprehendible.

15. The initiative to run the workshop came during the late 1990s, while the peace process was still under way. The project collapsed roughly a year after the outbreak of the Al-Aqsa *intifada*.

16. See Hafez 2000: 161 on the extensive usage of food and drink in Arab proverbs used in rural areas.

17. See Chu and Downes 2000; Chu and Downes 2002; Luria 1973; Sutton 2001; Young 1986.

References

al-Ahmadi, S. (2001), *The Palestinian Kitchen*, Jerusalem: unpublished: 4–5.

Almagor, U. (1990a), 'Odors and Private Language: Observations on the Phenomenology of Scent', *Human Studies*, 13: 253–74.

—— (1990b), 'Some Thoughts on Common Scents', *Journal for the Theory of Social Behaviour*, 20(3):181–95.

Anderson, B. (1991), *Imagined Communities*, London: Verso.

Appadurai, A. (1981), 'Gastro-politics in Hindu South Asia', *American Ethnologist*, 8(3): 494–511.

—— (1988), 'How to Make a National Cuisine: Cookbooks in Contemporary India',*Comparative Study of History and Society*, 30(1): 3–24.

Bahloul, J. (1996), *The Architecture of Memory*, Cambridge: Cambridge University Press.

Ben-Ze'ev, E. (2000), *Narratives of Exile: Palestinian Refugee Reflections on Three Villages, Tiret Haifa, Ijzim and 'Ein Hawd*, D.Phil submitted to the

Institute of Social and Cultural Anthropology, University of Oxford.

Chu, S. and Downes, J. (2000), 'Long Live Proust; The Odour-cued Auto-biographical Memory Bump', *Cognition* 75: B41–B50.

Chu, S. and Downes, J. (2002), 'Proust Nose Best: Odors are Better Cues of Autobiographical Memory', *Memory and Cognition*, 30(4): 511–18.

Classen, C., Howes, D. and Synnott, A. (1994), *Aroma: The Cultural History of Smell*, London: Routledge.

Cohen, H. (2000), *HaNifqadim haNokh'him: haPlitim haFalestinim biMdinat Israel me'az 1948* (The Present Absentees: The Palestinian Refugees in the State of Israel since 1948), Jerusalem: The Center for Research of the Arab Society.

Connerton, P. (1989), *How Societies Remember*, Cambridge: Cambridge University Press.

Darwish, M. (2002), 'A Love Story between an Arab Poet and His Land: An Interview with Mahmud Darwish', *Journal of Palestine Studies*, 31(3): 67–78.

Dundes, A. (1972), 'Seeing is Believing', *Natural History Magazine*, May.

Farah, R. (2000), *Crossing Boundaries: Popular Memory and Reconstructions of Palestinian Identity in al-Baq'a Refugee Camp, Jordan*, PhD, University of Toronto.

Feldman, A. (1991), *Formations of Violence: The Narrative of the Body and Political Terror in Northern Ireland*, Chicago: University of Chicago Press.

Hafez, S. (2000), 'Food as a Semiotic Code in Arabic Literature', in S. Zubaida and R. Tapper (eds) (1994), *Culinary Cultures of the Middle East*, London: Tauris, 257–80.

Kanafani, A. (1983), *Aesthetics and Ritual in the United Arab Emirates: The Anthropology of Food and Personal Adornment among Arabian Women*, Beirut: American University of Beirut.

Khoury, E. (1998), *Bab al-Shams*, Beirut: Dar al-Adab.

Luria, A. R (1973), *The Working Brain: An Introduction to Neuro-Psychology*, New York: Basic.

Miller, D. and Slater, D. (2000), *The Internet: An Ethnographic Approach*, Oxford: Berg.

Nora, P. (1989), 'Between Memory and History: Les lieux de mémoire', *Representations*, 26: 7–25.

Proust, M. ([1913] 1982), *Remembrance of Things Past*, Vol. I, *Swann's Way, Within a Budding Grove*, Translated from the French by C. K. Scott Moncrieff and T. Kilmartin, New York: Vintage.

—— ([1928] 1932), *The Past Recaptured*, New York: The Modern Library.

Qleibo, A. (2000), *Jerusalem in the Heart*, Jerusalem: Kloreus Publication.

Sakakini, H. (1987), *Jerusalem and I*, Jerusalem: Habesch – The Commercial Press.

Schechla, J. (2001), 'The Invisible People Come to Light: Israel's "Internally Displaced" and the "Unrecognized Villages"', *Journal of Palestine Studies*, 31(1): 20–31.

Seremetakis, C. N. (ed.) (1994), *The Senses Still: Perception and Memory as Material Culture in Modernity*, Boulder CO: Westview.

Slyomovics, S. (1998), *The Object of Memory: Arab and Jew Narrate the Palestinian Village*, Philadelphia: University of Pennsylvania Press.

Stoller, P. (1989), *The Taste of Ethnographic Things: The Senses in Anthropology*, Philadelphia: University of Pennsylvania Press.

—— (1997), *Sensuous Scholarship*, Philadelphia: University of Pennsylvania Press.

Sutton, D. (2001), *Remembrance of Repasts: An Anthropology of Food and Memory*, Oxford: Berg.

Young, J. Z. (1986), *Philosophy and the Brain*, Oxford: Oxford University Press.

Zubaida, S. and Tapper, R. (eds) (1994), *Culinary Cultures of the Middle East*, London: Tauris.

Zureik, E. (1996), *Palestinian Refugees and the Peace Process*, Washington DC: Institute for Palestine Studies.

Part III
Global Rules, Routes and Access

–9–

Grades and Standards in the Social Construction of Safe Food

Lawrence Busch

Adulteration: The action of adulterating; corruption or debasement by spurious admixture.

Oxford English Dictionary

Safety: The state of being safe; exemption from hurt or injury; freedom from danger.

Oxford English Dictionary

Introduction

Recently, I walked quickly through our local supermarket in East Lansing. East Lansing is part of a relatively small metropolitan area of about 300,000 people: it is certainly not New York or Los Angeles. Yet I found fresh clementines from Spain, fresh peaches and grapes from Chile, fresh tomatoes from Holland still on the vine, fresh starfruit from an unknown source, dried apricots from Turkey, kiwis from New Zealand, canned hearts of palm from Brazil, canned sardines from Norway, canned tuna from Mexico, coffee from at least ten nations, and a host of other food products from far away. The concentrated orange juice that I bought is made from a blend of US and Brazilian juices. The apple juice I bought contains juice from 'USA, Argentina, Brazil, Hungary and Turkey'. What is perhaps more astonishing is that this kind of global diet is becoming common not only in the high-income countries of Western Europe, Japan and the US, but also in middle-income nations such as Brazil, and in low-income nations such as China. In short, over the last several decades the food system has become truly global.

Of course, from the days of Columbus and even before, food has been transported around the world to meet the desires of the wealthy elites. Let us remember that Columbus undertook his dangerous and uncertain voyage to find an easier way to bring what were then exotic spices to Europe. European paintings of merchant families of the seventeenth century often include citrus so as to emphasize that the persons involved were comfortable enough to afford these semi-tropical delicacies. But, nevertheless, diets remained very local and seasonal in character. This is no longer the case for a significant and growing portion of the world's population: aside from the very important issue of control of this newly formed global food system, it poses a new set of issues with respect to food safety. Put briefly, the globalization of the food system poses a new set of food safety issues demanding that the very idea of safety be rethought.

In this chapter I first examine how the food system has changed as a result of the political realignments and reformulations collectively known as globalization. Then, I examine the apparent paradox of how food safety has become an issue just as food has become safer. Next, I examine how grades and standards are implicated in food safety and how they are used to impose a new discipline on food producers and processors, while concealing the origins of the problem. The case of HACCP is used to clarify the points made. I conclude by showing how food safety can only be fully understood when viewed as one among many conflicting worlds.

How Globalization has Changed Our Understanding of Food Safety

Time and space do not permit me to produce a detailed history of food safety. That is a work for another time. But what I can and will do here is to note, admittedly in somewhat abstract terms, how the food system has shifted over time and how our definition of and concern with food has changed from one of adulteration to one of safety as a result of this. As the epigraphs at the beginning of this chapter show, there is considerable difference between adulteration and safety. First, adulteration is a negative term, while safety is a positive one. Second, adulteration is an action. The term is metaphorically borrowed from adultery, voluntary sexual activity outside the bounds of marriage. In contrast, safety is a passive term, a state of being free from danger. Indeed, in its older definition, safety meant salvation. Those who want a perfectly safe diet still adhere to this older meaning. Thus, the shift from adulteration of food to food safety is more than a change of vocabulary; it reflects a fundamental shift in the behavior of those in the food chain, and simultaneously, a shift in perspective from searching for those *humans* who deliberately and knowingly tamper with food, to searching for the *non-humans* (microbes, chemicals, etc.) that taint the food supply. What I will try to uncover here is how and why the change occurred.

It appears that several intersecting transitions have occurred that have brought on the shift from adulteration to food safety. These include the transition from local to global markets, changes in what is shipped over long distances, changes in scale of production and processing, changes in production practices, changes in processing technologies, and the rise of industrialized food. These transitions are not the result of any natural process, but of the restructuring of agrifood networks by myriad actors, especially the agrifood giants. Let us examine each of these in turn.

From local to regional to global. Most obviously, what we buy today is no longer entirely or even largely locally produced and consumed. Indeed, in much of the industrialized world, and in the growing urban areas of the developing world, we have little or no idea who actually produces our food, in what manner it is shipped, or how it arrives on our supermarket shelves. In a word, we no longer have personal ties to producers, processors, or even retailers of our food. This is the case for two interrelated reasons.

First, the networks have been lengthened greatly as evidenced by my brief discussion of what I can find in my local supermarket. The very length of the chains makes personal relations between those who consume food and producers and processors virtually impossible.

Second, as the large producers, processors and retailers have come to dominate the scene, they have deliberately discouraged the social dimensions of exchange. They have made us into 'consumers', whose job in the system is to pick from the cornucopia of goods supplied in ever-increasing variety – there are 12,000 products for sale in the average American supermarket – without a lengthy chat with the grocer or butcher or baker that might distract from the process of exchange. Indeed, the modern supermarket enlists us in the very work process by having us retrieve the goods, place them in carts, bring them to the checkout counters, place them on the conveyor belts and put the purchased products in bags. This work, once done by the grocer, now falls to the consumer. Of course, we (arguably) do benefit through lower prices and greater variety, but there are perhaps other hidden costs as well.[1] Finally, I should note that those further upstream continue to maintain face-to-face relations. Food wholesalers almost always know their suppliers and their customers well. It is just at the very end of the process that the relations become impersonal, so as not to sully the exchange of money for goods with other less weighty matters.

Scale. At the same time, new technologies and new forms of social organization have led to an enormous increase in scale. In 1869 the first carload of California produce was shipped eastward, but most fruits and vegetables were still grown and eaten locally until about a decade later when improved rail service began to permit wider and wider marketing areas (Levenstein 1988). Consequently, much production was relocated to larger units further from metropolitan areas.

Giedion (1975) compares the Paris abattoirs of La Villette a century ago with those of Chicago at the same time. What is most dramatic about the differences is that in Paris each animal had its own stall and was separately butchered, while in Chicago the butchering process was already automated. Recently, I visited a hog-disassembly plant in Brazil. Built using the most modern technologies available, it typically slaughters 300 hogs an hour, although it could slaughter many more than that. Hogs are prodded down a chute. They are shocked, fall over onto a grated conveyor belt and have their throats cut. Their blood is drained and the carcasses are hoisted by one foot onto an overhead conveyor. The carcasses are then cut into pieces by numerous workers each of whom is assigned a specific butchering task. Clearly, no hogs passing through this plant are known individually to the butchers. The work is surprisingly clean, not at all like butcher shops of old. This has the peculiar effect of adding to the social distance that workers appear to have from the meat that passes by them.

Similar changes have taken place throughout the food system. Tomatoes, once a garden crop, are now grown in large fields in California or in hectare after hectare of glasshouses in the Netherlands. Kiwis, once the lowly Chinese goose-berry, are now grown on large farms in New Zealand, Italy and the United States. Brazil is the world's largest producer of concentrated frozen orange juice from fruit grown in huge orchards covering thousands of hectares.

Changes in production practices. Production practices have changed as well. Chickens, once the source of 'pin money' for American farm women, are now grown almost entirely in large barns with thousands of birds squeezed into small areas (Heffernan 1984; Sawyer 1971). Large feedlots contain thousands of cows on just a few acres. Dairy herds of 3,000 cows are no longer unusual. Hogs are now raised in confinement facilities on concrete floors. These are not merely changes of scale, but of entire production processes. Special measures must be taken to ensure that disease does not spread, rapidly killing the confined animals.

Moreover, feeds are no longer produced from whatever is locally available; they are the result of the careful mixing of ingredients from a wide range of sources so as to produce what animal nutritionists currently deem to be the best diet in terms of animal growth, cost and feed efficiency. When exotic materials are added to the feed, this may well lead to new disease vectors. Such is suspected for Bovine Spongiform Encephalopathy (mad-cow disease). Alternatively, it can lead to what Perrow (1984) referred to some years ago as 'Normal Accidents'. In Michigan some time ago fire retardant was accidentally mixed into cattle feed, resulting in enormous losses.

Similarly, crops are now more uniform, requiring greater applications of pesticides to keep the ever-evolving pest populations at bay. New crop biotechnologies are likely to introduce significant amounts of exotic material into crop plants in an effort to design more pest-resistant plants (Krimsky and Wrubel 1996). But humans have little or no experience with such 'wide crosses', so here too food-safety issues abound. And, all of these changes serve to help to transform the entire food system by raising new kinds of food-safety risks as well as by creating new fears among some consumers (see Heller, this volume).

Changes in processing technologies. Nor are the changes confined to the farm. The processing industry has introduced a wide range of new technologies over the last several centuries. The first of these new technologies was canning. Canning was developed by virtue of a prize offered by Napoleon for a way of preserving food for his troops. In response, Nicolas Appert developed what is now known as the canning process in 1809. A newspaper of the day, exclaiming wonderment at the new technology, noted, 'M. Appert has found a way to fix the seasons; at his establishment, spring, summer and autumn live in bottles, like those delicate plants protected by the gardener under glass domes against the intemperate seasons' (quoted in Toussaint-Samat 1992: 738). Although Appert himself failed to file for a patent and died a pauper, his technology spread widely such that canned foods were quite common by the end of the nineteenth century. They brought with them both the ability to move a wide range of foods across space and time and the potential for producing new kinds of foods. For example, in 1898, John T. Torrance, a PhD chemist, invented condensed soups and set up Campbell's Soup Company to sell them (Levenstein 1988). But canning also introduced a new set of potential food hazards, the most well-known of which is botulism. Toussaint-Samat (1992) reports that Americans now consume some 50–60 kg per year of canned food, although French consumption is considerably less.

In the late 1870s freezing technologies were invented, but they were rejected because they left the food spongy. Much later, Charles Birdseye learned the secret of effective freezing technologies: quick freezing. Soon, the food industry was again transformed and another group of foods, which lost flavor or changed color when canned, but which maintained color and flavor when frozen, could now be shipped worldwide.

More recently, we have seen the rise of what have been referred to as 'cold chains'. Starting with the banana industry a century ago, cold-chain technology has been gradually transformed such that it is now possible to ship fresh produce halfway around the world at relatively low cost with little spoilage. Thus, the clementines on the supermarket shelf that I mentioned above were much like the ones that I have seen and tasted in markets in Spain and Morocco.

Nor is change in processing confined to general technologies such as freezing and canning. For example, one brand of cookie sold in the United States claims that its firm outer layer and soft interior are just what grandma used to make. In fact, unless grandma had a 1,000°F (538°C) flash tunnel oven, she could never have cooked food in this fashion.

Finally, along with the new processing technologies, thousands of food additives have come into common use in an effort to (1) retard spoilage, (2) enhance color, (3) improve flavor, and (4) change the nutritional composition of the food we eat. While testing shows most of these to be individually harmless, no testing of *combinations* of additives has been done or is even possible given the current organization of the food system.

Changes in what is shipped long distances. Shipping distance is nevertheless an inadequate explanation for the increased concern about food safety. There have also been significant changes in what is shipped long distances. Let us consider several examples. Until the 1880s, beef in the United States was shipped on the hoof from stockyards in Chicago to slaughterhouses in New York. This was quite expensive as most animals lost weight on the trip and many died. Beef prices in New York reflected that fact. It was only through the inventiveness and persistence of Gustavus Franklin Swift that the system was changed. Swift developed and patented a refrigerator car, hung the carcasses on rails and over less than a decade completely transformed the industry by moving much of the butchering and nearly all of the hide production and tanning to Chicago (Giedion 1975). Thus, New York butchers who once could see the signs of certain diseases on live cattle before they slaughtered them, were presented with far less informational sides of beef. Instead, the Pure Food and Drug Act of 1906 required trained inspectors to examine each carcass to ensure that it was safe to eat.

Similarly, just a few years later, Harry L. Russell, Dean of the College of Agriculture at the University of Wisconsin, transformed the Wisconsin dairy industry by encouraging the development of tests for adulteration of milk and formulas for the production of cheese. Moreover, he was successful in convincing the State Board of Health to support his endeavors. As a result, Wisconsin cheese was transformed from a poor-quality product of largely local interest into a national and even international product with consistently high quality (Beardsley 1969).

Canning may well have 'fixed the seasons' as the reporter commenting on Appert's invention suggested. It also helped to increase the range of goods that could be shipped long distances in time and space. Later in the century, freezing had a similar effect. And, still more recently, cold chains extended the list still further. Today, for many foods, seasonality is a remnant of a forgotten past.

The rise of industrial food. Beyond the changes in processing technologies lies the rise of industrial food. For example, the apple juice noted above contains apples from five countries. This permits consistency of flavor and color. Hundreds of products now contain vegetable protein (usually from soybeans) as a filler. Other compounds are used as emulsifiers and thickeners in a growing array of snack foods. As a result, one can never really be sure just what ingredients are in a given food product, despite more detailed product labels.

At the same time, several new types of foods are emerging, by virtue of the large profits that they portend for their promoters. First, fresh prepared foods are now commonplace. These are foods that are fully cooked and ready to eat, sometimes sold hot, but often sold cold where only warming is necessary (often in microwave ovens). Such foods have existed for some time in continental Europe. French *traiteurs* (caterers) are commonplace in every village and city neighborhood. However, they are generally petit bourgeois enterprises where food is cooked on the premises and bought on the day of preparation. In contrast, the Anglo-American model, which is now expanding on the continent as well, consists of large, centralized kitchens in which fresh foods are prepared and packaged to be shipped to numerous stores for final sale. Thus, my local supermarket now sells a wide range of fresh salads, sliced meats, hot prepared chickens, and other fully prepared dishes which may be used as luncheon sandwich food or as a supplement to a dinner prepared at home. Since this food is prepared fresh and shipped considerable distances from the point of preparation, it is especially susceptible to spoilage. It must be kept hot or refrigerated until sold and it must be sold quickly before it spoils. Of course, at the same time, it permits corporate penetration into the fresh-prepared-food market, where value added is high.

Second, fabricated foods are beginning to appear on the market. In some sense the cold breakfast cereals invented at the turn of the twentieth century were the first of these as they contained a variety of ingredients mixed and prepared in unusual ways. (They also made extraordinary health claims – Grape-Nuts® promised a cure for consumption, malaria, and loose teeth (Levenstein 1988).) But now fabricated foods are beginning to appear in a wider variety of forms. For example, perfectly formed potato chips are produced by reducing potatoes to flour and reconstructing them in a precise form. Food components (I hesitate to use the word 'ingredients' as these are far more basic) are now available to food processors from which entire foods can be concocted. For example, one might choose to combine citrus fiber, soy protein, potato starch, 'natural' colors and flavors from various sources, and vitamins and minerals to make an entirely new food. These foods present a whole new sort of food safety problem on at least two levels: On the one hand, they must be meticulously watched to ensure product consistency as multiple ingredients that are often changed in response to short-term market prices are combined. Thus, packaged breads often note that they contain one or more of several edible oils. Each of these can be a source of contamination. On the other hand, they harbor the potential to create allergic reactions in unsuspecting consumers.

Third, fast foods are now found throughout the world. Fast food chains require great uniformity in their products. As such, the larger chains often ship goods over long distances. Moreover, since they are so large, they must buy from multiple sources, each of which can be a source of contamination of the food sold. Once the contamination occurs, the real challenge is to find its source. Given the length of the chains of supply, this is not necessarily a simple job.

In sum, the globalization of the agrifood system has also resulted in the complexification of the food supply and the global sales of a huge variety of food products once only available locally. Such systems are quite fragile and may be easily disrupted. Moreover, such vulnerability tends to raise food safety concerns to the national and even global level.

The Paradox of Food Safety: The Safer the Food, the More Concern about Safety

Before these changes, food safety was largely a local and even personal or family concern. Although it appears clear now that the health problems caused by food are not only a modern phenomenon – ergot was a common problem in rye throughout the Middle Ages, causing hallucinations among other things – unsafe food was not recognized as a problem until much more recently. Illnesses and deaths were rarely attributed (at least in any consistent way) to contaminated food at all. This was the case in part because poor communications made it well nigh impossible to determine if a disease or death in one place might have the same cause as a disease or death in another place. Furthermore, even if the link could be established, the food consumed in a given locale was usually from that locale (with the exception of spices and a few luxury foods). Therefore, even a case of food poisoning among a large number of persons would be local in nature. It could easily be attributed to the weather, to bad luck, to sorcery, or to any number of other equally plausible causes. This is still the case in many parts of the world. Thus, the earliest full-length work I have located that was devoted to food adulteration in the Western world was only published in 1820 (Accum 1820).[2]

Food safety could only come into existence as a conceptual category after some theoretical framework existed to link particular forms of contamination to particular diseases and symptoms. That had to await three developments. First, germ theory had to be developed in the late nineteenth century. And, germ theory was strongly resisted, first by surgeons who were encouraged to wash their hands, and then by physicians who saw hygienists as stealing their clientele (Latour 1984). Second, the addition of chemicals (as food additives, preservatives, flavorings, colorings) had to become common practice. Although chemical contamination was not unknown, it only became a concern with the industrialization of the agrifood system in the course of the past century. By that time many of the common microbial contaminants had been brought under control. Yet, ironically, many of the chemical contaminants were introduced in an effort to reduce microbial contamination. Third, toxicology had to enter the debate. In

other words, to move from adulteration to food safety, one had to develop a scientific basis for determining what was safe. Adulteration included such things as
adding water to milk or sawdust to flour. These sorts of thing were adulterants
but they were harmless and therefore not implicated in the newer discussion of
food safety. Only when regulatory science entered the debate could food safety
emerge. Thus, the earliest full-length document I was able to locate that talked
of food safety was published in 1958 (Joint FAO/WHO Expert Committee on
Food Additives 1958).[3]

Furthermore, the entry of regulatory science also changed the context of the
debate from whether a particular batch of food is contaminated to what the risk of
contamination is. That is to say, the 'scientification' of the problem shifted the
debate from specific food products – this milk, that piece of meat – to the world of
probabilities. It introduced notions of risk into food consumption as it did into all
other areas of social life. As Beck suggests, '*Risk* may be defined as *a systematic
way of dealing with hazards and insecurities induced and introduced by modernization itself*' (Beck 1992: 21).

Moreover, as food companies at all stages of the agrifood system have grown in
size, they have encouraged brand loyalty. Nabisco's Uneeda Biscuit was among the
first. Today, hundreds of brands are known around the world. But brand identification is a two-edged sword. It shifts quality concerns from the product to the producer (Eymard-Duvernay 1994). As such, it demands eternal vigilance on the part
of the producer. A single tainted bottle of Coca-Cola®, a single contaminated can
of Del Monte® peaches, can destroy brand loyalty. Thus, large companies see food
safety as important both in terms of building market share and as insurance against
harm to their reputation.

In sum, although far fewer persons die or become ill as a result of contaminated
food today than in the past, food safety concerns have increased among the general
public as well as among industry and government spokespersons.

The Role of Grades and Standards

Where do grades and standards fit into all this? Today, food safety is the result of
the practices of a variety of people who interact with food products in various
stages of development in such a way as to have them deemed safe. As such, food
safety is *simultaneously* dependent upon (1) the more or less predictable behavior
of chemical and biological entities including both foods and the microorganisms
that surround them, and (2) the behavior of human beings who perform various
more or less predictable activities that tend to ensure a certain level of safety that
is deemed adequate by a given society. Food safety, therefore, is neither a natural
process nor a social process. It is always *both* a natural and a social process; it is
what one might call a 'socionatural' process.

Producing food safety requires constant work – by scientists, engineers, farmers, food processors, wholesalers, retailers, and consumers among others – in order to serve the public good. This is the case as at each step in the production of food safety; there is always the possibility that something may go wrong. Thus, some human actors constantly monitor other human *and* nonhuman actors throughout each commodity subsector. For example, on the one hand, tests need to be made to determine the pesticide residues in fruit, while on the other hand, tests need to be made to determine the degree to which farmers and farm workers conform to standards for pesticide application. Similarly, tests need to be made on chicken to determine *salmonella* contamination, while inspections need to be made at chicken-processing plants to ensure that health standards are adhered to.

What should be apparent from the above example is that all tests of food safety are *simultaneously* tests of people and things (Latour 1987). These tests are designed to discipline human and nonhuman actors such that they perform in ways deemed acceptable (or correct or good) by whatever agency is in authority at a given point along a commodity subsector. Indeed, as I have argued elsewhere (Busch 2000), standards require standardization of things, workers, markets, and capitalists. Even the standards themselves must be standardized; thus, the Sanitary and Phytosanitary Agreement of the World Trade Organization requires that national standards conform to those set by the Codex Alimentarius unless scientific justification for a deviation can be provided.

However, since both human and nonhuman actors are interlinked in complex networks that are concerned with many other goals in addition to food safety, such disciplining may or may not be successful in particular circumstances. This is the case because, as Boltanski and Thévenot (1991) suggest, all of us live in multiple worlds where each has its own standards of greatness. In the world of food safety, careful monitoring of production to ensure safety is expected. The producer or processor whose foods never suffer from safety problems is lauded by consumers. But processors and producers also must live in the worlds of industry and commerce. In these worlds product excellence and marketability, respectively, are what count. For example, a food safety measure that adversely changes the taste of a product might be rejected by processors as it violates norms for product quality. Similarly, pressures to enhance profits may encourage retailers to continue to sell meat products when they know that they are no longer fresh. On the other hand, food safety may be compromised by changes in weather conditions that may increase spoilage of food products in ways unexpected by those concerned with safety. Note that in the former case, it is the human actors who do not measure up to the standards, while in the latter case it is nature itself that does not measure up. In addition, perceptions of what constitutes safety may differ between and among members of various scientific professions and the general public. These differing perceptions are often embedded in the standards.

Furthermore, food safety was and is used by larger industrial food processors as a means to increase their market share. Consider the famous case of the National Biscuit Company (now Nabisco) in the United States. As noted above, it introduced the 'Uneeda Biscuit' (You need a biscuit), the first biscuit packaged in a box and distributed nationwide. It soon replaced the older cracker barrels; with them, it was always possible that the biscuits you purchased were 'from the bottom of the barrel'. Such biscuits were deemed to be not only broken, but moldy, worm-ridden and unhealthy. Not much later, the United States Department of Agriculture convinced larger food processors to support food- and drug-safety legislation by noting how it would drive smaller processors out of the market. Publication of Upton Sinclair's, *The Jungle*, an exposé of the meat-processing industry, caused more outrage about food handling than it did about working conditions. Seizing upon the complaints, Armour Packing Company welcomed inspection of its meat-processing plants so as to increase its market share (Levenstein 1988). Similarly, pasteurization forced smaller dairy-products manufacturers out of business. The introduction of the bulk milk tank many years later, ostensibly a hygienic measure, had a similar effect. More recent examples are the current dispute between the European Union and the United States over the safety of genetically modified food, and between the US and France over the safety of unpasteurized cheese. In each case one party argues that the other fails to meet acceptable food safety standards. These illustrate the inseparability of cultural, economic, political, and technical aspects of food safety (see Busch 2002).

The standards themselves are subject to revision as a result of new scientific findings, needs and desires of subsector actors, and changes in the chemicals and microorganisms themselves. Standards that are too strict will have the effect of raising prices to unacceptably high levels, while standards that are too low will allow unacceptably high risks (usually to consumers). Moreover, there is rarely a single standard; multiple and even redundant standards along the entire subsector are far more common in producing food safety. Thus, pesticides are monitored in terms of what kinds can be produced, what kinds can be sold for use on particular crops, what dosages can be applied by whom at what points in the growing cycle, what kinds and amounts of residues can appear at the cannery, and what kinds and amounts can be left in the finished product. At each stage standards must be developed to test both the humans who handle the food and the food itself so as to ensure that all measure up to the tasks at hand (Busch 2000). Let us consider one case of particular importance that is currently the subject of much discussion, Hazard Analysis and Critical Control Points (HACCP).

The Case of HACCP

The introduction of the HACCP system in July, 1996 has begun to transform the US meat and poultry industries and may well transform the entire food-processing industry (Food Safety and Inspection Service 1996a). Until that date, meat was visually inspected by government inspectors. However, visual inspection was deemed inadequate to deal with bacterial contaminants.

In practice, HACCP is a very complex system of controls on whatever is being processed, such that it is highly unlikely that any contaminants enter the processed product. Of particular importance to HACCP is the development of Standard Operating Procedures that cover each Critical Control Point, detailed record-keeping to ensure that standards have been adhered to, and frequent verification. Also of note is that, for many products, it will be possible to identify the original source of each final product. In other words, a steak sold at the local supermarket should be linked to a particular cow that was raised at a particular ranch. In short, HACCP is a very effective system for disciplining all actors in a given commodity chain. However, HACCP may be equally useful in increasing the market share of larger companies and in reducing State intervention in food processing. Whether it will eliminate smaller processors remains to be seen, as no studies have addressed that issue as yet. However, the setting aside by the Secretary of Agriculture of approximately two million dollars for action research on the issue suggests that at least some persons believe that is the case (CREES 1997). EU observers make much the same point about small processors there (Taylor 2002).

In addition to the meat and poultry program mandated by USDA (United States Department of Agriculture), FDA (Food and Drug Administration) has implemented a pilot program for other food products with several manufacturers. In an FDA interim report on that pilot program, they note that firms with sophisticated quality-assurance programs have had little difficulty in implementing HACCP as it has involved only slight modifications to what has been done before. They quote a representative of a large industry as saying: 'We had a good control program before HACCP, and we look at HACCP as a refinement rather than a drastic change.'

In contrast, an FDA report quoted a representative of a small firm as follows:

> We did not have trained professionals in the QA [Quality Assurance] section at the firm who thoroughly understood the concepts of food safety control. We also lacked written procedures for our QA program and written monitoring records. Little formal QA training had been provided for line employees. (quoted in Food and Drug Administration, 1996)

In short, at least some smaller operations have greater start-up expenses and more record-keeping, and certainly need more education for their employees. But what needs to be emphasized is that smaller operations are not necessarily more likely to engage in practices that lead to unsafe food. Their very small size suggests that they are more likely to be intimately familiar with what they process – far more than a larger firm.

It is also worth noting that HACCP has another convenient feature from the industry's perspective: that of moving government regulation one step away from the processing plants. Under HACCP regulations, some of the day-to-day inspection is replaced by paper audits which ask questions about record-keeping rather than about safety. The auditors will assume that the papers provided to them accurately reflect the actual activities undertaken in a given plant, much the way that tax collectors request data on expenses and income in their work. In short, HACCP substitutes audits for visual inspections. As such, it may rightly be viewed as part of a larger, more widespread phenomenon: the creation of what Michael Power (1997) has called the 'audit society'. As Power suggests, auditing is not merely a solution to a technical problem, but a means of restructuring the practice of government. Thus, at its base, audits are highly political in nature, even when conducted with a view to objectivity.

Of course, there is little doubt that the revelation that audited records do not reflect accurately (to what degree?) the actual practices on the floor of the processing plant will bring severe penalties. Most firms will comply, both because of the penalties and because of the need to protect their reputations, and also because compliance may actually lower costs by reducing the volume of rejects. However, while direct State intervention into the affairs of the daily management of food-manufacturing plants is thereby reduced or avoided, HACCP pushes control further into the very structure of the plants that are audited. Put differently, businesses adopting HACCP must be organized in certain ways – not least in ways that permit audits to take place.

In addition, the very implementation of HACCP itself has become a business opportunity. As Beck (1992) notes, risk itself becomes a market opportunity. Thus, numerous firms now exist whose sole purpose is to provide training in HACCP implementation.

Furthermore, HACCP goes beyond older systems of inspection to remove human intentionality from the domain of food safety. It does this at several levels. First, it obscures the origins of food-safety problems in the organization of the industry itself. For example, *Salmonella* contamination, while it requires the presence of the organism that causes it, is also the result of particular practices including the transport of meat over long distances, speedups on the disassembly lines of meat-packing plants, and improper cooking in fast-food restaurants. These practices are not random occurrences but central to the industry's income- and wealth-seeking agenda. Stockholders praise them for that. But the ethical questions – How much should we modify the food system in our efforts to extract profits? How do we want to live? – are not asked.

Second, it tacitly argues that, if the procedures are followed and humans are affected adversely, it is the result of a chemical or a microbe. For example, if some new microbe should suddenly appear on the scene, despite the HACCP practices in place, that new microbe will be attributed to a never-before-seen mutation or some unusual climatological factors. It will not be attributed to the organization of production that restructures micro environments so as to encourage disease organisms to grow beyond threshold points and manifest themselves as a disease.

Finally, HACCP removes subjectivity even from the inspection system, by removing the inspector and replacing him or her with a meter reading or a set of routinized practices. Thus, food safety risks can be seen as entirely the result of the relations between machines and potential contaminants. The humans whose decisions and practices make the machines, design the production processes, inspect the machines that monitor the product and define food safety itself are all concealed behind the veil of scientific objectivity. The political is depoliticized (or at least concealed) as the politics of food safety is transformed into the technoeconomics of food safety.

Conclusions

In sum, food safety is not an inherent property of food, or even of the relations between people and food. The term did not even come into common use until less than 50 years ago. Instead, food safety is best understood as the result of the restructuring of the food system along industrial and scientific lines, and the consequent new problems that has posed for processors and the general public alike. Furthermore, the case of HACCP illustrates that food safety is a realm of negotiation between processors, governments, the general public, producers and others who have many goals they wish to optimize or maximize in addition to food safety itself.

Acknowledgements

This chapter is based on the 2003 article in Norwegian 'Klasser og standarder in den sosiale konstruksjonen av trygg mat', published in the book *Festskrift* to Reidar Almaas. It is published here in English with the permission of Tapir Academic Press.

Notes

1. These include the additional processing made necessary by a complex food system and the consequent dietary implications (e.g. increased salt, sugar and fat consumption). Furthermore, as noted below, food is now an element in the risk society.
2. There may well be earlier works. Nevertheless, it is indicative of the changing nature of the debate.

3. Indeed, most of the early work on food safety focuses on chemical contaminants.

References

Accum, F. (1820), *A Treatise on Adulterations of Food and Culinary Poisons, Exhibiting the Fraudulent Sophistications of Bread, Beer, Wine, Spiritous Liquors, Tea, Coffee, Cream, Confectionery, Vinegar, Mustard, Pepper, Cheese, Olive Oil, Pickles, and Other Articles Employed in Domestic Economy, and Methods of Detecting Them*, Philadelphia: Ab'm Small.

Beardsley, E. (1969), *Harry L. Russell and Agricultural Science in Wisconsin*, Madison: University of Wisconsin Press.

Beck, U. (1992), *Risk Society: Towards a New Modernity*, London: Sage.

Boltanski, L. and Thévenot, L. (1991), *De la justification: les economies de la grandeur*, Paris: Gallimard.

Busch, L. (2000), 'The Moral Economy of Grades and Standards,' *Journal of Rural Studies*, 16: 273–83.

—— (2002), 'The Homeletics of Risk', *Journal of Agricultural and Environmental Ethics*, 15: 17–29.

Cooperative State Research, Education and Extension Service (1997), *Fund for Rural America: Guidelines for Proposal Preparation and Submission*, Washington DC: USDA, photocopied.

Eymard-Duvernay, F. (1994), 'Coordination des échanges et qualité des biens,' in A. Orléan (ed.), *Analyse economique des conventions*, Paris: Presses Universitaires de France.

Food and Drug Administration (1996), *Hazard Analysis Critical Control Point (HACCP): Pilot Program for Selected Food Manufacturers. Interim Report of Observations and Comments*, Washington, DC: Food and Drug Administration, Center for Food Safety & Applied Nutrition, 19 June, http://vm.cfsan.fda.gov/~dms/haccp-1.html#intro

—— (1997), *FDA Warns Asthmatics, Other Sulfite-sensitive Consumers on Tuna*, Washington, DC: FDA Talk Paper T97–13, 7 March, http://vm.cfsan.fda.gov/~lrd/tunawarn.html

Food Safety and Inspection Service (1996a), *The Final Rule on Pathogen Reduction and Hazard Analysis and Critical Control Point (HACCP) Systems*, Washington DC: Food Safety and Inspection Service, US Department of Agriculture, July. http://www.usda.gov/agency/fsis/finalrul.htm

—— (1996b), *Key Facts: Economic Impact Analysis*, Washington DC: Food Safety and Inspection Service, US Department of Agriculture, July, http://www.usda.gov/agency/fsis/keyecon.htm

—— (1996c), *Key Facts: Impact of HACCP Rule on Small Businesses*,

Washington, DC: Food Safety and Inspection Service, US Department of Agriculture, July, http://www.usda.gov/agency/fsis/keysmall.htm

Giedion, S. (1975), *Mechanization Takes Command*, New York: W.W. Norton.

Heffernan, W. (1984), 'Constraints in the U.S. Poultry Industry', *Annual Review of Rural Sociology and Development*, 1: 237–60.

Joint FAO/WHO Expert Committee on Food Additives (1958), *Procedures for the Testing of Intentional Food Additives to Establish Their Safety for Use: Second Report*, Geneva: World Health Organization.

Krimsky, S. and Wrubel, R. (1996), *Agricultural Biotechnology and the Environment: Science, Policy, and Social Issues*, Urbana: University of Illinois Press.

Latour, B. (1984), *Les microbes: guerre et paix suivi de irréductions*, Paris: Editions A. M. Métailié.

—— (1987), *Science in Action: How to Follow Scientists and Engineers Through Society*, Milton Keynes: Open University Press.

Levenstein, H. (1988), *Revolution at the Table: The Transformation of the American Diet*, New York: Oxford University Press.

Perrow, C. (1984), *Normal Accidents*, New York: Basic.

Power, M. (1997), *The Audit Society: Rituals of Verification*, Oxford: Oxford University Press.

Sawyer, G. (1971), *The Agribusiness Poultry Industry*, New York: Exposition Press.

Sinclair, U. (1906), *The Jungle*, New York: Doubleday, Page & Company.

Taylor, E. (2002), 'HACCP, New Regulations and the Small Business Sector', *Health and Hygiene*, 23: 12–14.

Toussaint-Samat, M. (1992), *A History of Food*, Cambridge MA: Blackwell.

–10–

Dogs, Whales and Kangaroos:
Transnational Activism and Food Taboos

Marianne Elisabeth Lien

In May 2002, a couple of weeks before the World Cup Football Championships in South Korea, a demonstration was scheduled in front of the South Korean Consulate in Sydney to protest against what was referred to as the 'illegal dogmeat and cat juice trade that flourishes today in South Korea'. Similar demonstrations were launched by animal activist organizations in South Africa, Britain and the United States in attempts to use this global sports event to increase pressure on South Korea to put an end to what was seen by some as a 'barbaric culinary practice'.

Shortly afterward, as news media reported Norway's plans to resume the export of minke whale meat to Japan, Greenpeace launched a campaign to convince major international airlines to refuse to carry Norwegian whale exports, with an aim of securing a blockade of international trade. The power of such campaigns should not be underestimated. In Britain, an increased demand for Australian kangaroo as a safe alternative to beef after the outbreak of BSE was effectively curbed in 1998 as Viva! (Vegetarians International Voice for Animals) stepped up their campaigns against what they saw as a massive wildlife massacre. After extensive negative publicity, major British supermarket chains stopped supplying kangaroo meat, while the Australians increased their markets elsewhere.

These campaigns represent three different examples of transnational political activism that seeks to prevent certain animals from entering the commodity chain – that is, from being killed and consumed as meat. In other words, commonplace transformations from animal to edible were challenged on a transnational level. Classifications of food and edibility are intimately connected to cultural distinctions between society and nature, or between humans and animals, and linked to questions about what it means to be a morally responsible human being. In this chapter, I argue that these three campaigns all endorse a Euro-American view of human-animal relations on a global scale. I argue that such transnational activism implicitly promotes a universal morality which leaves little room for cultural variation.

My argument also concerns the emergence of what we may refer to as global food taboos, and their political enforcement at a transnational level. Why is it that certain ideas about what to eat and what to avoid travel so easily across the world? Why is it that some people's cultural notions that certain animals should be singularized gain such a momentum and suddenly become important to others?

The international campaigns against the consumption of dogs, whales and kangaroos are three ethnographic cases that could have been analysed in their own right. In this chapter, I will primarily draw attention to certain common dimensions: the globalization of particular classifications of nature and the human-animal relation, and the moral implications of this process for the distinction between animals that are edible and animals that are not. In this way I hope to enhance our understanding of what makes such campaigns so powerful.

In this analysis I use internet material and the media as my primary sources of data, while I rely on published ethnographic studies for contextual detail. I am particularly indebted to Walraven (2002) for his analysis of the Korean consumption of dogs, to Kalland (2001, 2002) and Einarsson (1993) for their analyses of anti-whaling campaigns, and to Morton (1990) for an analysis of the role of the kangaroo in Australian popular culture.

Food Taboos

Food taboos have been a central topic in the anthropology of food and a source of theoretical controversy (Leach 1964; Douglas 1975; Harris 1974). The term *food taboo* has been used by anthropologists and nutritionists alike to classify the wide range of instances in which substances that could potentially be consumed (and are of potential nutritional value) are avoided or classified as inedible. Typically, practices described as food taboos are those in which the avoidance of certain substances is deliberate and involves some degree of reflection by those involved. Sometimes, such reflections are triggered simply by the presence of an outsider, or by the awareness that things could have been otherwise. It is therefore useful to make a distinction between the terms *food avoidance* and *food taboo*: while *avoidance* denotes all acts of not eating something that could have been digested, the term *taboo* denotes those cases in which there is a conscious or premeditated act of avoidance .[1]

Because food is such a powerful medium for expressing group identity and social differentiation, the explicit avoidance of particular foods is an effective means to establish boundaries between self and others. Furthermore, food avoidance is sometimes associated with social rejection, and the act of refusing to eat something that others enjoy has the potential of disrupting social relations, even when that is *not* the intention.

Food avoidance is symbolically meaningful only insofar as it becomes the object of reflection. The fact that guinea pigs rarely appear on European dinner tables does not reflect any strong sense of social community; rather, it is a culinary option that is simply not considered. Thus avoidance of certain foods may be practiced without ever becoming a food taboo. However, as Europeans are confronted with the Ecuadorian culinary specialty '*el cuy*' (guinea pig) the edibility of guinea pigs may be considered, and if one chooses not to take part, what was previously a food avoidance becomes a food taboo.

Most people are surrounded by a wide range of technically edible substances that are never transformed into food, most of which never even enter the realm of substances classified as food. We are all selective eaters, but we are selective in culturally different ways. With intensified experiences of travel, migration and cross-cultural integration, one might expect that substances that are not classified as food either become edible or become the object of deliberate reflection and thus enter the realm of food taboos. Such transformations are the topic of this chapter.

In the three campaigns that are analysed below, the term *food taboo* is generally not used by the campaigners themselves. Rather, the campaigns focus on animal suffering[2] and animal rights, marine resources (whales), and environmental sustainability (kangaroos and whales). Yet, in spite of these overt concerns, the conflicts are for a large part played out in relation to the transformation of animal flesh to meat, a transformation which invariably implies a process of commoditization (Kopytoff 1986). As they seek to disrupt the production–consumption chain by challenging the use of animal flesh as meat, the construction or dissemination of a de facto food taboo becomes either a focus of the campaign, or – if the campaign is successful – one of its results. By analysing these cases as transformations from local cases of food avoidance to transnational food taboos, I wish to illuminate aspects of hegemony and power that are rarely addressed in research on transnational activism.

The World as a Political Arena: Nature as a Political Object

The main players in the campaigns against the commoditization and consumption of dogs, whales and kangaroos belong to the broad category of largely transnational activist networks[3] operating relatively independently of the nation state (Appadurai 2001). Often referred to as 'globalization-from-below', such networks are characterized by organizational structures that transcend the immediate locations of their members (Edelman 2001). According to UN estimates, the number of such associations was around 50,000 in the mid-1990s (Beck 1996).

Many networks make extensive use of the internet. However, the internet is more than a technological tool: it provides a space for political mobilization which is simultaneously a prerequisite for the activist network itself. Through the use of e-mail petitions and the production and maintenance of websites that are both informative and emotionally evocative, activists are able to draw upon and mobilize what we may describe as a transnational 'civil society'. Following Miller and Slater (2000) I suggest that we approach these networks as embedded in other social spaces, and thus inseparable from localized activities. Such activities may involve multi-sited demonstrations, TV performances, consumer boycotts or lobbying. I suggest that it is precisely the capacity of web-based technology to constitute a reality that is continuous with, yet slightly different from localized experiences, that accounts for the political significance of transnational activist networks.

Transnational activism is particularly important in environmental politics as a response to a growing understanding that environmental problems tend to operate on a global scale and require global solutions. As Kay Milton has argued, the identification of the human environment with the entire globe is closely linked to the idea of humanity as a single moral community (Milton 1996: 176). This implies that the experience of 'nature' under threat is, in most cases, a mediated experience, facilitated by images, statistics and text, and – not least – by the visual icon of the planet Earth, itself a symbol of global unity and shared vulnerability (Franklin et al. 2000). Through the use of global media (including the internet) we are invited to identify with environmental problems and animal suffering manifested *elsewhere*, usually far beyond the immediate surroundings of the people who actively campaign. The idea that humans are collectively responsible for what is increasingly perceived as a single ecosystem is crucial, as it provides the justification for sanctioning environmental practices of other people living in other places. As Macnaghten and Urry (1998) note, such transnational activist networks may therefore represent a 'new space for collective agency' and may eventually imply a 'transformed governance of global nature' (1998: 274–5; see also Sassen 2000).

Tactics used in the campaigns described below include both the participation in formal international fora (for example at public hearings and international meetings) and more informal strategies, such as demonstrations, boycotts, petitions, the enrolment of celebrities' testimonies and other strategies that mobilize individuals or put corporations and political institutions under pressure. Most activists refrain from the use of violence, but some apply physical force as part of their media tactics (cf. Sea Shepherd's direct interference in whaling activities).

Global sports events represent prime arenas for transnational activist networks seeking global attention and support. South Korea's hosting of the Summer Olympics in 1988 and of the World Cup Football Championships in 2002 were highlights in this regard. As we shall see, such events represent golden opportunities for activists to exploit the desire of sponsors, transnational sports organizations and national leaders to 'look good' and to appear to act responsibly vis-à-vis a global audience. In this context, the process of shaming is particularly important. This is salient in the campaign against dogmeat in South Korea, and demonstrates how the evocation of emotions such as disgust or revulsion may serve as a powerful tool in negotiating shame in international relations.

Rhetoric of Shame: Dog Meat in South Korea

In the South Korean case,[4] campaigns against the consumption of dogs are for a large part structured as an attack by 'the Civilized World' on a 'barbarian culture'. This is particularly evident in the web-material by international activists, which typically includes statements such as 'Koreans are barbarians who eat dog meat' (www.peta-online.org cited by Anti Dogmeat Movement Headquarters, www.admh.org), 'Korea – the sadistic country' (www.animals-hope.org), 'Korea is to cats & dogs what Hitler was to Jews' (www.animals-hope.org), and The Civilized World is disgusted at the thought of people eating 'Man's Best Friend' (www.dogbiz.com). To a considerable extent, the attacks on Korean consumption of dogmeat may be read (and are read) as attacks on Korean national culture, in spite of the fact that the consumption of dogs is not a very common activity in South Korea. According to a recent South Korean national survey, a majority of the respondents had never eaten dogmeat, or had tasted it only once or twice (Walraven 2002). When dogmeat *is* consumed, it is in part for medicinal purposes, prepared as a soup or invigorating tonic, and ceremonially associated with particular seasons (Walraven 2002: 102). However, within the discourse of the anti-dogmeat movement, the horror is hardly alleviated by reference to frequencies. Rather, the consumption of dogs evokes a very strong adversary reaction. Rhetorically, all South Koreans are made collectively responsible for the occasional practices of some.

The South Korean response to the anti-dogmeat campaigns took the shape of two opposing positions. On the one hand, there are the Korean animal activists, such as the KAPS (Korea Animal Protection Society) who are currently working to implement a new law to protect companion animals (dogs and cats) from being butchered.[5] This organization generally supports the view promoted by transnational animal activists. Like them they describe the eating of dogs as 'atrocious acts' – comparable to slavery and cannibalism – and argue that there is 'no place [for it] in modern society' (www.dogbiz.com/korean-dog-news .html). On the other hand there are those who feel that such critical remarks by foreigners result from their lack of understanding of Korean history and Korea's 'unique culinary custom', and interpret the criticism as an insult to all Koreans. In this category, we find both South Korean politicians[6] and groups organizing on-line petitions through the web (e.g. www.noorung.org)[7] arguing that the 'national and cultural integrity has been violated by [campaigners'] remarks'. Their key argument is first that dogmeat does not necessarily involve animal abuse (ethical slaughtering methods exist), and secondly that the killing of dogs is not essentially less morally justifiable than for example the killing of cows in France. The website makes a plea for a rational discussion, and even more for the acceptance of cultural diversity. In other words, attacks are countered by reference to a universal ethics of cultural relativism.

Between these two positions, there is an interesting middle ground which tries to uphold South Korea's honor as a modern nation by establishing a distinction between the shameful practices of the past, and a globalized modern South Korea. A typical example is the letter issued by the South Korean Embassy in the US and signed by Onhan Shin, the Counsellor of Health and Welfare, as a response to the criticism that the embassy receives. In the letter, emphasis is placed upon the marginal role of dogmeat in Korean daily life. According to the letter it is consumed very rarely, by very few people, and has been 'a marginal culinary tradition for generations'. The letter points out how South Korean society is changing fast as people experience tastes and influences from around the world, and argues that the 'Korean interest in the consumption of dogmeat, already marginal and exotic, will diminish further' (www.koreananimals.org/embassy.htm). Implicitly, the understanding of dogmeat as an old custom that has no place in the modern nations of the world is thus accepted. Rather than defending Korean cultural practice, the letter is a plea to be patient with South Korea, a country still in the process of becoming a morally accountable modern state. In other words, the process of shaming Korea has been successful, and the unsuitability of dog as meat is accepted.

Dogmeat is tabooed precisely because dogs have been domesticated in Europe and North America as a companion animal, pet or friend. Whale and kangaroo, on the other hand, are part of a charismatic mega fauna, previously hunted, but recently singled out as representations of a wilderness worthy of our protection. While dogmeat represents the violation of a deeply rooted and *already existing* food taboo among Euro-Americans, whale meat and kangaroo meat are rather *food taboos in the making*.[8] This could account for the emotional strength of the attacks against the Koreans, and for the partial submission of the official South Korean institutions to criticism from the West.

Located at opposite ends of the continuum between the domesticated and the wild, campaigns against dogmeat on the one hand and whale and kangaroo meat on the other might appear as entirely different phenomena. In the following, I shall argue that it is not that simple. In fact, a closer look at the campaigns against kangaroos and whales shows that all campaigns enforce a sense of moral responsibility by playing upon consumption of an image of dogs, whales and kangaroos as having human-like characteristics. Most importantly, all three campaigns appeal to our responsibility as 'global citizens' to act in accordance with certain allegedly universal distinctions between right and wrong. Let us first turn to the case of whales.

Our Brethren of the Sea: Anti-whaling Campaigns

When the International Whaling Commission (IWC) voted to stop commercial whaling in 1982, it was claimed that a temporary moratorium was needed until they had more information about the conditions of whale stocks, and until a new management scheme had been adopted (Kalland 2002: 207). Since then, there has been a general agreement that the stocks of minke whale are large enough to be sustainably harvested in the North Atlantic and in the Antarctic. In the meantime, a so-called revised management procedure has been developed, and has been recommended by the IWC's scientific committee. In spite of this, the moratorium has not been lifted by the IWC, and the IWC does not follow the advice of its own scientific committee to implement the revised management procedure. This is part of the reason why Norwegian whalers resumed commercial whaling in 1993. In 2001, Norwegian whalers caught about 550 minke whales, and in 2002 attempts were made to resume export of whale meat to Iceland and to Japan.

For the transnational anti-whaling activists – of which Greenpeace is probably the most prominent – the aim is, however, not *only* to protect the whales from extinction, but also to stop whaling altogether, through the establishment of a 'global whale sanctuary' (www.whales.greenpeace.org). This is the result of what Kalland (2001) has described as a significant shift in the anti-whaling discourse from a concern with ecology and sustainability to a concern with morality and animal rights.

In the early 1970s, when whales became a key issue in the environmental movement, the problem was defined in terms of environmental sustainability, and the initial solutions were sought within the realm of what was seen as scientifically informed knowledge. In the late 1980s, as more scientific evidence became available, a limited and carefully controlled whaling of certain species (e.g. the minke whale) became – at least in theory – a sustainable option. However, at the same time the focus of the debate changed, as scientific-based arguments gradually gave way to arguments based on moral or ethical concerns (Kalland 2001, 2002). Thus as Kalland points out, it was not difficult for the president of the Cetacean Society International to admit (around 1990) that science provided meagre support for the argument of extinction. 'Our arguments' he claimed 'now focus on ethical, aesthetic, and moral reasons for the protection of the individual whale, not the population or the species' (Shields 1992). A similar shift was evident about the same time in other organizations (for example the WWF and the US Marine Mammal Commission, cf. Kalland 2001), and even within the IWC (Einarsson 1993; Kalland 2001). In other words, there was a shift from what appeared as a scientifically informed effort to protect selected species, to an ethically informed effort to protect individual whales. Current websites of major anti-whaling campaigns provide numerous examples of the latter, and offer regular updates on the lives of individual whales, such as Springer, an 'orphaned orca transported from the waters of Washington State to be reunited with her family off Vancouver island' and her adoption by a whale known as Spike, who is the daughter of Sharky, who died in 1997 (www.wdcs.org.).

So what is going on? First, as many authors have pointed out, this is an example of the strategic use of anthropomorphism.[9] Kalland describes how the anti-whaling rhetoric has created an image of a 'super-whale' by lumping together traits found in a number of different species, masking the great variety that exists among the 75 species of cetaceans (Kalland 2002: 209). In this way, all traits that we would like to see in our fellow humans (playfulness, caring, kindness, having a family) and other traits that may call for special treatment (being the largest animal on earth, having the largest brain, being endangered) are combined to create an image of whales in general as morally and intellectually superior beings.

Secondly, the whale itself has become a symbol of the environmentalist movement (Kalland 2001; Einarsson 1993). As a prominent figure in the anti-whaling movement pointed out: 'If we can't save the whale we can't save anything' (quoted in Einarsson 1993:80). At the same time, the whale *as a symbol* has become a commodity within the environmental movement, and a basis for fund-raising activities. 'Adopt-a-whale' and other programs offer sponsorships to businesses that want to display a 'green image' (Kalland 2002). For transnational corporations, such sponsorships are ways of demonstrating environmental concern at a low cost, as the burden of a total stop of whaling practices will only be felt by very few and politically marginal groups of people.

To summarize, the campaigns against the commoditization of whales are *not* only about saving threatened whales from extinction. If that were the case, the revised management procedure would probably have been adopted several years ago. Instead, the recent and ongoing debate indicates that the rhetoric used in anti-whaling campaigns is just as much an effort to present an alternative perspective on the position of whales in nature, an effort to singularize the whales as different from other species, and to reconfigure the relationship between humans and whales. In other words, anti-whaling campaigns – like anti-dogmeat campaigns – are critically engaged reflections on the human-animal relation. As such they are culturally based reflections upon Nature.

Hunting the 'Friend Ever True': The Case of Australian Kangaroos

Kangaroos[10] have been a source of food in Australia for thousands of years, and the European invasion did not significantly change that. In spite of the fact that they became the totemic emblem of the Australian nation-state, kangaroos were still prey to hunters and kangaroo meat is still part of the Australian menu.

For Europeans whose knowledge of kangaroos is influenced by the children's TV series about 'Skippy' – the animal companion of a freckled Australian boy – the presence of kangaroo on Australian dinner tables may seem a bit odd. In the TV series, 'Skippy' the 'bush kangaroo' is not only a great playmate for a kid on a remote Australian outpost, he is also intelligent and caring, undoubtedly 'a friend ever true'. This image as a child's companion is also a recurrent theme in several Australian children's stories, including the famous *Dot and the Kangaroo* by Ethel Pedley published in 1899 (Morton 1990).The physical appearance of kangaroos serves to strengthen their resemblance with humans: Kangaroos place their weight on their two hind legs, which gives them an upright position. The pouch of a female kangaroo, which is vital for its offspring's survival, strengthens the image of the adult kangaroos as a protective and caring species, and evokes a certain resemblance with human nursing practices.

In the Australian bushland, kangaroos are neither pets nor friends, but part of the Australian native wildlife often referred to as 'charismatic mega fauna'. As native wildlife they have been hunted, shot and eaten by the Europeans since the days of Captain Cook.[11] But during the same period, they have also been counted, managed and legally protected. In fact, fears that kangaroos may become extinct were expressed as early as in 1822 (Low 2001), and comprehensive management programs are now established in order to 'ensure conservation . . . by promoting harvesting which is ecologically sustainable' (www.ea.gov.au/biodiversity). Such management plans represent efforts to deal with what is increasingly seen as a problem in the Australian bush: namely the high density of kangaroos in certain areas. Having proliferated as a result of the transformation of bush to pasture, kangaroos now represent a major threat to grazing and farming properties. In and around national parks, their easy access to water and protection from human and non-human predators have allowed kangaroos to increase their numbers. As a result, kangaroos are now seen to represent a major threat to several native plants, and thus a threat to biodiversity (Low 2001). This is the background for the Australian management plan which sets an annual harvest quota of 4–6 million kangaroo per year. This, in turn, provides the legal framework for an export-oriented kangaroo industry promoting both meat and leather to countries overseas.

The BSE crisis in Great Britain in 1996, followed by the European ban on British beef, may have appeared as a golden opportunity for Australian exporters struggling to promote kangaroo on the European market. British consumption of

beef fell dramatically and, for a while, game that had been raised in remote surroundings was in high demand (Lien 1997). However, the success of kangaroo
meat in Britain turned out to be brief, as Viva! soon launched a massive campaign
to stop the sales of kangaroo meat from supermarkets in the UK. The campaign
involved demonstrations and extensive use of the internet, and was very successful: By 1999 all major supermarkets had withdrawn kangaroo from their
shelves, and Australian export of kangaroo meat to the UK fell from a million-
dollar industry to nearly nothing.[12] Since then, the Viva! campaigns have shifted
attention from the use of meat to the use of kangaroo skin by suppliers of footballs
and football boots. Adidas has now become a main target, along with their spon-
sored world champion player David Beckham, while major world football championships have become triggers for transnational political events.

Viva's campaign focuses primarily on the cruelty involved in the hunting of kangaroos. Calling attention to the 'largest massacre of wild land animals the world
has ever known' the Viva! home page turns directly to a vivid description of the
death of a kangaroo and her joey. The introduction reads:

> Imagine this. A mother kangaroo with her beautiful joey at night in the vast outback.
> It's a scene millions of years old. What's new is the roar of a four-wheel drive. She turns
> towards the noise and is transfixed by a searchlight. A rifle cracks and a bullet tears a
> hole in her neck. She falls, in pain and unable to save her joey, who retreats into her
> pouch for safety. The first thing the hunter does is to search the pouch and, feeling a
> joey inside, pulls him out. The hunter tosses him to the ground and stamps on his head.
> The joey writhes in agony. The mother struggles as her leg is slit open and a hook
> inserted through it. She is hauled up on to the truck and slowly dies. The scene is
> repeated all night long. Older joeys frantically hop away when their mother's are shot
> – to die a slow and lonely death from cold or starvation. This is the reality of kangaroo
> killing. But the killing continues. (www.savethekangaroo.com)

Viva! also questions the validity of the scientific evidence underpinning the
Australian management plans, but this is not their main focus. Rather than discussing sustainable management of Australian wildlife, the campaigns use the case
of the kangaroos to expose one of the most fundamental ethical dilemmas involved
in the consumption of meat – that is, the need to kill in order to consume. In this
way, the campaign against the consumption of kangaroos is simultaneously an
invitation to consider the suffering of animals. The killing of mother and joey represents, as it were, the killing of all animals, and serves to mobilize a sentiment
against the consumption of meat, which is the main foundation of the organization
Viva!

The most important strategy applied by Viva! appears to have been the mobilization of British consumers against supermarket chains in the UK. Following a
series of demonstrations outside supermarkets, Tesco, Sainsbury and Safeway gave

in to Viva!'s requirements. The effectiveness of this strategy must be seen in light of the fact that kangaroo was a peripheral product in the British meat counters in the first place. Thus, removing kangaroo from the shelves could be done without a significant loss to the supermarket chain.

Unlike the campaign against dogmeat in South Korea, the Viva! campaign did not primarily blame Australians. To the extent that Australian parties were blamed, the criticism was directed at the industry and at the Australian government, while the Australian public was mostly called upon simply for support. Furthermore, unlike the Korean case, it was the potential expansion of markets overseas that was the primary concern, while domestic consumption received less attention.

The Viva! campaign hits Australia on a sore spot. Hunting a national emblem is clearly problematic, and the legal commercial culling of kangaroos is fraught with ambivalence (Morton 1990). In Australia, the conservationist movement is divided. While many environmental organizations support a regulated commercial harvesting of kangaroos,[13] the animal rights organization Animal Liberation opposes the culling on ethical grounds, and the Australian Wildlife Protection Council questions the sustainability of culling from a scientific perspective. However, the Australian websites are generally less evocative than Viva! Rather than focusing primarily on the kangaroo hunt as a cruel act, they point for example to the disadvantages of kangaroo meat from a cost-benefit perspective, the uncertainty of scientific guidelines and the effects of selective killing of large animals on the kangaroo population (cf. http://www.animalliberation.org.au/commuseum.html and http://www.awpc.org.au). Thus, while the Viva! position reflects an unconditional ethical principle against the killing of kangaroo, the Australian debate is more nuanced. In this way, the harvesting of kangaroo in Australia differs from whaling by Norwegians and Japanese, which seem to a greater extent to escape the public attention in the respective home countries, and seldom trigger massive protests at a local or national level. Nevertheless, the campaign against the commoditization of kangaroos is yet another case in which a local classification of an animal as food is challenged and politicized on a transnational level. Thus, the case is also a battle over the proper ways of perceiving and engaging with nature.

Transnational Politics and Global Food Taboos

The campaigns against the consumption of dogs, whales and kangaroos are all part of the broad category of transnational activist networks often referred to as 'grassroots globalization' or 'globalization-from-below' (Falk 1993; Appadurai 2001).[14] In contemporary literature on globalization, such transnational networks are seen as a significant form of civil resistance against more institutionalized forms of global power such as world capitalism. Appadurai maintains, for instance, that successful transnational activist networks are seen by many as having the potential to offset the effects of runaway capital (Appadurai 2001: 17). This view concurs with the general image of transnational activist networks as democratic, non-hierarchical and anti-elite. Thus, transnational activist networks may be seen as filling a gap with regard to global corporate accountability, as they serve to impede forces of economic globalization that are beyond the reach, politically, of any single nation state. However, a closer analysis of the three cases (campaigns against use of meat from dogs, whales and kangaroos) reveals that what appears as a 'bottom-up' battle of transnational civil society against transnational economic forces, is, in fact, much more complicated. In order to evaluate the counter-political power of such campaigns we need to unpack targets, tactics and alliances, and we need to make a distinction between campaign tactics and long-term objectives.

All three cases involve protests against the practice of killing and consuming certain animals. Yet their respective long-term objectives differed: While the anti-dogmeat campaigns focused simply on preventing the killing and consumption of dogs, the anti-whaling campaign served in addition as a flagship of the environmental movement. The campaign against the killing of kangaroos, in turn, had vegetarianism as an overarching objective. In spite of these differences, the focus on the need to protect certain animals from entering the commodity chain remains a shared explicit aim. In order to achieve this, arguments were underpinned by rhetorical strategies which tended to expose instances of cruelty and animal suffering while at the same time highlighting resemblances between the animals and human beings. In this way, species that are generally associated with the wild (whales, kangaroos), were symbolically transformed into pets, companions or close kin – what Leach (1964) would refer to as the creatures of the house. Bypassing the realm of domestication which most clearly implies edibility, whales and kangaroos are thus reclassified from being wild game or prey to being human-like creatures in need of protection.

Such processes of reclassification are aptly captured by the term 'ontological politics' (Mol 1999). If 'ontology' defines what belongs to the real, or the conditions of possibility we live with, then 'ontological politics' suggests that the conditions of possibility are not given, or, as Mol writes: 'That reality does not precede the mundane practices in which we interact with it, but is rather shaped within these practices' (Mol 1999: 74–5). Defining an animal as unfit for human consumption is a particularly powerful way of redefining reality, precisely as it contests the classification of food: Intimately linked to the body and the self, food is an effective medium for expressing identity and social differentiation, and for mobilizing strong emotions (Lupton 1996). In a sense then, the symbolic transformations of kangaroo and whales from (edible) game to (inedible) companions may be seen as a way of fueling environmentalist arguments with evocative concerns that are more intimately linked with notions of morality than with the far more sober scientific-based argument about sustainability. The transnational enforcement of food taboos may thus be analysed as a strategy which has the effect of mobilizing even stronger support for key environmental issues.

How are these transformations achieved? In order to mobilize public support on a transnational level, issues must be presented in a way that emphasizes a clear enemy and a sense of urgency (Kalland 2002). This is not always easy. Dogs have been consumed in Korea for generations, and hardly represent an ecologically threatened species. Certain species of whales, by contrast, *are* threatened and this provides the sense of urgency. But who is the enemy? In the case of kangaroos, the question of sustainable management is contested, and may thus substantiate claims for urgency. However, as the issue is highly controversial, the question is who is to blame?

Those who actually perform transformations of dogs, whales and kangaroos into meat are neither transnational nor particularly powerful actors. In the case of Viva!'s crusade against the commoditization of kangaroo, one of the enemies is 'Lenah Game Meats', a relatively small Tasmanian meat producer that tries to make a living through the export of wallabies within a state with high unemployment. Similarly, when Greenpeace's anti-whaling campaigns try to obstruct Norwegian whaling, the implications are most strongly felt among a small network of fishermen in a remote part of Northern Norway. South Korean suppliers of dogmeat are hardly more powerful, struggling to make profit on what is by now a fairly peripheral commodity. Yet, with the exception of Sea Shepherd's confrontations with whalers at sea, the campaigns rarely mobilize directly against these parties. Instead, they enroll, as we have seen, far more powerful transnational and national corporations and organizations as 'co-conspirators' on the enemy's side. By shaming, blaming or boycotting FIFA, Lufthansa or Tesco, campaigns seek to hold these corporations indirectly responsible for activities that are, in fact, only marginally connected to their business activities. Yet, precisely because these activities *are* marginal, a corporate decision to comply with the campaigners' demands can be made at a low cost, or even represent an opportunity for boosting the company's image. Thus by enrolling transnational companies in the battle, the activists not only enroll actors that evoke bottom-up, anti-elite feelings among the general public, they enroll actors that are acutely aware of the importance of a good public image, and also large enough to make decisions that could make a difference.

To the extent that consumer boycotts are involved, such transnational activism could be seen as the victory of the consumer as a political agent, and thus as a partial alleviation of what is often referred to as a 'democratic deficit' in world politics and global capitalism (cf. Miller 1995). However, as we have seen, the relation between victory and defeat (or between accuser and accused) is far more complex. What was essentially a conflict between certain activists and a range of small or medium-sized local meat suppliers is transformed, through campaign tactics, into a conflict between consumers and transnational corporations. Sensitive to world opinion, such organizations cannot afford to ignore the implications of 'losing face'. Thus, what appears as a victory of transnational activists against 'global capital' may in fact turn out to be the victory of a hegemonic Euro-American view of the human-animal relation at the expense of more marginal local views.

The emergence of transnational campaigns contesting the routes of certain animals through the commodity chain represents another turn in the globalization of food politics, as they target actors at a cultural and geographic distance. Yet, there is hardly any space for foreign diplomacy. Instead, the conflict is played out in relation to a public of largely Euro-American consumers, often without the presence of the accused. Thus, the cultural context of the accused remains blurred, and the cultural significance involved in the acts exposed as bad practice is rarely allowed to surface in the debate. Consequently, what may appear on the television screen as British consumers' victory over large corporations such as Tesco, of air-travelers' fight against European airlines, or of a global civil society fighting transnational companies such as Adidas are, in fact, examples of cross-cultural conflicts masquerading as protests against 'world capitalism'.

Mononaturalism and Multiculturalism

Recent theories of nature and society remind us that nature is socially and culturally constructed. There is no singular nature as such, only natures – and such natures are historically, geographically and socially constituted (Macnaghten and Urry 1998: 15). Through its historical emergence on the North Atlantic rim two key characteristics of the idea of nature may be singled out. First, the concept of nature emerged in opposition to the concept of society. According to Macnaghten and Urry, the juxtaposition of society and nature was most fully developed in the nineteenth century, and formed the basis for the idea of wilderness in England, North America and Australia, where wilderness presupposes a minimum of human interference. It was also the basis for modern natural sciences: the study of nature became the study of a reality set apart, and the laws of nature became the laws of physics and biology (Macnaghten and Urry 1998: 10–11; see also Latour 1993, 2002).

The second characteristic of the cultural construction of nature on the North Atlantic rim is that nature, once it was set apart from society, was attributed with a range of fundamental values, and became the object of worship. Following the romantic movement and the industrial revolution, the term 'unnatural' became a way of describing the ill-effects of urbanization, markets and immoral behavior. Nature became, and is still regarded as a guide and a source of beauty and truth, as exemplified through the anti-whaling campaigns. Lately, this perception of nature has been associated with vulnerability, and has given rise to sentiments of responsibility (Macnaghten and Urry 1998: 12–15).

Our perception of Nature is continuously maintained, re-enacted and negotiated through our relationship with – and classification of – animals. Thus, the presence of food-avoidance practices or of food taboos is based upon culturally defined classifications within the overarching order through which we perceive and interpret Nature and our place in relation to it. As I have tried to emphasize, these are not universal perceptions of nature, but cultural perceptions that have emerged at a specific time and place – that is, on the North Atlantic rim during the last few centuries. Why then, is it that this view appears to gain such momentum just now, and from where does it derive its power to affect or shame nations and people who do not necessarily subscribe to such views in the first place?

One of the unique achievements of modernity, according to Latour (2002) is that it bestows us with the belief that *we* are people with privileged access to reality. While other people see natures through their various cultural representations, *we* are able to grasp Nature objectively. Boosted with scientific achievements, we believe our perceptions of Nature to be valid way beyond our immediately experienced surroundings. We not only believe to know how to sustainably manage whales in the Antarctic oceans or kangaroos in vast Australian bushlands, we even know when Koreans are trespassing a moral boundary that they themselves don't even see.

According to Latour this notion of a privileged access to Nature, in the singular, is part of the reason why multiculturalism has gained some ground as an ideology in the West. He writes, slightly ironically:

> Different cultures existed, with their many idiosyncrasies, but at least there was only one nature with its necessary laws … Differences of opinion, disagreements and violent conflicts remained, but they all had their source in the subjectivity of the human mind without ever engaging the world, its material reality, its cosmology or its ontology, which by construction … remained intangible. (Latour 2002: 6)

As the examples above show, this truce – this relatively peaceful tolerance of other peoples' natures – is now dramatically threatened. And the contemporary quests are no longer some sort of objective scientific truth against some prescientific symbolic belief. Rather the conflicts are between cultural representations of nature, including on the one hand those who present themselves *as if* having some privileged access to universal truths about Nature in the singular, and on the other hand those whose practices and rhetoric in relation to nature are forever seen as being locked in the 'cultural'. The former includes transnational activist networks, but also social science research to the extent that it ignores the cultural foundation of transnational environmental discourse. The latter includes, among many others, Norwegian whalers, Australian farmers and hunters, and Koreans who like to eat dogmeat. As the environment is increasingly interpreted as a single ecosystem, conflicts involving the power to define Nature are bound to intensify. Through such controversies, food and edibility enter the sphere of politics.

I suggest that it is precisely the symbolic significance attributed to Nature that makes it compelling for transnational activists to engage morally in issues involving planet earth, even if it implies direct interference in the daily practices and livelihood of people living very far away. As long as mononaturalism prevails, an ideology of multiculturalism and cultural tolerance can only be sustained up to a point. When people who live their lives elsewhere interfere with animals and ecosystems that are increasingly interpreted as part of 'our common future', cultural tolerance may yield as a result. The result could be a global order based on a new form of eco-imperialism.

Acknowledgements

This chapter is inspired by ongoing projects that are part of the research program 'Transnational flows of concepts and substances' at the Department of Social Anthropology, University of Oslo. Thanks to program collaborators for good discussions, and to Eivind Jacobsen, Thomas Hylland Eriksen, Marit Melhuus and Brigitte Nerlich for useful comments to an earlier version.

Notes

1. Food taboos may be permanent, or they may be temporary, applying only to certain stages of the life cycle. They can apply to all members of a community, or they can apply to only some. In some cases, the avoidance of certain foods is conditional: some vegetarians will argue that if animals were treated better they would resume eating meat. Others claim an absolute ethical principle with regard to the killing of animals, in which case the avoidance is unconditional (Frey 1983).

2. All campaigns criticize the use of slaughtering methods, many of which are seen as very painful, and many campaigns offer photos and videos to support their claims. I will not elaborate on this theme, as the campaigns are not primarily about improving the methods of hunting or slaughtering (in which case they would be a case of conditional avoidance), but rather aim to put an end to killing as such (see below).

3. Anti-whaling campaigners include Greenpeace, the International Fund for Animal Welfare (IFAW), the Whale and Dolphin Conservation Society (WDCS), the Cetacean Society International (CSI), Sea Shepherd, the Environmental Investigation Agency (EIA), and Save the Planet. Campaigns against Kangaroo-meat were launched by VIVA! (Vegetarians International Voice for Animals) and the World League for the Protection of Animals and

are supported by the Australian Wildlife Protection Council (AWPC) and Animal Liberation. Anti-dog-meat campaigners include In Defence of Animals (IDA), the World Society for the Protection of Animals (WSP), People for the Ethical Treatment of Animals (PETA), People Against Companion Animal Slaughter (PACAS), International Aid for Korean Animals (IAKA), Advocates for Animals and Animals Hope Organization.

4. Information was gathered on the Internet in May and July 2002 by searching the terms 'dog', 'eat' and 'Korea'. In addition to web-based information from the organizations mentioned, I rely on internet versions of newspaper articles, petitions and material accessible via the web-pages www.dogbiz.com, and *Anti-Dogmeat Movement Headquarters*. Similar information gathering strategies were used for the cases of whales and kangaroos, although in these cases my presentation relies even more on the use of published secondary sources.

5. Although the base of supporters of KAPS is relatively small, only 1,800 in a country of more than 46 million people (source: www.koreananimals. org/history.htm), they have overseas support through the international sister organization IAKA (International Aid for Korean Animals). The leader of IAKA, Kyenan Kum, is the sister of the founder and current director of KAPS, Sunnan Kum, who also runs a shelter for stray dogs and cats (www.dogbiz.com/korean-dog-news.html).

6. A prominent figure in this camp is congressman Kin Hong-Shin of the Grand National Party.

7. The term *noorung* is the common Korean term for dogs that are used for foods, as distinguished from dogs used as pets, who have singular names. (source: www.noorung.com).

8. Note, however that the avoidance of dogs and cats as food in Europe is a relatively recent historical phenomenon. I am grateful to Inger Johanne Lyngø for drawing my attention to recent archeological excavations in Bergen which indicate that dogs and cats were consumed in a Hanseatic town in the Middle Ages.

9. Such strategic use of anthropomorphism should not be interpreted too literally, as an indication of blurred boundaries between human and animals. Rather I see it as a rhetorical effort to evoke empathy and moral engagement through the use of human metaphors. In other words, the attribution of what is commonly thought of as human characteristics to mammals may simply reflect an effort to allow a certain degree of subjectivity to species that are not human. I am grateful to María Guzman for bringing my attention to this distinction (cf. Guzman 2003).

10. Kangaroos are also referred to as macropods, of which there are 48 different species, including wallabies, wallaroo and pademelon. In accordance with the terminology used in public debate, I will refer to the macropods in general as kangaroos.

11. According to public surveys in Australia referred to by the industry, more than 50 per cent of all Australians have tried kangaroo meat, while about 75 per cent agree that kangaroos are a valuable source of meat (www.kangaroo-industry.asn.au).

12. Sources: www.savethekangaroo.com/Report/, *Guardian*, 6 March 1999.

13. These include the Australian Wildlife Management Society, the Ecological Society of Australia, and the Wildlife Preservation Society of Australia.

14. The term was introduced by Falk to refer to a global civil society linking 'transnational social forces animated by environmental concerns, human rights, hostility to patriarchy, and a vision of human community based on the unity of diverse cultures seeking an end to poverty, oppression, humiliation, and collective violence' (Falk 1993: 39).

References

Appadurai, A. (2001), 'Grassroots Globalization and the Research Imagination', in A. Appadurai (ed.), *Globalization: A Millennial Quartet Book*, Durham NC: Duke University Press.

Beck, U. (1996), 'World Risk Society as Cosmopolitan Society? Ecological Questions in a Framework of Manufactured Uncertainties', *Theory, Culture and Society*, 13: 1–32.

Douglas, M. (1975), *Implicit Meanings*, London: Routledge.

Edelman, M. (2001), 'Social Movements: Changing Paradigms and Forms of Politics', *Annual Review of Anthropology*, 30: 285–317.

Einarsson, N. (1993), 'All Animals are Equal but Some are Cetaceans', in K. Milton (ed.), *Environmentalism: The View from Anthropology*, London: Routledge.

Falk, R. (1993), 'The Making of Global Citizenship', in J. B. Childs, J. Brecher and J. Cutler (eds), *Global Visions: Beyond the New World Order*, Boston: South End.

Franklin, S., Lury, C., and Stacey, J. (2000), *Global Nature, Global Culture*, London: Sage.

Frey, R. (1983), *Rights, Killings and Suffering*, Oxford: Basil Blackwell.

Guzman, M. (2003) 'Når dyr blir kjøtt' ('When Animals become Meat'), in E. Jacobsen et al. (eds), *Den Politiserte Maten (Politicized Food)*, Oslo: Abstrakt.

Harris, M. (1974), *Cows, Pigs, Wars and Witches: The Riddles of Culture*, New York: Random House.

Kalland, A. (2001), 'Fiendebilder i hvalfangstdebatten' ('Images of Enemies in the Anti-whaling Debate), in A. Kalland and T. Rønnow (eds), *Miljøkonflikter: Om bruk og vern av naturressurser (Environmental conflicts)*, Oslo: Unipub.

—— (2002) [1993], 'Whale Politics and Green Legitimacy: A Critique of the

Anti-whaling Campaign', in J. Benthall (ed.), *The Best of 'Anthropology Today'*, London: Routledge.

Kopytoff, I. (1986), 'The Cultural Biography of Things: Commoditization as Process', in A. Appadurai (ed.), *The Social Life of Things: Commodities in Cultural Perspective*, Cambridge: Cambridge University Press.

Latour, B. (1993), *We Have Never been Modern*, New York: Harvester.

—— (2002), *War of the Worlds: What about Peace?* Chicago: Prickly Paradigm Press.

Leach, E. (1964), 'Anthropological Aspects of Language: Animal Categories and Verbal Abuse', in E. H. Lenneberg (ed.), *New Directions in the Study of Language*, Cambridge: Cambridge University Press.

Lien, M. (1997), 'Nation, technology and nature: Constructions of Safe Food in the Market', in R. Almås (ed.), *Social Construction of Safe Food; Health Ethics and Safety in Late Modernity*, Workshop report no. 5, Trondheim: Centre for Rural Research.

Low, T. (2001), *The New Nature: Winners and Losers in Wild Australia*, Camberswell, Victoria: Viking.

Lupton, D. (1996), *Food, the Body and the Self*, London: Sage.

Macnaghten, P. and Urry, J. (1998), *Contested Natures*, London: Sage.

Miller, D. (1995), 'Consumption as Vanguard of History', in D. Miller (ed.), *Acknowledging Consumption*, London: Routledge.

—— and Slater, D. (2000), *The Internet: An Ethnographic Approach*, Oxford: Berg.

Milton, K. (1996), *Environmentalism and Cultural Theory*, London: Routledge.

Mol, A. (1999), 'Ontological Politics. A Word and Some Questions', in J. Law and J. Hassard (eds), *Actor Network Theory and After*, Oxford: Blackwell.

Morton, J. (1990), 'Rednecks, Roos and Racism; Kangaroo Shooting the Australian Way', *Social Analysis*, 7: 30–49.

Sassen, S. (2000), 'Excavating Power: In Search of Frontier Zones and New Actors', *Theory, Culture and Society*, 17: 63–170.

Shields, L. (1992), 'Be Careful what You Wish for . . .', *Whales Alive!* CSI Publication, 1(2).

Walraven, B. (2002), 'Bardot Soup and Confucians' Meat: Food and Korean Identity in Global context', in K. Cwiertka and B. Walraven (eds), *Asian Food; the Global and the Local*, Hawaii: Curzon/University of Hawaii Press.

–11–

The Political Economy of Food
in an Unequal World

Keith Hart

If you ask why they are not employed, they tell you because commerce is not in the country: they talk of commerce as if it was a man, who comes to reside in some countries in order to feed the inhabitants.

Sir James Steuart, *Principles of Political Oeconomy*

The population of a country in which commodity economy is poorly developed (or not developed at all) is almost exclusively agricultural. This, however, must not be understood as meaning that the population is engaged solely in agriculture: it only means that the population, while engaged in agriculture, itself processes the products of agriculture, and that exchange and the division of labour are almost non-existent.

V. I. Lenin, *The Development of Capitalism in Russia*

The most important item on the agenda of development is to transform the food sector, create agricultural surpluses to feed the urban population and thereby create the domestic basis for industry and modern services. If we can make this domestic change, we shall automatically have a new international economic order.

W. Arthur Lewis, *The Evolution of the International Economic Order*

Introduction: The Problem of Development

All the above authors assumed that development starts, if at all, in a rural world dominated by agriculture, that the economy becomes more differentiated with the growth of towns and that commerce activates exchange between the two. If that is what development is, why is it so difficult today to bring commerce and division of labor to feed the poor countries of our world? After all, half of humanity now lives in cities and, in the twentieth century, even the most backward regions experienced massive urban growth. What did Arthur Lewis mean when he said that, in order for poor countries to develop by the traditional method of domestic rural-urban exchange, it would take nothing less than a world revolution? I will approach this question first through an anecdote (Ottawa, 1982):

> I was once asked my opinion of a Canadian development agency's aid program for rural Mali. They proposed to supply steam-pumps for irrigated rice production, even though dry upland rice is the norm there. I asked why they didn't imitate Western agricultural policies and give the money to the government to subsidize farm-gate prices for rice without raising food prices in the city. Malian farmers would gain an incentive to produce more commercial rice and the risk of urban riots would be averted. The officials thought a bit and eventually agreed that this was the most direct way of stimulating rural development in Mali. Then one of them said, 'Wait a minute! If the farmers in Saskatchewan hear that we are using taxpayers' money to help Third World producers compete with them in the world food market, they will raise hell and get us closed down.'

There are several characteristic features of this story. Inappropriate aid projects geared more to offloading surplus industrial products than to local needs. The idea of paddy rice cultivation as a step forward for Africa. State subsidies to Western farmers, but not to their poor counterparts. The threat of the urban mob being stronger than that of the peasantry. Weak governments obliged to feed their cities at the lowest cost – that is, with subsidized Western food. The power of Western farmers as a political lobby in their own countries. The ineffectiveness of aid bureaucracies. A skewed world market for food. And so on. The result is that farmers in places like Mali cannot compete with foreign suppliers of food and the development of rural–urban exchange there is thwarted. Commerce does not come to feed the inhabitants. How did all this come about and what is needed for it to be changed? Here I will take a long view of the problem in order to throw light on the pathologies of a world society growing more unequal even as humanity has potentially solved the question of food supplies for the first time

We stand poised between agrarian civilization and the machine revolution (Hart 2001). Failure to use technology to make a decisive break with unequal society will ruin us all. We live by a rhetoric of modernity, where democracy and science hold sway. But in reality we are like the first primitive farmers using digging sticks on the way to inventing an agriculture whose potential they could not yet understand. For 5,000 years, the Eurasian land mass was dominated by urban elites ruling agricultural societies. In the last 200 years, the human population has increased six times and the rate of growth of energy production has been double that of the population. Many human beings work less hard, eat better and live longer today as a result. Whereas about 97 per cent of the world's people lived under rural conditions in 1800, half of humanity lives in cities today. This hectic disengagement from the soil as the chief object of work and source of life was made possible by machines, converters of inanimate energy for useful purposes. Before 1800 almost all the energy at our disposal came from animals, plants and human beings themselves. In the process, we have brought humanity together into a much more integrated social network.

World population doubled between 1960 and 2000 (from 3 billion to 6 billion). Countries like France, Japan and Italy were still half peasant in 1945, but by the millennium agriculture accounted for less than 10 per cent of the workforce in all the rich countries. Most of the increase in the world's urban population after 1945 took place in the poor countries. Food production was fully mechanized for the first time and the world now ate the produce of a few heavily subsidized Western farmers. By the end of the century half of the 100 largest economic units on the planet were business corporations, thirty-five of whom had an annual turnover ($30–50 billion) greater than the GNP of all but eight countries. If the world became a single interactive network in this period, it was mainly as a network of markets on which everyone's livelihood now depended in some degree.

Increased human connection has gone hand in hand with escalating inequality. According to the United Nations *Human Development Report* (UNDP 1998), the world's 225 richest men then owned more than a trillion dollars, the equivalent of the annual income of the world's 47 per cent poorest people. The West spent $37 billion a year on pet food, perfumes and cosmetics, almost the additional cost of providing basic education, health, nutrition, water and sanitation for those deprived of them. The rate of car ownership in industrial countries was 400 per thousand, but 16 per thousand in all developing countries. World consumption increased six times in 20 years; but the richest fifth accounted for 86 per cent of it. Almost half the world's people live on less than $2 a day.

Disparities of life experience on the planet are vast. The rich countries, those of the OECD club that includes North America, Western Europe and Japan, account for about 15 per cent of the world's population. The rest must reconcile their relative poverty with an unfinished history of racism, a hangover from the nineteenth century when Westerners used their new machines to take over the globe. Over a third of humanity still works in the fields with their hands; a similar number have never made a phone call in their life. A remote elite of white, middle-aged, middle-class men, 'the men in suits', rules masses who are predominantly poor, dark, female and young. The rich countries, who can no longer reproduce themselves, frantically erect barriers to stem the inflow of migrants forced to seek economic improvement in their midst. In most respects our world resembles nothing so much as the old regime in France before the revolution (Hart 2002).

How could that be? The form of emergent world society is not yet disclosed to us, but the reason it is so unequal stems first from the role of agriculture in human evolution and from agrarian civilization in particular; then latterly from the social forms that emerged to control the machine revolution from the top – public- and private-sector bureaucracies linked by a culture of nationalism. Now there is an attempt to restore classical liberalism as the foundation of world economy; but this favors strong actors over the weak. An earlier mercantilist model of development (Vaggi and Groenewegen 2003) provides a more plausible framework for thinking about global economic realities today. Who provides for the losers in an unequal competition? We need a political economy of food that protects the interests of the weak for the general good. National solutions to economic disaster in mid-century, such as the New Deal and Keynesian macro-economics (Keynes 1936), should be adapted to the scale of world economic problems today. But the hybrid entity that still dominates our world, the nation-state, along with the giant corporations that have flourished under a regime of state capitalism, pose immense difficulties for the achievement of a more equal world society.

Agriculture in Human Evolution

In his *Discourse on the Origins and Foundations of Inequality among Men* (1754) Jean-Jacques Rousseau was concerned, not with individual variations in natural endowments, but with the artificial inequalities of wealth, honor and the capacity to command obedience that he derived from social convention. In order to construct a model of human equality, he imagined a pre-social state of nature, a sort of hominid phase of human evolution in which men were solitary, but healthy, happy and above all free. This freedom was metaphysical, anarchic and personal: original human beings had free will, they were not subject to rules of any kind and they had no superiors. At some point humanity made the transition to 'nascent society', a prolonged period whose economic base can best be summarized as hunter-gathering with huts. This second phase represents his ideal of life in society close to nature.

The rot set in with the invention of agriculture or, as Rousseau puts it, wheat and iron. Cultivation of the land led to property institutions whose culmination awaited the development of political society. The formation of a civil order (the state) was preceded by a Hobbesian war of all against all marked by the absence of law. He believed that this new social contract to abide by the law was probably arrived at by consensus, but it was a fraudulent one in that the rich thereby gained legal sanction for transmitting unequal property rights in perpetuity. From this inauspicious beginning, political society then usually moved, via a series of revolutions, through three stages.

> The establishment of law and the right of property was the first stage, the institution of magistrates the second, and the transformation of legitimate into arbitrary power the third and last stage. Thus the status of rich and poor was authorized by the first epoch, that of strong and weak by the second and by the third that of master and slave, which

is the last degree of inequality and the stage to which all the others finally lead, until new revolutions dissolve the government altogether and bring it back to legitimacy. (Rousseau 1984: 131)

This subversive parable ends with a ringing indictment of economic inequality which could well serve as a warning to our world.

It is manifestly contrary to the law of nature, however defined ... that a handful of people should gorge themselves with superfluities while the hungry multitude goes in want of necessities. (ibid.: 137)

Surely the stale odor of corruption that so revolted Rousseau is just as pervasive today.

The force propelling humanity to a new relationship with the natural world is the use of machines as converters of inanimate energy sources. From a modern perspective, human history seems to be divided into three periods – our own two centuries of mechanization, the ten millennia when agriculture dominated world production and the vast tracts of prehistory before we settled down on the land. Until very recently all economic activity rested on harnessing the energy stored in plants and animals, including the work of human beings themselves (energy fueled by consuming plants and animals). Other inanimate energy sources – water, wind, fossil fuels – and machines driven by them made a negligible contribution. The significance of agriculture lies in the way it changed the balance of human to non-human sources of animate energy deployed in production. Before the invention of agriculture, human beings conserved their own efforts by letting plants and animals do most of the work involved in bringing products to the point of consumption. They moved to the locations where these sources grew naturally, leaving only the tasks of collection and processing to be performed by human labor. People who live this way today ('hunter-gatherers') allow large spaces to accommodate small mobile bands and the food quest does not seem to absorb very much of their time. Marshall Sahlins (1972) has called them 'the original affluent society', rich in leisure because they limit their material wants.

Agriculture is perhaps best thought of as a system of food production in which the growth of plants and animals comes increasingly within the control of human beings. Human work is progressively substituted for natural processes of reproduction. By settling down in one place, human communities are obliged to protect animals and plants from threats to their well-being. The resulting pattern of irrigation, pest-scaring and weeding involves an intensification of labour inputs with diminishing returns. That is, people have to work harder for proportionately less reward. This logic of development through *intensification of labor* would not be freely chosen by producers themselves; and indeed society came to be polarized between the powerful beneficiaries of this system and those who did most of the work. This lent to agriculture a dynamic of inequality that eventually reduced the bulk of the population in most advanced centers to a life of coercion and servitude (slaves and peasants working under varying degrees of unfreedom). Thus the richest civilizations of the world in the late eighteenth century, Western Europe and China, rested on peasantries that could barely stay alive. Chinese peasants were once compared to people standing in a lake with the water fractionally below their noses: the merest ripple and they drown. This was also the time when Robert Malthus (1798) developed a theory of population for Europe in which life and death were regulated by short-term fluctuations in the food supply.

Because we are used to the neat hedgerows and paddy fields of 'civilized' agriculture, it comes as something of a shock to learn that the untidy confusion of so-called 'swidden' agriculture (shifting cultivation of plots often undertaken in semi-cleared forest by tribal peoples) conceals much higher levels of labor productivity, since so much of the work involved is left to natural regeneration and the amount of protection required is less (Conklin 1957). When peasants work for absentee landlords, the emphasis is on maximizing yields from the land area owned, regardless of the drudgery involved in its cultivation. It is a long way from the neolithic revolution (the expulsion from the Garden of Eden) to China's half-drowned peasants. Yet the contrasts of pre-industrial civilization, with splendid urban enclaves erected on the backs of impoverished country-dwellers, are entailed in the origins of domestication. The social forces necessary to bring animals and plants within a sphere of human regulation were also deployed to compel some parts of the population to work harder than their own immediate reward would justify. It took time; but eventually what we take to be civilizations were built on the systematic neglect of the interests of large sections of the workforce.

This argument has obvious affinities with Rousseau's. Like him, I locate the turning point of human history in agriculture as a mode of production. I also join Marx (1867) in supposing that the mechanization of production holds out some hope for humanity. For the machine revolution introduced the possibility of releasing us all from the drudgery of village life, even if, as Marx showed, its immediate consequence was to make matters even worse for many workers. Nevertheless, increased resort to mechanical converters of inanimate energy did reverse the direction of the agricultural regime. Now human beings were able to produce much more for less work; more abundant means have been generated with less back-breaking toil. It is hardly surprising that peasants worldwide have voted with their feet to join the life of greater freedom afforded by machine production in cities. At first, mechanization was almost exclusively an urban phenomenon and slow to penetrate agriculture. In fact people were initially displaced from farming in Britain by horses. Animals also dominated many sectors of transport throughout the nineteenth century, giving rise to the term 'horsepower' as a measure of a machine's strength. Only since 1945 have machines reorganized agriculture in some parts of the world. The pursuit of human freedom, the idea that society is set on a course of material improvement, the rise of modern personality and of subjectivity itself – all this is reinforced by the substitution of inanimate energy sources for human labor.

Agrarian Civilization and State Capitalism

We think of agricultural societies who lack rulers as egalitarian. The majority of them are based on kinship and they only look equal because of the extremes typical of agrarian civilization. Usually age and gender stratify societies organized through kinship, so that older men control the labor and products of women, young men and children (Meillassoux 1981). About halfway through agriculture's dominance of the human economy, some 5,000 years ago in Mesopotamia, there occurred what Childe (1954) called 'the urban revolution'. Small town-like settlements, such as Jericho and Çatal Huyuk, appeared in the Middle East almost as soon as the invention of agriculture. But here, in the lands between the two great rivers, the Euphrates and the Tigris, genuine cities emerged and with them a complex of institutions that we think of as constituting 'civilization'. The majority of people still produced food on the land, but in the new urban settlements and in great houses scattered through the countryside a wholly different lifestyle developed. This involved centralized government, the state and bureaucracy, writing, long-distance trade, markets using money, a complex division of labor, a priestly class and temple organization, landlordism, more elaborate buildings and art – all of it sustained by the transfer to the main centers of agricultural surpluses generated by more intensive technologies, notably the plough and irrigation. The inequality that separated luxurious urban elites from the drudgery of the rural masses became culturally formalized as class distinctions and reproduced through exclusive patterns of kinship and property transmission (Goody 1976).

The leading societies of Europe, the Mediterranean and Asia all grew out of this invention of agrarian civilization and took its original form. Africa south of the Sahara apparently missed out on these developments, even though the continent's northern fringe was one of the first areas to adopt the new institutional package. Childe got the basic framework for his urban revolution from L. H. Morgan's *Ancient Society* (1877) which some have seen as the origin of modern anthropology. This was made more widely accessible by Engels as *The Origin of the Family, Private Property and the State* (1884). But the source of this 'anthropology of unequal society' is still Rousseau.

The history of agrarian civilization hinged on the changing balance of power between city and countryside – that is, on whether military control of the land or money gained from water-borne trade predominated. The struggle for political supremacy between warrior aristocracies and maritime merchants, between property in land and property in money, countryside and city, lasted a thousand years in the ancient Mediterranean – from the Assyrians and Phoenicians, through the Persians and Greeks, the Peloponnesian war and Alexander's conquests, until the Romans, in defeating Carthage, made their world safe for landlords for almost another two thousand years. In that period, all the main Eurasian civilizations ensured by various means that money and markets were kept at the margins of mainstream society (Polanyi 1944; M. Weber 1981). And this was particularly so in feudal Europe, where rural illiterates almost destroyed the cultural legacy of ancient civilization. Starting with the Italian Renaissance and the Northern Reformation, Europe's urban middle classes began a sustained drive to replace this rural society with one reflecting more closely their own interest in commerce. This culminated in the political and intellectual revolutions of the seventeenth and eighteenth centuries. The new science of political economy, inaugurated by Adam Smith (1776), sought to demonstrate that the wealth of nations would grow if revenues were diverted from rents to profits – that is, from the courts of aristocratic land-owners to democracies informally dominated by owners of money, capitalists.

This middle-class revolution looked poised for a decisive victory over agrarian civilization, when its nineteenth-century offspring, industrial capitalism and the nation-state, combined to subvert its original liberal premises. Perhaps the last authentic expression of the liberal revolution was the free-trade movement in Britain, culminating in the 1840s. A wide coalition of capitalists and popular interests, based in Manchester, successfully mobilized to change the corn laws that had hitherto protected British landlords. In the process the Tory Party was split and food prices fell in the face of cheap foreign imports. At this time workers' wages were so closely tied to their food needs that the price of wheat was taken to be a good proxy for labor costs. But the concentration of machine production in a few large cities raised unprecedented problems of crowd control for the traditional rulers. And the capitalists themselves were made sharply aware of the threat posed by both disaffected workers and the 'dangerous classes', criminal gangs who lived in the city largely beyond the law (Asbury 1927).

In the mid-nineteenth century there was almost no intellectual support for the idea that the state could control commercial society. The restless energies of vast crowds, of cities, markets and machines, could hardly be directed from a fixed central point, in the way that small urban elites had extracted surpluses from the slaves and serfs of dispersed agricultural societies. Had not political economy shown that decentralized market economy was a force for development superior to the *dirigisme* of monarchs and their courts? Yet there was already an uneasy accommodation between capitalism and the traditional powers. And, faced with an ungovernable urban workforce, the middle classes thought again and committed to a more whole-hearted alliance with the representatives of agrarian civilization. It is hard to overstate the significance of this shift, a genuine counter-revolution against the principles of the liberal revolution, especially since the hegemonic ideology remained more or less the same.

The grounds for this new phase were already prepared by the rising tide of nationalism. Perhaps as a reaction against the speed of political and technological change induced by the French and industrial revolutions, European societies began to embrace a national logic. Nationalism was an escape from modern history, from the realities of urban commercial life, into the timeless rural past of the *Volk*, the people conceived of as a homogeneous peasantry, living in villages near to nature, unspoiled by social division, the very archetype of a community bound together by kinship. It reflected a dominant worldview that has the whole of humanity pigeonholed as separate tribes, each the owner (or would-be owner) of a hybrid entity, the *nation-state*. In the eighteenth century, before we began to think of ourselves as nations, Western intellectuals compared their societies with the city-states of the ancient world (Thom 1995). Now they fabricated myths of their own illiterate ethnic origins in primeval forests. This cultural move prepared the way for a new class alignment in which the values and lifestyle of rural aristocracies gained new legitimacy alongside the modern movement to embrace money, markets and liberal democracy.

Capitalism always rested on an unequal contract between owners of large amounts of money and those who make or buy their products. This contract depends on an effective threat of punishment if workers withhold their labor or people fail to pay what they owe. The capitalists cannot make that threat alone: they need the support of governments, laws, prisons, police, even armies. Perhaps Karl Marx's most vivid contribution to our understanding of the modern world was his characterization of capitalism as feudalism in drag, with the owners of the means of production still extracting surplus labor from workers under threat of coercion. By the mid-nineteenth century it became clear that the machine revolution was pulling unprecedented numbers of people into the cities, where they added a wholly new dimension to traditional problems of crowd control. Capitalists and the military landlord class now joined together to form states capable of managing industrial workforces, that is, to keep the new urban masses to an unequal labor contract.

This was a stark reversal of the opposition between capitalists and landowners that had fueled the liberal revolution in the seventeenth and eighteenth centuries. Through a series of linked political upheavals in the 1860s (of which the greatest was the American Civil War) all the leading nations in the century to come acquired the institutional basis to control industrial capitalism from the top. Bureaucracies were formed to manage public life and private production. Mass production and consumption shaped new national societies. The majority of the middle classes abandoned their predilection for commerce in order to staff the professions. Out of this compromise between agrarian civilization and the machine revolution came renewed imperialism and the terrible destruction of the twentieth century's wars. The world economy was still in its infancy: in 1870 the share of GNP attributable to international trade was not more than 1 per cent for most countries (Lewis 1978).

I call the phase of world society inaugurated by the revolutions of the 1860s 'state capitalism', the attempt to manage markets and accumulation by means of national bureaucracies. Germany and Japan provided the clearest examples of this new pattern. It became general as a result of the First World War and it may or may not be decaying in the face of globalization today.

Despite a consistent barrage of propaganda telling us that we now live in a modern age of science and democracy, our dominant institutions are still those of agrarian civilization – territorial states, embattled cities, landed property, warfare, racism, bureaucratic administration, literacy, impersonal money, long-distance trade, work as a virtue, world religion and the nuclear family. This is because the rebellion of the Western middle classes against the old regime that gave us the scientific revolution and the Enlightenment, as well as the English, American and French democratic revolutions, has been co-opted by state capitalism and, as a result, humanity's progressive emancipation from unequal society has been reversed in the last century and a half. The myopia of nationalism prevents us from seeing how contemporary world society replicates the old regime from which the liberal revolutions were supposed to have emancipated humanity.

Africa is the most poignant symbol of this unequal world. Having entered the twentieth century with an extremely sparse population and next to no cities, Africans leave it having undergone a population explosion and an urban revolution of unprecedented speed and size. In 1950 Greater Europe (including Soviet Central Asia) had twice the numbers of Africa. Today Africa has a population 120 millions larger than Europe and Central Asia and is projected to be well on the way to double their size by 2010. Although the conventional image of Africa is of starving peasants ravaged by war and AIDS, the new social reality is burgeoning cities full of young people looking for something to do. It is the case that Africa largely missed out on the first and second stages of the machine revolution and is far behind in the present one associated with digitalization. Today development there as likely as not consists of irrigation and ox-plough agriculture. In other words, sub-Saharan Africa, especially in the last half-century, has been going through Childe's urban revolution, erecting state bureaucracies and class society on the basis of surpluses extracted from the countryside. This is not without contradiction, given the pretensions of modern governments, the rapidly expanding population and the widespread failure to mechanize production (Hart 1982).

The USA and Britain recently invaded Iraq, which is of course another name for Mesopotamia. The irony of state capitalism battling to control the original home of agrarian civilization was missed by most commentators. The struggle to displace agrarian civilization from world society is not yet won because state capitalism incorporated its main features into what had been until then the middle-class revolution against the old regime. Consider what happened to all the wealth siphoned off as taxes by Western states since the Second World War, the largest concentrations of money in history. It went on subsidizing food supplies and armaments, the priorities of the bully through the ages, certainly not those of the urban consumers who paid the taxes. No, as Bruno Latour (1993) says, we have never been modern. We are just primitives who stumbled recently into a machine revolution and cannot yet think of what do with it, beyond repeating the inhumanity of a society built unequally on agriculture. This is why agriculture must lie at the core of any strategic attempt to bring about general economic development and world peace.

The Mercantilist Model of Development in a Liberal World Economy

Sir James Steuart was a Jacobite exile who brought the term 'political economy' from France into the English language. His book (1767) was published less than a decade before his countryman's *Wealth of Nations* (Smith 1776) and was quickly overshadowed by it. But Steuart's mercantilist model of economic development was more subtle than Smith's and in many ways more realistic. He was convinced that the successful transformation of an agricultural society required a benevolent and effective state. Conditions in the poor countries today are closer to the economic structures of pre-industrial Europe than to modern Western economies. For Steuart the problem was how to get some farmers off the land so that they could generate demand for commercial foodstuffs supplied by those who remained behind. This meant migration to the city. People complain, he said, about the urban riffraff in Edinburgh and Glasgow; but, as long as this riffraff can exist by any means (we might say, through the 'informal economy', Hart 1973), they provide a market for the country's food farmers. With the money they earn from these sales, the farmers in turn generate demand for the manufactures and services produced in the towns. Rural-urban exchange based on division of labor is the motor of development. But getting there is not easy.

Steuart observed that economies of the sort he was familiar with prospered under a regime of high food prices. These stimulate the bulk of producers, the farmers, to realize a portion of their output as commodities. They need a market of local consumers, protected from cheap imports, and the money they earn will be spent on the products of local industries, provided that they too have some respite from foreign competition, so that they can afford the relatively high costs imposed by local food prices and by their own inexperience. This protected exchange of agricultural and industrial products was necessary in order to generate a dynamic commercial division of labor in a country whose economy was initially backward and stagnant. When the infant commodity-producing sectors grew stronger, they could be exposed to the downward spiral of prices and costs that Adam Smith made so much of, a spiral thought to accompany laisser-faire conditions of international competition. Then the cry would legitimately be for low food prices, thereby reducing the cost of local wage labor and enhancing the competitiveness of some local firms in world markets. This transition is very hard to achieve; but it begins with high agricultural prices. A similar principle underwrote food policy in post-war Europe, but here vast tax surpluses were available to subsidize prices.

Classical liberalism downplayed the protectionist role of states in promoting a system of free-trade that encouraged each country to specialize according to its comparative advantage (Ricardo 1817). But state capitalism led to a synthesis of these two positions, with the big powers competing under the umbrella of a gold standard imposed on world trade by Britain. For a century after the victory of the free-trade movement, Europe – and especially Britain – was fed by the temperate lands of new settlement. But the Second World War interrupted Atlantic sea lanes and devastated the granaries of the East. Starvation was commonplace during and after the war. It is sometimes forgotten that an organization like Save the Children was originally saving European children. The Marshall Plan restored food supplies to some extent; but, when the Western Europeans began to form an economic and political union, regional food security came first on the agenda. The Common Agricultural Policy has notoriously absorbed the bulk of the European budget ever since. The result of so much public money being thrown at farmers was predictable – the mountains of unsold butter and corn that are from time to time dumped at giveaway prices on the world market. These subsidized food surpluses were augmented by the coming at last of the machine revolution to agriculture – not just mechanization, but pesticides and genetic engineering, culminating in the notorious GMOs. What had still been largely a peasant activity in 1945 now became a hi-tech industry combining large amounts of capital with a dwindling but highly productive labor force.

The farmers also revealed themselves to be a particularly effective political force, blocking ports with their equipment and lighting bonfires on motorways. They gained legitimacy as the embodiment of the countryside's distinctive way of life on which national ideology drew so heavily (Gellner 1983). In consequence, despite the overwhelming demographic majority of urban consumers in the rich countries today, the farmers' share of the public purse has been almost untouchable for the last half-century, distorting domestic political economy and, of course, world food markets. They were joined there by the Americans, the Canadians, the Australians and the other countries who fed Europe in the second half of the nineteenth century, but who now had to find other customers, given

Europe's new self-sufficiency in food. Here too the combination of public subsidy and mechanization, allied to the vast open spaces of the prairies, supported a revolution in production that translated into cheap food. Well-publicized famines in the Third World made it seem almost an act of charity to dump food there. Whether sold or donated, cheap food from the West has repeatedly frustrated the development of commercial agriculture in poor countries by pricing local farmers out of the market.

In the nineteenth century, the growth of cities closely followed industry (A. Weber 1899). But recent urbanization in much of the Third World has taken place without substantial industrialization. Instead the concentration of public expenditure in a few large centers of government has drawn massive crowds out of a depressed agriculture. Steuart's urban riffraff can now be counted by the millions and they do sustain themselves in the city, largely by informal means. Here then is the opportunity for the commercial food producers of the hinterland. All that is needed is a temporary regime of high agricultural prices for a classical rural-urban exchange. But food is already available from overseas at giveaway prices. The governments are weak and dependent on foreign creditors, so they have no chance to play the benevolent far-sighted role envisaged by Sir James. They cannot protect their own farmers because Western farmers are so heavily protected. And that includes especially international trade negotiations, where conflict between the Europeans and Americans over food markets is endemic and the interests of the rest are largely neglected.

Arthur Lewis (1978) makes a plausible case that the twentieth-century world economy was constructed as an order of racial inequality in the decades leading up to the First World War. At this time, fifty million Europeans ('whites') left home to settle the temperate zone, while a similar number of Indians and Chinese ('coolies') were shipped to the tropical colonies as indentured laborers. These two streams of migrants had to be kept apart since, although their work was often similar, Europeans were paid nine shillings a day on average and Asians received an average of one shilling per day. In those areas where Asian workers were allowed to settle, the price of local wage-labor was driven down to the same one-shilling level. Lewis goes on to argue that the division of the world by Western imperialism into countries of dear and cheap labor had profound consequences for their subsequent economic development. High-wage economies sustain higher levels of demand than their low-wage counterparts. World trade has been organized ever since in the interests of the better-paid, with tax-rich states subsidizing their farmers to dump cheap food overseas at the expense of local agriculture, while simultaneously preventing the poorer countries' imported manufactures from undermining the wages of industrial workers at home. South Africa and the United States were two countries that allowed heavy immigration of working-class Europeans while seeking to retain a reserve of poorly paid, mainly black labor. The resulting dualism is inscribed on their shared twentieth-century history of racist urbanization (Hart and Padayachee 2000).

Origins of the Neo-liberal Economic Crisis

What is 'new' about neo-liberalism? It is a world economic order based on selective freedom, on the freedom of money to move where it will (but not people, machines, products or information) and on the freedom of strong states to impose their will on the weak. This describes our world well enough, but it could just as well be described as neo-mercantilism and is no newer than the invention of state capitalism a century and a half ago. Then the economic superpower setting the rules for hypocrisy was Britain; today it is the United States. It is hardly surprising that an international economy run by and for states would be unequal. For states were invented in order to supervise the unequal society of agrarian civilization and they were co-opted for their crowd-control functions by owners of money who cloaked coercion and inequality in the old rhetoric of liberal democracy (Polanyi 1944). The state comes with a whole institutional package – a focus on landed property and territorial rule, on the organized use of force at home and abroad, on bread and circuses, on writing and bureaucracy, on control of the money supply and taxation of trade, on ethnic definitions of citizenship and natural symbols of identity. And this does not fit well with freedom of movement, as we all know too well.

Inequality is intrinsic to the functioning of the modern economy at all levels from the global to the local. The rich and poor are often separated physically, kept apart in areas that differ greatly in their standards of living. It is impossible to prevent movement between the two areas in any absolute sense, if only because the rich need the poor to perform certain tasks for them on the spot (especially personal services and dirty work of all kinds). But movement of this sort is severely restricted, by the use of formal administrative procedures (state law) or by a variety of informal institutions based on cultural prejudice. These rest on systems of classification of which racism is the prototype and still the single most important means of inclusion and exclusion. Apartheid is the general name for how we live in world society today (Hart and Padayachee 2000).

There is a great lie at the heart of modern politics. We live in self-proclaimed democracies where all are equally free; and we are committed to these principles on a universal basis. Yet we must justify granting some people inferior rights; otherwise functional economic inequalities would be threatened. This double-think is enshrined at the heart of the modern nation-state. Nationalism is racism without the pretension to being as systematic or global. So-called nations, themselves often the outcome of centuries of unequal struggle, link cultural difference to birth and define citizens' rights in opposition to all-comers. The resulting national consciousness (Fanon 1959), built on territorial segmentation and regulation of movement across borders, justifies the unfair treatment of non-citizens and blinds people to humanity's common interests. So, apart from the state as a social form, one problem to be overcome is its culture. The cultural content of nationalism was made up largely by urban intellectuals who based the idea of national unity on the presumed authenticity of the village (Gellner 1983). Traditional rural society was conceived of as being outside the social forces making the modern world, in both time and space. Rural imagery thus shaped the inner core of a nation aiming to resist the outside forces of modernity by slowing down the changes generated by urban industry and political revolution. Its slogan is 'stop the world, I want to get off'. This is why Western farmers, and agriculture more generally, carry a political weight far beyond their contemporary economic importance (Bryden and Hart 2003). And this too prevents a global solution to world food markets, with countries of the West squabbling among themselves over who subsidizes agriculture the more outrageously. So the world's two billion or more poor farmers continue to be locked out of world markets.

There have been two general crises for global capitalism in the last century, and we may be entering a third now. They were the 1930s and the 1970s (Hardt and Negri 2000; Hart 2001). Each stimulated a major reconstruction of capitalism's political economy and each has shaped the conditions we face now. In the Great Depression, Maynard Keynes (1936) offered a solution (deficit spending) to national elites overwhelmed by the mass of poor and unemployed. Roosevelt's New Deal was the most practical program at the time and the USA promoted welfare-state economies among its industrial allies after 1945. This welfare-state consensus underlay the long postwar boom. The rich minority are today similarly cast adrift in a sea of human misery that includes most people alive, but especially the inhabitants of Africa, India and China. Marx used to say that capitalist markets could not organize machine production for the benefit of society as a whole. Today the world market is supervised by the United Nations and the Bretton-Woods institutions (still dominated by the USA) which likewise inhibit the evolution of more appropriate economic forms. They also prevent the alleviation of world poverty by means of a Keynesian redistribution of purchasing power (Stiglitz 2002).

There is a watershed in postwar history and its moment is the mid-1970s (Hart 2001, chapter 4). Cracks were already beginning to show in the West's postwar boom when the Vietnam War introduced financial instability to world markets. The oil-price rise of 1973 then threw the world economy into a depression from which it has never recovered. If this was bad for the industrial countries, it was a full-scale disaster for the non-oil-producing Third World countries. These had been encouraged by the World Bank and other donors to concentrate on exporting a few primary products. The resulting oversupply kept prices down, while rapid urbanization there raised demand for industrial manufactures. As a result the terms of trade between the two blocs were worsening from the perspective of the poor agricultural economies. The oil shock depressed demand in the rich countries for Third World exports; yet when the latter were faced with increased energy bills, all they could do was try to sell more of their traditional exports, thereby driving prices even further downward.

Into this desperate situation came the Western banks looking for ways of lending on the oil surplus. They found takers, of course, usually corrupt leaders of bankrupt governments. The money went into private Swiss bank accounts or the projects failed, as most 'development' projects did at the time (Hart 1982). By the end of the 1970s there was a huge banking crisis, since Third World debtors were in no position to pay off the loans. The dollar was undermined and the Federal Reserve responded by raising interest rates to nearly 20 per cent. From around 1980 massive transfers of money drained the means of development from the poor countries to the rich at an unprecedented rate (George 1990). At the same time, the International Monetary Fund and World Bank imposed draconian measures known as 'structural adjustment', designed to open up capital movements and to reduce each government's powers of economic intervention. The threat to the Western banking system was averted by a combination of rescheduling agreements (which only increased Third World liabilities) and covert support to the most vulnerable banks. The governments of poor countries had long ago exchanged representing their own people's interests for dependency on their foreign creditors.

This catastrophe is the specific context for the impoverishment of most of Africa, Asia and Latin America today. The international agencies meanwhile quietly dropped the idea of 'development', being concerned only for the survival of governments whose task is to supervise the flow of money into the coffers of Western banks and corporations. Aid levels have been much reduced since the 1960s; indeed non-governmental organizations of a bewildering variety have stepped in to perform functions that neither Third World states nor their international sponsors are prepared to undertake any more. The obscene transfer of wealth from the poor to the rich in the last two decades, honoring debts contracted under dubious circumstances, reveals how far world society has degenerated from the high ideals of mid-century following the defeat of fascism and colonial empire.

Food in a New Economic Order

I divide these conclusions into general reflections and specific recommendations concerning markets, machines, states and capitalists, small farmers and organic food.

General Reflections

If we are serious about tackling global economic inequality, it would be reasonable to start with the shortcomings of the institutions and powers that currently govern our world, focusing on the USA, the EU, the multilateral agencies and the transnational corporations (Bello 2002). But I have chosen here to take a longer view. For decades nation-states have been losing some of their monopolistic controls over subject populations as a consequence of 'globalization', so that humanity is now somewhat stranded between weakened national societies and a world society that is still embryonic. Although we often portray ourselves as moderns emancipated from a rural past, we have not resolved the tension between the legacy of agrarian civilization and a machine revolution that has so far failed to support genuinely democratic societies. Capitalism is itself divided, some parts siding with the old governing interests, others pushing beyond the political institutions of unequal society toward a global framework for trade.

The question is, if capitalism is out of control today, what political units and strategies are adequate to making it more democratically accountable, at least on the scale achieved in the Great Depression and after? There are three main places to stand: to put our faith in strengthened global institutions and networks; to seek to reinforce the powers of the nation-state against globalization; and to develop regional federations, such as the EU and ASEAN. The problem is that each of these options makes bedfellows of interests that have been traditionally opposed as right and left. Thus a global strategy juxtaposes the strongest states, the big corporations and the Bretton-Woods institutions with democratic associations representing popular interests everywhere, such as the World Social Forum. Nationalism throws together greens, the unions and racist anti-immigration groups. In regional federations the voices of popular interest groups are drowned by those of the member-states and big money. 'Civil society' is thus split between all three levels, thereby adding to the general political confusion.

Which interests are likely to push for a new world economic order? Surely not the existing nation-states. How about the transnational corporations? Are they moving to a stage of capitalism beyond the nation-state? Before we admit such a possibility, the old question of capitalism's unequal contract has to be answered. Who will enforce contracts on threat of punishment, if not the established governments? The balance may be shifting, but an alliance between states and capitalists is still functional. Perhaps radical global change will be driven by the same impulses that led to the formation of welfare states in the general crisis of the 1930s and after. These are basically the fear of the rich and powerful that they will lose everything if they make no concessions to the poor. Only a major deflationary crisis could induce such a development.

Food is important in all this, mainly because over a third of humanity still work in the fields with their hands, and drawing them into the circuit of commodity exchange would go a long way toward ending the stagnation of world economy that began in the 1970s. But also because world society is still in the throes of disengaging itself from the institutional logic of agrarian civilization. The world wars of the last century almost brought victory to extreme variants of unequal society, just as the Romans put the lights out on the bourgeois revolution begun by the Phoenicians, Athenians and Carthaginians. We still have a long way to go before commerce can be said to have truly displaced the forces of war. So, what is to be done?

Markets The main drift of my analysis has been that world markets for food constitute the main obstacle to the development of poor countries. The farmers of these countries need some measure of protection so that a regime of higher producer prices might be established, without substantially increasing costs to consumers and non-agricultural producers. Local commerce would then be stimulated by the rural-urban division of labor. At present, in the name of free trade, the rich countries dump cheap food on the rest, while raising barriers to their exports. Clearly world markets have to be radically reorganized in the interests of the poor. The lesson of my initial Canadian anecdote is that ideally the existing subsidies made to Western farmers by tax-rich states should be diverted to the governments of poor countries for similar purposes. Why ever would the world's powers do that? Perhaps if the fear of violence and mass emigration from underdeveloped areas persuaded them that something drastic had to be done to improve their domestic economies. A powerful inducement to that end would be to make international movement a human right, so that citizens of rich countries could no longer rely on the power of their states to keep the others out. In return, the beneficiary governments would have to accept certain political obligations, not only to their own citizens, but to the rest of the world.

Machines The past half-century has seen a radical improvement in the global food supply. This was largely a result of the mechanization of agriculture, not just the use of machinery, but also that of pesticides and high-yield varieties. Machines are converters of inanimate energy, which today means oil. The Green Revolution came out of Rockefeller-funded research institutes in Mexico and the Philippines as a way of making Third World agriculture dependent on petrochemicals as fertilizer (Lipton and Longhurst 1989). Now GMOs are being patented by large chemicals corporations in order to tie farmers to their brand of pesticide and seeds. The ecological threat of a hi-tech agriculture driven by financial considerations has been well advertised. Beyond that, the aggressive privatization strategies of the leading bio-chemical corporations undermine one of the key planks of the cultural commons – our right to borrow the means of growing food from each other. The fact that many still go hungry, despite the increased supply of food, is a function of distribution mechanisms, not of the machine revolution in agriculture as such. Somehow the benefits of mechanization have to be diffused without the abuses.

States and Capitalists Humanity's inability to redress these abuses is partly due to a state capitalist synthesis that divides us into so many competing tribes. This synthesis is now being eroded by globalization. I think that, if the terms can be meaningfully separated, states are more dangerous than capitalism. Territorial states will persist as building blocks of world society; but their powers ought to flow upward into global and regional federations and downward to local and more diffuse associations. Nor is it good enough to denigrate capitalism as such. The production of cheap commodities by profit-making firms is intrinsic to economic progress. The markets, transport and communication systems on which we depend cannot function without them. The classical liberal revolutions against the old regime were fueled by the bourgeoisie, and some capitalists will play a similar role in future. It is a question of their relationship to the status quo. We need to be more discriminating about the forms of capital. Thus Red Hat Linux has been lobbying for the adoption of its software in India's schools on the grounds that it is cheap, flexible and robust. Microsoft has been campaigning there on its track record in helping governments to regulate access to the internet. Hewlett-Packard has targeted the four billion poorest people as a market. If all those excluded from the digital revolution are to join, existing firms will be needed to develop the required infrastructure. This is why putting money into the hands of the poor benefits the rich too.

Small Farmers The French make a great deal of *terroir* (soil), the specifics of local environment, in asserting local identity against the corrosion of globalization. Commercial agriculture there covers a wide range of scales, but the farmers still refer to themselves as 'peasants'. The German Marxist leader, Karl Kautsky (1899) found that Europe's small farmers were far from being wiped out by capitalism. Certain commodities benefited from the natural protection of local conditions and markets: viticulture, dairy products, market gardening. But also, peasant producers have often proven to be more efficient and durable than larger-scale specialized operations. Now, following an ancient pattern of pluriactivity (see the Lenin quote above), rural areas have diversified away from agriculture into services such as tourism (Bryden and Hart 2003). The gap in lifestyle between city and countryside has been much narrowed. The world's poor need more than agriculture as a way of participating in the world economy. The growing market is for cultural commodities in fields like entertainment, information services and education. Most of these will be produced in cities, not villages; but here too, small producers should be able to compete effectively with the giant corporations.

Organic Food Faced with what often seems a runaway world (Leach 1968 [1967]), where remote forces threaten to overwhelm our fragile claims to identity, the idea that natural things are good for us finds fertile ground, especially when it comes to food. Of course, after 10,000 years of domestication, the idea of something being natural is highly relative (or organic, if you prefer Greek to Latin). The appeal to nature was already incorporated into nationalism as a sort of reaction to the speed of modern change. The current wave of resistance to GMOs has echoes of this Luddite rejection of machine civilization. Nevertheless, several themes in this chapter find echoes in the movement to promote organic agriculture. It can provide a measure of local protection from global producers; it is often small-scale and more compatible with existing peasant practice; it avoids the excesses and risks of hi-tech production; and, as the existence of an international association shows,[1] it may support a grassroots democratic politics. If the Western middle classes embrace natural food with the enthusiasm with which they have returned to natural fibres for their clothing (Schneider 1994), organic farmers will gain an important global ally in their struggle for economic equality.

I began with Lewis's observation that a new international economic order is needed if the development prospects of the poor countries are to be substantially improved. Would-be revolutionaries first have to decide which is the greater enemy of human progress, the persisting legacy of agrarian civilization or a capitalism built on machines. State capitalism is a hybrid of both. To target one element while turning a blind eye to the other is a recipe for political failure in the long run. State socialism in the twentieth century tried to outlaw markets, with ruinous consequences. Now the neo-liberals, in the name of universal private property and free trade, promote the interests of the strong over the weak by emasculating their states. If we want a more democratic and equal world, we need a more comprehensive view of the problems facing humanity as a whole.

Note

1. A version of this chapter was presented as a keynote speech at a conference held in Bangkok, 6–8 November 2003, by the International Federation of Organic Agriculture Movements (IFOAM).

References

Asbury, H. (1927), *The Gangs of New York*, New York: Alfred Knopf.
Bello, W. (2002), *Deglobalization: Ideas For a New World Economy*, London: Zed.
Bryden, J. and Hart, K. (2003), *Why Local Economies Differ*, Lampeter: Edwin Mellen.
Childe, V. G. (1954), *What Happened in History*, London: Penguin.
Conklin, H. (1957), *Hanunoo Agriculture*, Rome: FAO.
Engels, F. (1884), *The Origin of the Family, Private Property and the State*, London: Lawrence & Wishart.

Fanon, F. (1970 [1959]), *The Wretched of the Earth*, London: Penguin.

Gellner, E. (1983), *Nations and Nationalism*, Oxford: Blackwell.

George, S. (1990), *A Fate Worse than Debt*, London: Penguin.

Goody, J. (1976), *Production and Reproduction*, Cambridge: Cambridge University Press.

Hardt, M. and Negri, A. (2000), *Empire*, Cambridge MA: Harvard University Press.

Hart, K. (1973), 'Informal Income Opportunities and Urban Employment in Ghana', *Journal of Modern African Studies*, 11: 61–89.

—— (1982), *The Political Economy of West African Agriculture*, Cambridge: Cambridge University Press.

—— (2001), *Money in an Unequal World*, New York and London: Texere.

—— (2002), 'World Society as an Old Regime', in C. Shore and S. Nugent (eds), *Elite Cultures: Anthropological Approaches*, London: Routledge.

Hart, K. and Padayachee, V. (2000), 'Indian Business in South Africa after Apartheid: New Old Trajectories', *Comparative Studies in Society and History*, 42: 683–712.

Kautsky, K. 1988 (1899), *The Agrarian Question*, London: Zwan.

Keynes, J. M. (1936), *The General Theory of Employment, Interest and Money*, London: Macmillan.

Latour, B. (1993), *We Have Never Been Modern*, Amsterdam: Harvester.

Leach, E. (1968), *A Runaway World?* London: BBC (lectures 1967).

Lenin, V. I. (1956 [1899]), *The Development of Capitalism in Russia*, Moscow: Progress Publishers.

Lewis, W. A. (1978), *The Evolution of the International Economic Order*, Princeton, NJ.: Princeton University Press.

Lipton, M. and Longhurst, R. (1989), *New Seeds and Poor People*, London: Unwin Hyman.

Malthus, R. (1992 [1798]), *An Essay on Population*, Cambridge: Cambridge University Press.

Marx, K. (1968 [1852]), 'The Eighteenth Brumaire of Louis Bonaparte', *Marx-Engels Selected Works*, London: Lawrence & Wishart.

—— (1970 [1867]), *Capital (volume one)*, London: Lawrence & Wishart.

Meillassoux, C. (1981 [1975]), *Maidens, Meal and Money*, Cambridge: Cambridge University Press.

Morgan, L. H. (1964 [1877]), *Ancient Society*, Cambridge MA: Bellknap.

Polanyi, K. (1944), *The Great Transformation*, Boston MA: Beacon.

Ricardo, D. (1971 [1817]), *Principles of Political Economy and Taxation*, Cambridge: Cambridge University Press.

Rousseau, J.-J. (1984 [1754]), *A Discourse on Inequality*, London: Penguin.

Sahlins, M. (1972), *Stone-Age Economics*, Chicago: Aldine.

Schneider, J. (1994), 'In and Out of Polyester', *Anthropology Today*, 10(4) (August): 2–10.

Smith, A. (1961 [1776]), *An Inquiry into the Nature and Causes of the Wealth of Nations*, London: Methuen.

Steuart, J. (1767), *Principles of Political Oeconomy* (two vols), London: Miller and Caddell.

Stiglitz, J. (2002), *Globalization and its Discontents*, New York: Norton.

Thom, M. (1995), *Republics, Nations and Tribes*, London: Verso.

United Nations development Program (1998), *Human Development Report*, New York: UNDP.

Vaggi, G. and Groenewegen, P. (2003), *A Concise History of Economic Thought: from Mercantilism to Monetarism*, Basingstoke: Palgrave.

Weber, A. F. (1965 [1899]), *The Growth of Cities in the Nineteenth Century*, Ithaca NY: Cornell University Press.

Weber, M. (1981 [1921]), *General Economic History*, New Brunswick NJ: Transaction Books.

Epilogue:
On the Legacy of *The Politics of Food*

Anne Murcott

Introduction

> Both food and politics are fundamentals in human society . . .
> Without food an individual eventually dies; if too many do so, whole groups die out . . .
> Power, and its (mal)distribution, is an ever-present feature at all levels of the social . . .

So profound, so integral to human society, is the significance of both politics and food that at times the intimacy which connects the two can get overlooked, rendered invisible and become taken for granted. Of course, what commonly illuminates matters that have become so familiar that they continue unnoticed is a novelty, a change, or, especially perhaps, an emergency. Genetically modified foods are nothing if not novel. Bovine spongiform encephalopathy (BSE) was, and maybe remains, nothing if not the threat of a major emergency.[1] And the increasing prevalence of risk discourse in public commentary is nothing if not a notable development of the last ten or so years, one to which social anthropologists and psychologists, economists and geographers, political scientists and sociologists have all come to pay extensive and energetic attention.

In some respects, this book is not simply a product of, but is itself also integral to, these changes. By way of appreciating its timeliness, the editors are to be congratulated for their initiative in convening the original workshop (held in Copenhagen in August 2002 as part of the annual conference of the European Association of Social Anthropologists) and for continuing that work by putting this collection together. As Marianne Lien makes clear in her Introduction – and as exemplified by the contents – the *politics of food* has been transformed. No longer, she remarks, is the field so easy to define. No longer is it limited to quite a short list of typical topics. New ground has been broken.

Like Lien's discussion, this endpiece also adopts the long view and, like hers, also reflects on the novelty represented by this book. It takes the form of a short essay whose point of departure is the very title of this volume, *The Politics of Food* – a title which, though neatly to the point, is not original. Even if the law provides for authors to hold copyright in the title of their books, in practice they seem not to. For, well before the present volume was mooted, there were already three items (Darling 1941; Cannon 1987; Henson and Gregory (eds) 1994) on my own book-shelves with the identical name – give or take the definite article. Indeed, it turns out that, as a book title, *The Politics of Food* is not even particularly recent: the oldest of my trio, that by George Darling, was published more than half a century ago, during the Second World War. In any case, my three are not alone: a quick search identified a couple of successors also with the same name (Green 1975; Mitchell 1975), two more simply transposing the words (Balaam and Carey (eds) 1981; Nestle 2002) and several additional books and articles whose titles represent variations on very closely related vocabulary (Hadwiger and Browne 1978; Winkler 1987; M. Smith 1991; Mills 1992; D. Smith (ed) 1997; D. Smith and Phillips (eds) 2000).[2]

Based on an unpardonably selective dip into this small array of like-titled examples, what follows attempts a short sketch of the field in order to illuminate certain facets of the preceding chapters' distinctive place in it. Several novelties will already be evident to the reader: novelties of topic – the politics of food as risk, the implications of a global reach – and intellectual approach – the emergence of analysing discourse and rhetoric – all of which indicate future directions ripe for further study, directions such as the conjunction of the politics of science with the *politics of food* or the introduction into the field of the dissection of the nature of experts (Collins and Evans 2002). Here, however, I shall ponder on the idea that Lien and Nerlich's edited collection signifies an emerging social-scientific profes-sionalism that allows a contrast between activism and scholarship to become more clearly evident. The editors and contributors to this volume, have – whatever their party political allegiances, whatever their stance on the power of the food industry and its relation to governments, whatever their reactions to radical lobby groups of various persuasions – stepped aside from activism to develop thoroughgoing analyses in political science, linguistics, sociology and social anthropology and thereby take important steps on the newly broken ground in the *politics of food*. At the same time, continuities remain, and these too deserve careful attention, estab-lished by beginning chronologically with the wartime example.

A Venerable Tradition in *the Politics of Food*: Campaigners

The case of an island nation in mid-twentieth-century wartime threw into ex-ceedingly sharp relief questions of the adequate supply of a suitable range of foodstuffs, as commentators of the period graphically illustrated (see for example Le Gros Clark and Titmuss 1939; Orr and Lubbock 1940; and also Boyd Orr 1966: 120). And it is to a discussion of such questions about the United Kingdom at war that Darling's 1941 *The Politics of Food* is devoted. George Darling, the upwardly socially mobile son of a Co-op shop assistant, having taken a degree from Cambridge University was to enter Parliament in 1950 with later elevation to the Upper House on his creation as a life peer in 1974. At the time that his *The Politics of Food* was published, he had been a journalist on *Reynolds News*[3] for some four years. His is an activism that worked through existing, institutionalized, some might say conventional routes. Though it deals with technicalities of the food supply, his book was written for a popular readership. And, as will become clear, Darling had a practical, political case to make.

In the process, Darling's book also lucidly illustrates that longer-established denotation of the *politics of food* in which, as Lien observes, food is a source of necessary nutrients and politics is what political institutions do. This approach is neatly summed up on its dust-jacket:

The author first exposes capitalism's failure to feed the people adequately either in peace or war. He traces the failure to its root cause, and points out that this nation has never had a food policy. Finally he shows how policy could be re-cast on a co-operative basis to meet the conditions resulting from the war.

For Darling, politics is what political institutions fail to do unless his remedies are adopted, while his concern with food assumes nutritional necessity in revolving around the (in)adequacy of supply, and thus happens to represent a negative version of the two dimensions which, as Lien indicates, distinguishes earlier work in the field.

In drawing attention to the absence of a food policy, Darling's book also identifies one of the recurrent themes of later commentaries in the politics of food. In one of these, for instance, Michael Franklin, a former Permanent Secretary at the Ministry of Agriculture who had retired by the time he was writing, took the view that the UK 'scarcely had a recognisable food policy' until the middle of the 1980s (Franklin 1994). And, sure enough, during the decade in question, the sub-head provided for Jack Winkler's article 'Food is a Political Issue' was: 'It is time a national food health policy was developed' (Winkler 1987). Winkler, be it noted, is a trained sociologist but he has probably spent more of his career working either as a journalist, or an activist. Fellow activist Tim Lang lists him among a new generation which, he proposes, has helped create 'a new context for food policy decision-making by taking food issues to the public' (Lang 1997: 238). Lang does not, however, compare the new generation of activists with its wartime predecessors, any more than he mentions Darling's book. In the previous year the Labour

Party, then in opposition, had already issued a Consultative Paper entitled 'A Food Policy: a Priority for Labour' (Labour Party 1986) whose opening paragraph contains a sense of historical urgency:

> Food policy has always been an issue of great importance to the Labour movement. Our aim in this document is to *re-open* the debate on this critical issue, taking into account new scientific evidence, and to provide the background for a major *restatement* of Labour's policy on food. (The Labour Party 1986:1, emphasis added)

To determine how closely that Labour Party document is in line with Darling's political philosophy would require further investigation. The latter's brand of radicalism is readily evident in his proposed solutions to immediate wartime emergencies. To take a very clear-cut example, Darling does not simply castigate government for the wholly inadequate provision for people made homeless by air-raids.[4] He calls for them to be provided with free food, paid for (in part) from – and herein lies his distinctive radicalism – the profits to be made from reorganizing and taking into state ownership the wholesale section of the food chain (Darling 1941: 103, 160).

The same radicalism is also evident in his scorn for the wartime Ministry of Food. Certainly, he prefaces his analysis by acknowledging that a Minister cannot 'control Britain's food trades single-handed' and that the 'advice of men and women who know how food supplies are bought, stored, processed, shipped, transported and sold' has to be sought. Certainly, he praises the integrity, expertise and unquestioned abilities of those appointed as Head Controllers – he names all thirteen of them – in charge of commodities from condensed milk to bacon and ham, from canned fish to sugar. But, 'the trouble is,' Darling writes, 'they were doing it in the wrong way' (Darling 1941: 58). Since, quite simply, these Controllers faced a predictable clash between the interests of the state and the interests of the businesses to which they hoped to return, he judged that they were all too liable to resolve that clash in favor of the latter. Again, Darling's political economy is just as evident in his didactic observation that: 'it is clear to anyone who knows anything about the food trades that a single selling agency operating in a controlled market can effect considerable economies in selling costs' (Darling 1941: 62). So, instead of turning them into profits for traders who made up needless sections between production and retailing, those economies of scale are to be passed on in lower prices to the public, achieving greater equity in access in the process. What is more, state control of the food industry, he declares, must be intensified and extended after the war ends.

Once more anticipating a theme in later contributions to the field, Darling's call for shortening supply chains and above all taking the whole out of the hands of big business is a goal echoed several decades later in respect of a markedly different nation. Provoked by the combined power of government and agribusiness represented in a report by the Canadian Federal Government's Task Force on Agriculture, Don Mitchell – in another of the books called *The Politics of Food* – offers a dozen proposals. One of the most notable suggests that 'Food processing could be integrated (through public ownership) with the production and marketing priorities of basic agriculture' (Mitchell 1975: 224). Although they are centered on such contrasting nations – a dwindling agricultural sector in a small overcrowded country that was first to industrialize against a vast and highly diversified landmass with great potential for food production – the analyses Darling and Mitchell present have much in common,[5] never mind representing that longer established *politics of food* which Keith Hart's chapter does much to sustain. But there is a certain difference of emphasis in the means they urge for the achievement of their radical solutions. Mitchell has no illusions as to quite how much needs to happen before his alternatives could begin to be implemented. Among his preconditions is the creation of a class-based political party to respond to working-class interests, coupled with the need to convince Canadians 'that the food resource is too socially vital to be left to private-marketing' (Mitchell 1975: 226).

Darling, on the other hand, relies on the model of the English Cooperative movement to represent those interests. It is striking that in the process, he freely refers to 'consumers'. This makes his vocabulary sound much more like that of early twenty-first century usage where the word has replaced reference to a wide array of social roles (for example those occupied by health-service patients, rail passengers, people who buy insurance) as well as increasingly commonly serving as a synonym for the general public or the population at large. Darling, though, is more specific, addressing himself primarily, in the style of the period, to 'the housewife'; he does not need to mention that it is she who is responsible for shopping, domestic organization and cooking whereby, in his words, the war is brought right into her kitchen. The effects, he insists, of ever-increasing concentration in the food trades into fewer and more powerful hands may well result in lower prices and more abundant supplies. But, he emphasizes, a penalty is exacted both in ceding power to the big firms over the 'housewife's selection of foods and (in) the reduction of quality which frequently accompanies mass production of foodstuffs' (Darling 1941: 205). He is quite clear. Housewives need not only to learn the lessons about the form and structure of the food supply, they need 'to realize that they have the *power* to demand and get an efficient Food Service controlled by the public to serve the public' (Darling 1941: 211, emphasis added).

Darling's book is a compelling historical document, every page redolent of its period. Yet many of his concerns continue to run, barely changed, through discussions on food policy ever since. For instance, a version of his analysis of the penalties paid for cheap food comprises a significant part of the semantic field portrayed in Brigitte Nerlich's chapter in the opening section of this book. And it needs only a slight alteration in viewpoint to recognize that his concerns with the housewife's power as consumer are paralleled by questions on which Bente Halkier enlarges in her chapter in the same section – representing, perhaps, a bridge between an older political economy tradition and newer themes in political sociology.

Chronologically located between Darling and Halkier, is a contribution by Wyn Grant to the 1994 item entitled *Politics of Food* on my shelves. He identifies a shift which sheds light on that bridge. It is a shift from a politics of production – primarily revolving round the employer/employee relationship – to a politics of collective consumption – a politics of collective concerns which, in the case of the food industry, takes the form of a 'shared perception of a particular type of product as morally or physically dangerous or both' (Grant 1994: 22). All the same, his ensuing discussion of (UK-based) pressure groups concerned with such perceptions remains located in a longer-standing approach in political science to forms of political activity, from which Halkier's discussion represents a considered departure.

Among the pressure groups Grant lists is one headed by Geoffrey Cannon whom he describes as a 'long standing campaigner on food issues' (Grant 1994: 25). Cannon is the author of the second of my trio of items bearing the title *The Politics of Food*. Like Darling, he has worked as a journalist, writing for several of the major British newspapers as well as more specialized magazines.[6] Cannon's topic, his choice of title, the directness of his style and his stance – akin to exposé journalism – are succinctly represented on his very first page:

> Why is British food and health so bad? When did the rot set in, and who is responsible? How can we – consumers and citizens, whoever else we are – transform the quality of the British food supply, and thus the national health? These are all political questions, and are the reasons why I decided to write *The Politics of Food*. (Cannon 1988: 2)

And, like Darling's, this book is also addressed to the general public. Darling's is a hardback and has the occasional footnote but carries neither bibliography nor index. Cannon's was first published in hardback in 1987; a year later, however, it appeared as an abridged and updated paperback, with an index but without its bibliography and appendices. Cannon has a note in the acknowledgements referring readers who want such details to the hardback edition. His concern to reach a wide audience with a shorter, and presumably lower-priced, paperback meant he was willing to forgo having all editions carrying the evidence to support his arguments.

By contrast, Marion Nestle's *Food Politics* (Nestle 2002) (published a year later in paperback), one of the most recent contributions, carries not just an appendix and an extensive index but also some fifty pages of notes and references. Examining the American case, the book is aptly summarized in its subtitle: 'How the Food Industry Influences Nutrition and Health' – concluding that it does so legally, via public relations, vigorous lobbying but with the interests of share-holders taking precedence over the public health; possibly most telling of all, however, it does so almost invisibly. The book's springboard is, in the words of the dust-jacket, Nestle's own 'rare dual perspective afforded by government service and academic expertise' as a senior academic nutritionist, professor and chair of her department at New York University as well as editor of the *Surgeon General's Report on Nutrition and Health* (1988) and more besides.

Like Darling and Cannon before her, she is at pains to reach as wide and general a readership as possible (Nestle 2002: viii). Unlike Darling and Cannon she addresses the question of sources and evidence explicitly and in some detail. Dealing with concerns about the food industry that are hardly discussed in aca-demic or public circles, she thus deemed it important to document her sources more than might seem absolutely necessary. Not only, as her own book reveals, does much that food companies do in order to create a favorable sales environment for their products take place out of public view, documents about associated activ-ities are also subject to confidentiality agreements and cannot be quoted. Consequently she has had to rely more heavily than is common practice on her own extensive experience, on grey literature and on other non-academic sources. More striking perhaps, is her comment that: 'I could not find *anyone* who would speak to me "on the record" for this book' (Nestle 2002: ix, original emphasis). She received numerous offers of help from colleagues in government, the industry, and universities, but always with the proviso that she use the information unattrib-uted.

Both Nestle and Cannon conclude with well-elaborated suggestions for action that are a considerable advance on Darling's solely pointing out to the housewife her power as consumer. In the US, Nestle proposes learning from what she calls 'tobacco wars', anti-smoking campaigns that focus not just on individual smokers but also on the tobacco industry: she discusses limiting lobbies' access to Congress and regulatory bodies; and she considers tax and pricing policies in addi-tion to continued efforts at education. Cannon recommends a long list of reforms many of which, though first published at the end of the 1980s, have in all proba-bility not been adopted or implemented. In particular he recommends that his UK readers write to their Member of Parliament explaining that their support is influ-enced by his or her views on food and health.

Such a sentiment has a faint echo in one of the earlier books entitled *The Politics of Food* by Daniel Green (1975) aimed just as much for the general reader. He summarizes his educational purpose as follows:

> If this book is able to leave the reader with the thought that there may, after all, be some connection between yesterday's vote and tomorrow's dinner then it will have fulfilled whatever didactic purpose it holds. (ibid.: xi)

Like Darling, Green studied at Cambridge University and he too was born into and has practical experience of the industry; but where Darling's was at the distribution end of the food chain, Green's was in farming. With different experiences prompting them – Green was a prisoner of war in the Second World War – they were nonetheless both led to a powerful awareness of the internationality of the food supply:

> (N)o country exists and evolves its traditions in isolation least of all when it comes to matters of food. To an ever increasing degree the food producers and the food consumers of this world are tied to each other in a complicated nexus that has long since ceased to be regional or national or even multi-national in its scale. Food, in short, has now become the most international of all commodities. This is why the food politics of any one country must be the concern of us all. (Green 1975: ix)

Green's discussion deals with the globalization of the food supply – to which Part III of the present book is devoted – before the widespread adoption of that expression. Similarly, Green anticipates several other topics considered here. So, for instance, the first chapter of his book is devoted to a set of generalizations about 'man the hunter'. Here Green talks of the way people are unthinking about what they continue to eat, and he introduces a somewhat perplexing idea of morality in food – making rather sarcastic remarks about the immorality of rare foods such as pheasant and port, dubbing them immoral because they are rare. In key respects this chapter is a homespun mix of amateur anthropology and intelligent personal opinion. All the same, he touches on several themes taken up by Lien and Nerlich's contributors when he notes that:

> A country's food traditions, like its political traditions, evolve slowly, often with no apparent logic. They are influenced strongly by the vagaries of climate and history. These in turn are reflected in such things as its farm structure, its legal system, its demography, its economy and in that generalised psychological attitude best described as a national culture. (ibid.)

There is, however, one notable respect in which Green's *The Politics of Food* differs significantly from the others. Quite unlike Darling before him, however, unlike Mitchell at around the same time, and unlike either Cannon or Nestle afterward, Green's politics look to be right-of-center. That they are so is rather less interesting for the present discussion than the manner in which he couches his opinion. The Conservative Party, he reckons, is most likely to come up with the best solutions to world hunger and suitable provision for Britain because they exercise *common sense*.

> (C)ommon sense is an even more desirable quality than pragmatism in the politics of food. Pragmatism implies, to a certain extent, having no policies beyond those of the

immediate situation. Common sense allows a longer-term more global view to be held and to be held to especially when there are no limitations of dogma or sectional interest to get in the way of the sense. (ibid.: 185)

In all likelihood to their mutual puzzlement, Cannon seems to share with Green a view of common sense as a virtue when he writes:

Common sense suggests that the quality of food and health is a function of class and money: that the working class and the poor eat worse food and have worse health than people with comfortable middle-class jobs. (Cannon 1987: 26)

It is not completely clear, incidentally, how far the wide dissemination of a century and a half of research on inequalities in health[7] has led to its acquiring a popular that is, common-sense – currency. A possibly short historical view allows Cannon to contrast common sense with – and apparently to prefer over – more systematic investigation. At the risk of over-interpreting what these campaigners share, it is possible that such a preference signals an impatience with the slower speed, the stepping aside from a call to arms of the academic and scholarly.

An Emergent *Politics of Food?*: In the Academy

The point at issue here is not solely that common sense is what science is not: common sense is what science is to supersede; common sense is to be left behind by science which can overturn it; common sense is what science investigates, and science produces dependable results that show up the limitations of common sense. Einstein is reputed to have declared that 'common sense is what we have learned by the age of eighteen: science is what takes us beyond common sense'. In vital respects, a novelty represented by the preceding chapters in this book is that they represent a *break* with common-sense understandings. This sort of break is in direct contrast with what Darling, Cannon, Green, Nestle and other such campaigners have in mind. However much their politics may vary, or their style of solution or source of inspiration differ, these authors present their politics of food not as scholarship but as a program for action, a discussion dedicated to exposing the need for change. By contrast, the chapters in this book pave the way for investigating what is held to be common sense, rather than invoking common sense as a part of a call for change. To this extent, they signify a version of a professional academic (social-) scientific attitude – albeit one which remains unspoken.

In effect, it is proposed, Lien and Nerlich and their contributors adopt an intellectual attitude that opens up a space between scholarship and activism. A *consequence* of scholarly analysis may well be to inform activism, but the ostensible rationale for embarking on academic analysis is primarily to further understanding

– that is, being learned – rather than providing a program for action. Engagement as an activist or with some campaign may well be to prompt a separate scholarly enquiry, but the *original* engagement is primarily to effect some change – that is, an example of political practice – rather than emphasizing detailing types of understanding.

A good many familiar observations deserve to be made about drawing a distinction between scholarly analysis on the one hand and activism on the other. Just in case anyone is tempted to think otherwise, so doing does not rely on an assumption that some value-free anthropological, sociological or political-scientific analysis is possible. Equally, making this distinction does not mean analysts are to blind themselves to political or campaigning implications of their work – in principle, this too is not possible, else we stand charged with being ingenuous or disingenuous, one as unfortunate as the other in a scholar. In any case, debating such a distinction has a history as long as the existence of discussions of politics, knowledge and science. The present proposal is not to claim some general world-shattering novelty, but to mark a significant enough contemporary incarnation in the particular field to which Lien, Nerlich and their collaborators devote their efforts. In this sense the novelty of their achievement is in addition to, and has the potential to carry beyond, the innovations of substance, topic and reach which Lien discusses in her introduction.

It must ever be noted that a distinction between scholarship and activism is perilous. Even in simple terms, it is not hard and fast. In sketching the historical place of *The Politics of Food* in its field, it is important to recognize that it maintains continuities on the one hand and, even where claims can be made for its manifestly breaking new ground, there are identifiable precursors on the other. Perhaps the most marked instance of affinity if not continuity with campaigning predecessors in this book is Keith Hart's chapter. It well displays the value, to which Lien points, of a holistic approach that attends to continuities between food and those institutions which, at first sight, seem to be unrelated to the politics of its provision. His is also a compelling piece, difficult enough for those schooled in other disciplines and analytic perspectives to square with their own; difficult morally for those whose position in an unequal world gives them the comfortable full belly that is the freedom not to have to think about the fact or source of that comfort; difficult politically, since, unless it is to disappear into sands of cynicism or despair, his analytic approach urgently implies action. Chaia Heller adopts a different tack. Electing to expose in her chapter the manner in which risk and contrasting types of expertise are framed, she steps aside from her publicly proclaimed persona as variously a writer, activist and educator, and also an eco-feminist, radical and left-libertarian. Her chapter could, but does not, discuss the activist uses to which her analysis could be put. Like Heller, other contributors concentrate on scholarly analysis, stopping short of considering any campaigning implications of their chapters. Bente Halkier could urge people to act as the good consumer Darling proposes, but does not. Haldis Haukanes concludes that expert advice in respect of BSE was not heeded, and could have, but does not go on to propose a campaign such as one Darling might applaud, to ensure that it was. Jacobsen details some of the mechanisms – though that word is too crude and the imagery of a machine too unsubtle to do his analysis justice – of the politics of words, the rhetoric adopted by powerful vested interests in food production and provision. He could, but does not take his discussion further as a basis either for 'arming' campaigners against industrial interests or for 'arming' industrial interests against campaigners. And so on for the other co-contributors' chapters.

Of itself, none of this is new. Simply, and on the basis of this ruthlessly selective inspection of like-titled volumes, that fragile distinction between scholarship and activism can yet again be noted as a significant consequence of Lien and Nerlich's efforts. But the distinction as made here is intended to do nothing more than reflect a division of labor. The job of campaigning – to the extent there is a job – is to act. The job of an academic is intellectual analysis, from a devotion to learning to the selection and examination of topics from all kinds of angle and to being alert to the range of consequences, whether or not there is scope, virtue or danger in actively promoting, or campaigning against, one or other of them. Perhaps this contrast is most relevant, and most delicate, among the social rather than the biological or physical sciences. Be it noted, that even where authors of the earlier items entitled *Politics of Food* took an initial degree in one of the social sciences, many moved on from scholarly work to write about politics and food from *outside* the academy, *explicitly* seeking to reach an audience beyond its boundaries, with the main purpose of proposing modes of effecting change. By contrast, all the contributors here have, primarily if not exclusively, embarked on academic careers, and elected to write as scholars for present purposes. Instead of offering discussions of the politics of food in which analysis and activism coincide, Lien, Nerlich and their authors concentrate on the former, and remain silent on the latter. It is in this sense that their combined efforts open up a space between activism and analysis.

Yet, reference to a division of labor is all very well. It will not do, however, to neglect its political economy. So the significance of a distinction between activism – of no-matter-which political or ideological complexion – and scholarship is also to highlight the politics of academic research, in the politics of food as in anything else. Explicit thoughtfulness about the relationship between scholarship and campaigning extends to consciousness of service into which research, to a greater or lesser extent, is pressed. Such service to *governments'* policy, is, in varying guises, increasingly emphasized in the UK, Australia, the US and other countries as a condition for the award of research funding – a stern reminder, if one be needed, that standing aside from activism cannot per se, necessarily be treated as tantamount to political nonalignment. Such a reminder is but a short step to another: governments' relationship to industry in whatever sector, including food, is not only investigable but is, by implication, at some level a potential fact of research life.

Researchers have to deal with adverse criticism from those scornful of attempts at open-minded nonalignment that simultaneously strives to remain honest and as faithful as possible to the integrity of the discipline they profess. It is neither comfortable nor easy. But, in putting their collection together, Lien and Nerlich not only urge a more mature, 'holistic' intellectual appraisal of the field but also, in effect, reintroduce us to the perpetually irresolvable issue of where researchers are to stand in the vital matters of the politics of food. As signalled at the beginning of this concluding commentary on their *The Politics of Food*, the manner in which their and their contributors' work departs from venerable traditions in this field is more than the substantive developments to which Lien refers, more than an attempt to focus on connections. It also departs from such traditions in respect of paving the way for a developed sense of the place of research in the politics of food in that self-same increasingly politicized arena whose analysis is a key theme of this book.

Acknowledgements

I am most grateful to the editors for inviting this contribution to their book and for their kind understanding in waiting for it. I also wish to thank Bente Halkier, Pru Hobson-West, Christine Hogg, Virginia Low, Dominic Murcott, Toby Murcott, Steve Rayner, Lindy Sharpe, David Smith and Corinne Wales for conversations, references and thought-provoking chance remarks.

Notes

1. The so-called human variant of the disease, Creutzfeld-Jacob Disease (vCJD), is particularly unpleasant and, at the time of writing, invariably fatal. And although the number of known cases is still just below 150, given the pace of development of both diseases, the threat of a major epidemic, although judged to be reduced, cannot yet be unequivocally ruled out.
2. Of interest, though beside the present point, is the variation in emphasis and/or part of the so-called food chain to which these volumes refer; Balaam and Carey, for example, emphasize primarily agriculture and food production, Mills dwells on the policy analysis of health and nutrition policies, as does Smith who also includes a history of the political activities of professionally trained nutritionists – a strong tradition to which Nestle's work is a very recent addition.
3. A newspaper founded in 1850 by a supporter of Chartism.

4. It will be recalled that the UK's modern welfare state only became a practical reality after 1945.
5. Both authors are also graduates in economics, of the Universities of Cambridge and Saskatchewan, Regina respectively.
6. Notably as one of the founder members of the now defunct *New Society*, a left-of-center weekly founded in the 1960s devoted to social issues and problems.
7. The earliest I have been able to locate is Villermé's investigation of Paris whose 1828 studies are discussed by Richard Shryock (1979: 225).

References

Balaam, D. N. and Carey, M. J. (eds) (1981), *Food Politics: The Regional Conflict*, London: Croom Helm.

Boyd Orr, L. (1966), *As I Recall*, London: MacGibbon and Kee.

Cannon, G. (1987), *The Politics of Food*, London: Hutchinson.

Collins, H. and Evans, R. (2002), 'The Third Wave of Science Studies: Studies of Expertise and Experience', *Social Studies of Science*, 32: 235–96.

Darling, G. (1941), *The Politics of Food*, London: George Routledge & Sons.

Franklin, M. (1994), '*Food Policy Formation in the UK/EC*', in S. Henson and S. Gregory (eds), *The Politics of Food: Proceedings*, Reading: University of Reading.

Grant, W. (1994), 'Food Policy Formation: The Role of pressure groups', in S. Henson and S. Gregory (eds), *The Politics of Food: Proceedings*, Reading: University of Reading.

Green, D. (1975), *The Politics of Food*, London: Gordon Cremonesi.

Hadwiger, D. F. and Browne, W. P. (eds) (1978), *The New Politics of Food*, Lanham MD: Lexington.

Henson, S. and Gregory, S. (eds) (1994), '*The Politics of Food: Proceedings of an inter-disciplinary Seminar held at the University of Reading, 7 July 1993*', Reading: Department of Agricultural Economics & Management, The University of Reading.

Labour Party (1986), 'Food Policy: A Priority for Labour', London: Labour Party.

Lang, T. (1997), 'Going Public: Food Campaigns during the 1980s and early 1990s', in Smith: 238–60.

Le Gros Clark, F. and Titmuss, R. M. (1939), *Our Food Problem and its Relation to our National Defences*, Harmondsworth: Penguin.

Mills, M. (1992), *The Politics of Dietary Change*, Aldershot: Dartmouth.

Mitchell, D. (1975), *The Politics of Food*, Toronto: James Lorimer & Co.

Nestle, M. (2002), *Food Politics: How the Food Industry Influences Nutrition and Health*, Berkeley CA: University of California Press.

Orr, J. and Lubbock, D. (1940), *Feeding the People in War-Time*, London: Macmillan.

Shryock, R. H. (1979 [1936]), *The Development of Modern Medicine*, Madison WI: University of Wisconsin Press.

Smith, D. (ed.) (1997), *Nutrition in Britain: Science, Scientists and Politics in the Twentieth Century*, London: Routledge.

Smith, D. and Phillips, J. (eds) (2000), *Food, Science, Policy and Regulation in the Twentieth Century: International and Comparative Perspectives*, London: Routledge.

Smith, M. J. (1991), 'From Policy Community to Issue Network: *Salmonella* in Eggs and the New Politics of Food', *Public Administration*, 69 (Summer): 235–55.

Winkler, J. (1987), 'Food is a Political Issue', *The Health Service Journal*, 6 August: 910.

Index

CPSIA information can be obtained at www.ICGtesting.com
Printed in the USA
LVOW08s2210020216

473362LV00006B/105/P